Securing the Belt and Road Initiative

Alessandro Arduino • Xue Gong
Editors

Securing the Belt and Road Initiative

Risk Assessment, Private Security and Special Insurances Along the New Wave of Chinese Outbound Investments

palgrave
macmillan

Editors
Alessandro Arduino
Shanghai Academy of Social Sciences
Security & Crisis Management
Program
Shanghai, China

Xue Gong
S. Rajaratnam School of International
Studies (RSIS)
Nanyang Technological University
Singapore, Singapore

ISBN 978-981-10-7115-7 ISBN 978-981-10-7116-4 (eBook)
https://doi.org/10.1007/978-981-10-7116-4

Library of Congress Control Number: 2017961565

Cover Image: MYALA88 / Alamy Stock Photo

Printed on acid-free paper

This Palgrave imprint is published by Springer Nature
The registered company is Springer Nature Singapore Pte Ltd.
The registered company address is: 152 Beach Road, #21-01/04 Gateway East, Singapore 189721, Singapore

Acknowledgments

The core chapters of this volume are based on the draft papers presented during the 'Securing the Belt and Road Initiative: Risk Assessment, Private Security and Special Insurances along the New Wave of Chinese FDI' (28 October 2016) workshop co-organized in Singapore by the China Programme of the S. Rajaratnam School of International Studies (RSIS) at Nanyang Technological University (NTU) and the Shanghai Academy of Social Sciences–University of Turin (SASS–UNITO) Joint Security and Crisis Management Program.

The editors desire to acknowledge the intellectual contribution of all the workshop discussants and the support given during the editing of the volume by all the chapters' authors and the understanding editor Mr. Jacob Dreyer. The workshop and the volume are fortunate to benefit from the insights and extensive experience of Dr. Cindy Smith, director of the United Nations Interregional Crime and Justice Research Institute (UNICRI).

Deepest thanks go to all the supportive staff from RSIS, the Communications Department at SASS and the Chinese Studies Department and International Relations Office at UNITO.

Last but not least, the editors would like to express their gratitude to Professor Gianmaria Ajani, Rector of UNITO; Professor Li Yihai, Secretary General of the Think Tank Foundation at SASS; and Professor Li Mingjiang, Director of the China Programme at the Institute of Defence and Strategic Studies (IDSS) at RSIS for their continuous support and strategic vision.

Contents

List of Contributors

Alessia A. Amighini is Co-Head of the Asia Research Programme and Senior Associate Research Fellow at Istituto Per Gli Studi Di Politica Internazionale (ISPI) in Italy. She is also Associate Professor of Economic Policy at the University of Piemonte Orientale and Catholic University of Milan, and a Senior Fellow at SDA Bocconi China Lab. Professor Amighini was previously Associate Economist at the United Nations Conference on Trade and Development (UNCTAD). She holds a PhD in Development Economics at the University of Florence, a Master in Economics and a BA in Economics from Bocconi University. She is editor and author, with Alex Berkofsky, of *Xi's Policy Gambles: The Bumpy Road Ahead* (2015), *China Dream: Still Coming True?* (2016) and *Belt and Road: A Game Changer?* (2017), all for ISPI. She is also author of more than 60 scientific articles in top international peer-reviewed journals including *China Economic Review*, *World Development*, *The World Economy*, *International Economics*, *China and the World Economy*, *European Journal of Comparative Economics*, *Regional Studies*, *Seoul Journal of Economics*, *Frontiers of Economics in China* and chapters in books by Edward Elgar, Harvard University Press, Oxford University Press, Palgrave and Routledge.

Professor Amighini is the scientific coordinator of research projects on EU-China economic and trade relations for the European Parliament, Italian Ministry of Foreign Affairs and International Cooperation and Italy-China Business Forum. She is a senior expert for the Council on Global Problem-Solving (Kiel), the International Centre for Trade and Sustainable Development (Geneva) and the Italy–China Foundation.

Alessandro Arduino is the co-director of the Security & Crisis Management program at the Shanghai Academy of Social Sciences (SASS-UNITO) and external affiliate at the Lau China Institute, King's College London. Dr. Arduino's two decades of experience in China encompass security analysis and crisis management. His main research interests include China's political economy, Sino-Central Asia relations, Sovereign Wealth Funds, Private Military Security Corporations and China's energy security and foreign policy. He is the author of several books and has published papers and commentaries in various journals in Italian, English and Chinese. His most recent book is China's Private Army. Protecting the New Silk Road (2017). He was appointed Knight of the Order of the Italian Star by the president of the Italian Republic.

Sebastian Booth is a PhD Candidate at the University of York. His current research focuses on the post-crisis regulation of the UK private security industry.

Kerry Brown is Professor of Chinese Studies and Director of the Lau China Institute at King's College, London. From 2012 to 2015, he was Professor of Chinese Politics and Director of the China Studies Centre at the University of Sydney, Australia. Prior to this, he worked at Chatham House from 2006 to 2012 as Senior Fellow and then Head of the Asia Programme. From 1998 to 2005, he worked at the British Foreign and Commonwealth Office, as First Secretary at the British Embassy in Beijing, and then as Head of the Indonesia, Philippine and East Timor Section. He lived in the Inner Mongolia region of China from 1994 to 1996. He has a Master of Arts from Cambridge University, a postgraduate diploma in Mandarin Chinese (Distinction) from Thames Valley University, London and a PhD in Chinese politics and language from Leeds University. Professor Brown directed the Europe China Research and Advice Network (ECRAN), giving policy advice to the European External Action Service between 2011 and 2014. He is the author of more than ten books on modern Chinese politics, history and language, the most recent of which are *The New Emperors: Power and the Princelings in China* (2014), *What's Wrong with Diplomacy: The Case of the UK and China* (2015) and the *Berkshire Dictionary of Chinese Biography* (in four volumes; 2014–2015). His *CEO China: The Rise of Xi Jinping* was published in 2016 and was an *Economist* book of the year. *China's World* will be published in late 2017.

James M. Dorsey is a Senior Fellow at the S. Rajaratnam School of International Studies and co-director of the University of Würzburg's Institute for Fan Culture. An award-winning journalist and political analyst, Dr. Dorsey is the author of the acclaimed *The Turbulent World of Middle East Soccer* blog as well as a syndicated column and several books.

Xue Gong is a Research Fellow with the China Programme at S. Rajaratnam School of International Studies (RSIS), Nanyang Technological University (NTU) of Singapore. She received her PhD from NTU in 2017. Her main research interests include China's economic diplomacy, the Belt and Road Initiative, China's economic relations with Southeast Asia, China's state-owned-enterprises (SOEs) reforms and corporate social responsibility. She has contributed to one peer-reviewed journal article in *Harvard Asia Quarterly* and one book chapter to *China's Economic Statecraft: Co-optation, Cooperation, and Coercion* (2017). She has also contributed to other op-ed articles.

Khuram Iqbal is a distinguished authority on terrorism in Pakistan and author of *The Making of Pakistani Human Bombs* and co-author of *Pakistan Terrorism Ground Zero* and *Negotiating the Siege of Red Mosque*. After receiving a doctorate degree in Policing, Intelligence and Counter-Terrorism from Macquarie University (Australia) he joined the National Defence University of Pakistan as an Assistant Professor of Counter-Terrorism and created Pakistan's first university-based centre of excellence on counter-extremism. Previously, he served as Research Coordinator at Pak Institute for Peace Studies (Islamabad), where he planned and executed a number of research projects on radicalization and terrorism in Pakistan. A graduate in Strategic Studies from the S. Rajaratnam School of International Studies (RSIS), Singapore, Dr. Iqbal has also worked as Senior Analyst at the International Centre for Political Violence and Terrorism Research (ICPVTR), Singapore. He is a member of the Council for Asian Transnational Threats Research (CATR), an international body of leading Asian experts on counter-terrorism and transnational crimes.

Alica Kizeková is a Senior Researcher at the Institute of International Relations Prague, the Czech Republic. She lectures at Mendel University in Brno, the Czech Republic. She holds an Honorary Adjunct Research Fellowship at the Center for East-West Cultural & Economic Studies at Bond University, Queensland, Australia. Previously she worked as Adviser to the Speaker of the Chamber of Deputies at the Parliament of the Czech Republic, Head of Department of Asian Studies at Metropolitan University

Prague, a Teaching Fellow at Bond University and she was a National contact point for the Slovak Republic in the European Union communitary program—IDABC (Interoperable Delivery of European eGovernment Services to Public Administrations, Businesses and Citizens). Her research interests include Shanghai Cooperation Organization, Russian and Chinese regional politics, regionalism and great power relations in Greater Central Asia and the Asia Pacific, Track One-and-a-Half and Track Two Diplomacy, security and soft balancing.

Tuan Yuen Kong received his PhD in Industrial Economics from the National Central University, Taiwan. He had taken part in Taiwan's economic research projects during his postdoctoral fellowship at the Research Centre for Taiwan Economic Development, and joined Epson in turn, a Japanese multinational enterprise in Malaysia, to conduct business management and financial analysis. During his service with Epson, he was sent to Japan to investigate on Toyota's production system and manufacturing automation. His current research interests include China's industry development, especially strategic emerging industries, and China-ASEAN relations. He has published his works in *Review of Global Politics*, *Applied Econometrics and International Development*, *Journal of Overseas Chinese and Southeast Asian Studies* and *Energy Sources.* He also frequently contributes commentaries to Singapore's Lianhe Zaobao and MediaCorps's Capital 95.8FM radio station.

Guanie Lim is a Postdoctoral Fellow at Singapore's Nanyang Centre for Public Administration, Nanyang Technological University. He received his PhD in Geography from the National University of Singapore in 2016. His research interests include value chain analysis, transnational corporations in Southeast Asia and the political economy of China's engagement with Southeast Asia.

Cindy J. Smith became Director of the United Nations Interregional Crime and Justice Research Institute (UNICRI) in 2015. At the time of her appointment, she was Senior Coordinator for International Programs in the Office to Monitor and Combat Trafficking in Persons at the US Department of State. Prior to this, she served as a Lead Foreign Affairs Officer (Criminal Justice Programs) in the Bureau of International Narcotics and Law Enforcement Affairs and as Assistant Director of Corrections for the Civilian Response Corps. From 2006 to 2008, she was Chief of the International Center of the National Institute of Justice in the US Department of Justice, and was the department's representative to the United Nations Crime Prevention and Criminal Justice Programme Network of the

Commission on Crime Prevention and Criminal Justice. In this same period, she was research consultant to the UN Office on Drugs and Crime for the country assessment of human trafficking in Lebanon. She served as an expert in the development of the UN Rules for the Treatment of Women Prisoners and Non-custodial Measures for Women Offenders (the Bangkok Rules). From 2005 to 2006, Dr. Smith was a Fulbright Senior Researcher in Turkey, conducting research and training at the National Police Academy. In the early 1990s, she was involved for five years in a juvenile detention and commitment facility. Dr. Smith was Associate Professor in Criminology and Criminal Justice at the University of Baltimore and the University of Illinois-Springfield. She was Director of the Masters in the Criminal Justice Program in Baltimore. Throughout her career, she conducted extensive research on policing, courts and corrections, adult and juvenile drug treatment, human trafficking, terrorism, juvenile sex offenders, gender issues and strategic planning and program development. She holds a Doctorate of Philosophy in Social Ecology from the University of California Irvine, a Master's of Science in Education Administration from the National University, Irvine and a Master's of Science in Justice from the American University in Washington, DC.

Pinjie Sun is a lecturer at Shanghai University of Political Science and Law, School of International Relations and Public Administration. After receiving his PhD from the Department of Sociology at Shanghai University, he has been working on the issue of social identity. His area of study particularly focuses on the identity formations among ethnic groups in China. He intends to draw on the geographical, cultural and political implications of these groups and study their impact on extremism. In terms of international relations, his study focuses on international security cooperation in cyberspace. He has a strong interest in studying the mechanisms of cooperation and trust building across countries in terms of fighting against cyberterrorism and associated problems in the "real" world.

Zhimin Tang received his PhD from Cambridge University, UK. He is currently Dean of International College and Director of China ASEAN Studies in Panyapiwat Institute of Management, Thailand. The academic and professional career of Professor Dr. Tang in the past 20 years spanned across Europe, Australia, South East Asia, India and Great China. His recent research interests include market entry strategy in China and ASEAN Economic Community, Chinese Overseas Direct Investment and Multinational Corporations in Thailand, and internationalization of Renminbi.

Farkhod Tolipov graduated from Tashkent State University. From 1994 to 2005, he taught at the University of World Economy and Diplomacy in Tashkent, from which he received a PhD in Political Science. From 1998 to 2002, he was a chief consultant for the Presidential Apparatus of Uzbekistan. From 2005 to 2010, Dr. Tolipov taught at the National University of Uzbekistan. His courses included World Politics, and International Security. Currently, he is a director of the non-governmental research institution Bilim Karvoni (Caravan of Knowledge) in Tashkent. Dr. Tolipov specializes in geopolitics, regional security and regional integration in Central Asia, nationalism and democratization in Central Asian countries. In 2003–2004 Dr. Tolipov was a National Professional at the OSCE Center in Tashkent. He was a Fellow at the NATO Defense College (Rome) in 1997 and 2013; a Fellow at Harvard University (USA) in 1999; a Visiting Professor at the University of Georgia (USA) in 2004; a Visiting Professor at the Middle East Technical University in 2015 (Ankara, Turkey); Visiting Researcher at the Atilim University in 2016 (Ankara, Turkey); a lecturer at the George Marshall European Center for Security Studies (2004, 2005), and Geneva Center for Security Policy (2008, 2009, 2010, 2011); and a lecturer at the OSCE Academy in Bishkek (2004, 2009, 2012). Dr. Tolipov extensively publishes his articles on Central Asian topics in several international scientific journals. He is an author of the monograph "Grand Strategy of Uzbekistan in the Context of Geopolitical and ideological Transformation of Central Asia." Dr. Tolipov is a member of the international editorial board of the journal *Central Asia and Caucasus*. He is also a member of the senior advisors board of the China-Eurasia Forum and Central Eurasian Studies Society. Dr. Tolipov is also a member of the expert group of the journal *Security Index* of the PIR-Center (Russia). He speaks English, Russian, French, Turkish and Uzbek (native) languages.

Sarah Y Tong is Senior Research Fellow at the East Asian Institute. She obtained her PhD in Economics from the University of California at San Diego and held an academic position at the University of Hong Kong before joining National University of Singapore (NUS). Her research interests include international trade, foreign direct investment, economic reforms and industrial restructuring. Her publications have appeared in journals such as *China: An International Journal*, *China and the World Economy*, *China Economic Review*, *Global Economic Review*, *Journal of International Economics* and *Review of Development Economics*. In addition to contributing more than dozens of book chapters, Dr. Tong co-edited several book volumes including *China's Great Urbanization* (2017), *China's Evolving Industrial Policy* (2014) and *China's Economy in Transformation under the New Normal* (2017). She served as editor for *Globalization, Development, and Security in Asia*, Vol. 2 of *Trade, Investment and Economic Integration*.

HaoMing Zhou leads Asia Construction Practice and Project Risk Management for Brit, a market-leading global specialty (re)insurer. Dr. Zhou began his career as an engineer in China in 1982 and holds a PhD in Civil Engineering from Delft University of Technology of the Netherlands. He has taken senior underwriting management roles with some world leading (re)insurers including RSA, Swiss Reinsurance Company. He was CEO of Aon in China, a global leading risk management company. He has worked in (re)insurance markets in Singapore, Sydney, Hong Kong and China, and his geographic coverage includes Asia, Pacific and Middle East and Asia Interest Worldwide. He was Chartered Insurer of Chartered Insurance Institute in the United Kingdom. The combination of his technical knowledge and experience and his international perspective has made him an expert for project insurance and project risk management under the Belt and Road Initiative.

List of Figures

List of Tables

PART I

Introduction

CHAPTER 1

Introduction

Alessandro Arduino and Xue Gong

The Belt and Road Initiative (BRI), formerly known as One Belt, One Road, is a signature foreign policy priority of Chinese President Xi Jinping. BRI consists of two aspects: the Silk Road Economic Belt, a land route starting in western China that goes through Central Asia and on to the Middle East (SREB) ending in the European Union; and the 21st Century Maritime Silk Road, a maritime route that connects Southeast Asia, the Persian Gulf and the Horn of Africa (MSR) also ending in the EU. It outlines five major goals of the BRI: policy coordination, facilities connectivity, unimpeded trade, financial integration and people-to-people bonding. All in all, it includes more than two thirds of world population and more than one third of global economic output, and could involve Chinese investments that total up to $4 trillion.[1]

On 14–15 May 2017, China held a grand forum to burnish its international leadership credentials under the well-known but little-understood BRI. The Forum has provided Chinese leader Xi Jinping a stage to demonstrate China's role in connecting with the world, while much of the

A. Arduino (✉)
Security & Crisis Management Program, Shanghai Academy of Social Sciences (SASS-UNITO), Shanghai, China

X. Gong
S. Rajaratnam School of International Studies (RSIS), Nanyang Technological University, Singapore, Singapore

A. Arduino, X. Gong (eds.), *Securing the Belt and Road Initiative*,
https://doi.org/10.1007/978-981-10-7116-4_1

West is looking inward, especially with United States President Donald Trump withdrawing from the Trans-Pacific Partnership and announcing his 'America First' posture to the rest of the world, and the European Union progressively reducing international reach. The Forum also reaffirmed China's and the participating countries' commitment to an open economy, inclusive trade and opposition to all forms of protectionism. One lasting implication of the Forum would be the economic power and influence accruing to China when the BRI's objectives are fully realized. The Forum has clearly shown that the BRI, which had begun under Xi's predecessors' 'March Westward' (Wang) development of the Xinjiang Uyghur Autonomous region, can serve as an integrative platform for global connectivity (Gong 2017b).

In general, BRI is designed to meet Chinese objectives both at home and abroad. Domestically, Chinese leadership hope BRI will help ease industry overcapacity and spur growth in its underdeveloped border regions, especially the West. As the labour costs of China rise, BRI is expected to move its labour-intensive and low value-added manufacturing facilities overseas. Nevertheless, the promise of increasing efficiency and interconnectivity with low-volume, high-value good shipments by the BRI railway connections, from the Chinese western cities of Xi'an and Chongqing to the European dry ports of Duisburg and Lodz, still have to be fulfilled. Further promises of sustainable development and cooperation in infrastructure building are facing reality checks.

BRI is also one of the economic diplomatic tools through which China can wield its economic power to advance diplomatic and strategic objectives (Li 2015; Blanchard and Flint 2017; Blanchard 2017). Such considerations fan existing fears in the region that BRI will help China accrue influence and leverage on these countries. In this logic, China is expected to exploit economic power for political objectives at the cost of autonomy of other countries. For countries that are suspicious of China's BRI, such as India, Japan and the United States, BRI is considered as a threat to their regional interests (Palit 2017). Although China has intended to downplay the strategic dimensions of this initiative, many scholars, including Chinese scholars suggest that the plan is indeed a response to the US strategic rebalance to Asia. It is a reflection on the 'Look Westward' proposal made by some foreign policy elites in China a few years ago (Li 2015).

The Chinese leadership have paid close attention to how the initiative itself is marketed and perceived in the region and have adjusted their approach accordingly. In the Forum, Xi reiterated that 'BRI would not repeat the old geopolitical competition game but open the new approach for win-win cooperation'.[2] However, implementing BRI will not be easy and the geopolitical challenges will be the biggest hurdle in the region. For example, along the SREB route, Central Asia as a regional grouping in political and security terms remains widely divided with serious internal conflicts caused by unresolved boundary, water and energy disputes, regional rivalry, deep mistrust and differences in political, diplomatic and security policies (Zhang 2015). In MSR, China finds it more difficult to implement projects as geopolitical concern is more serious, particularly reactions of Southeast Asian countries towards China on the disputed South China Sea.

For most countries participating in BRI, they are motivated more by a practical recognition of its relevance for advancing their own economic and development goals. It is especially so in promoting foreign investment or improving infrastructure in their own country. Following the financial and economic crisis that has forced the European Union and the United States to look more inward, China is among only a few countries that are able to provide financing without many requirements.

Security Challenges

Despite China's aspirations to provide an open economy and trade system, there are numerous challenges ahead. While the Chinese State-Owned Enterprises (SOEs) are expanding their international reach capabilities, they still do not have the capacity to assure adequate security along the Belt and Road. As countries along the route are either unstable or fraught with ethnic and religious tensions, and there is a lack of legal protection for investors to uncertainties regarding local regulations, Chinese infrastructure and personnel could be subject to political risks and criminal violence. While the threat related to the use of violence is not common over all the BRI, several other crises may arise, such as social confrontation, environmental degradation and an overall lack of corporate social responsibilities. The rise of new models of risk assessments, prevention and mitigation, Corporate Social Responsibility (CSR), private security corporations and big data analysis provide a wide range of capabilities that can benefit the overall BRI's security.

Risks Challenges

Economic returns and control of risks are generally two aspects of outbound investment activities. The security environment is evolving globally and more attention is given for other than military threats. They are a major concern related to internal and external security of any country as such risks are evolving across national borders.

Since China launched the Going Out investment policy, its FDI has spread all over the world. In terms of infrastructure and energy investments, the Chinese outbound economic footprint largely concentrates on the developing countries such as the African ones. As a latecomer, China usually invests in countries with religious tensions and militant groups where Western companies are absent. Therefore, insurgents, rebels and militants are already targeting the massive Chinese infrastructure investments altogether with the influx of Chinese personnel. The concept of 'One Belt, One Road' is vulnerable for attacks along the land and sea. Therefore, non-traditional security threats are posed to curb the progress of regional economies and social development (Arduino 2015).

Many countries along the BRI are facing security threats from extremism and terrorism, such as the self-proclaimed Islamic State. China has remained very cautious of getting involved in the complexities of politics and conflict of other countries. But as Chinese citizens and properties are threatened, the Chinese leadership realizes the necessity of increasing its capability of protecting overseas investments and personnel. The Xinjiang Uyghur Autonomous Region as the link of Central Asia and the mainland of China is a place vulnerable to Islamic extremists and disruptive forces. Moreover, the China-Pakistan Economic Corridor (CPEC) presents extreme risks as the political environment in Pakistan has proven unstable and terrorist attacks are the norm.

In addition to political risks, some of the projects Chinese companies have been undertaking are exposed to dangers that are based on unsustainable debt or lax social and environmental standards. Such projects are vulnerable to the economic situation and public perceptions. Indeed, a number of BRI projects have already experienced social protest, such as the suspension of the Sri Lankan port of Hambantota.

The BRI has to deal with risks challenges where a shared understanding on security, and the role of China in security is needed. The question is to what extent the outside world will feel comfortable with China's participation in protecting its overseas investments. After all, China's role in security challenges is largely dependent on how other countries view China's intention and the purposes of the BRI.

Corporate Social Responsibilities Challenges

China's efforts in cultivating close economic ties with developing countries, particularly its neighbouring countries, have been a key element in its regional strategy. The Chinese government has launched strong supporting policies in encouraging Chinese companies to make overseas investments, from 'Going Out' to 'BRI'. China has wielded its economic clout via a sovereign wealth fund, state-owned investment banks and huge amounts of foreign reserves to seek investments in energy, technology, finance and infrastructure in both developed and developing economies.

However, China's growing presence in the international investment markets has resulted in mixed responses. On the one hand, Chinese investment brings benefits to the host country as a new source of investment while capitals from traditional developed countries dry up. On the other hand, Chinese overseas business activities faced a number of governance problems that resulted in resistance in host countries: claims of neo-colonial motives in the developing world; irresponsible operations in the investment destination; defiance against labour rights and so on. China's perceived poor records in the environment and corporate governance have triggered further concerns. The appeal of China's state-led business model to the developing countries is believed in the West to undermine international attempts to promote governance and transparency. At the same time, other countries may find the 'Capitalism with Chinese characteristics' a viable model after the 2008 financial meltdown.

China's economic statecraft is also inconsistent. Despite its declaration of becoming a responsible global player, it continues to collaborate with 'pariah' states in pursuit of its own economic interests. Such contradictory behaviour undermines its foreign policy goal of becoming a more responsible power (Canning 2007). This has led some to question China's capacity for corporate governance and its intention of becoming a responsible player in promoting sustainable development. Several valuable deals have gone awry, resulting in huge loss of profits, criticism and resistance from many target countries in Africa, Europe, Latin America and Southeast Asia for various reasons (Gong 2017a).

Stated in the Forum, China has been putting efforts to stress the open, inclusive and collaborative nature of the BRI. It also intends to address questions regarding standards and transparency, which have been under criticism for decades. China has made incremental progress in accordance with international norms on environmental and social impact assessment for financing. The birth of the Asian Infrastructure Investment Bank (AIIB) along with other funding sources like the Silk Road Fund and the New Development Bank, which encourage the source of financing from a third party and apply international standard for funding the projects, demonstrates China's determination of improvement. However, it always comes to the question of its capability of implementation and the enforcing degree that Beijing can assert on the SOEs operating abroad.

Although the connectivity goal of 'people-to-people bonding' was emphasized before the Forum, it was less visible in its actual implementation. Owing to the fact that people from several of the BRI countries are generally wary about the negative impact of massive Chinese investments, the Forum also included people-to-people and think-tank exchanges to improve interpersonal interaction along the Belt and Road route. Nonetheless, it remains to be seen how the Chinese companies, managers and workers engage with the local communities where the BRI projects touch. After all, it is not the government but the business actors who will be implementing the Belt and Road projects.

There are different questions about BRI with so many security and governance issues along the routes. Would an initiative like BRI ever enable states to act in a more shared way, despite different interpretation and expectations from BRI? How China can be involved and how it is able to engage other countries in these security and governance issues? Despite different expectations, could BRI ever lead to a better consensus between China and others on security issues? This is an important question, especially because the security trust between China and other countries is lacking, for example, in the South China Sea. At the moment, despite the common threats that many BRI participants' nations face, there seems to lack signs of cooperation in the security area.

To address these questions, it needs shared understanding of what security and governance involve and what they aim to achieve. As security, economics and governance are inextricable, this book aims to provide a holistic perspective on China's BRI. This book consists of three sections that analyze the BRI challenges moving from China to the European Union across the land and sea new silk roads.

Sebastian Booth and **Cindy J. Smith** provide an overview of legislative and regulatory frameworks in ASEAN member states. It is underpinned by the assertion that the Belt and Road Initiative will increasingly rely on domestic private security services, whose quality and effectiveness are improved by the existence of statutory frameworks. It has demonstrated that these frameworks amount to an uneven patchwork of regulatory requirements and restrictions across the region. While it appears that private security is receiving increasing media and governmental attention, significant limitations and problems still exist. Authors of this chapter explain regulatory loopholes across Southeast Asia, which raises concerns of the safety of Belt and Road projects that cross jurisdictions. They further suggest greater economic and political integration require the harmonization of regulatory frameworks and strengthening of institutional capacities across the regions.

Alessandro Arduino argues that Chinese corporations just started to acknowledge that the risks associated with outbound foreign direct investments carries a higher failure rate due to intertwined factors such as: economic crises, conflict, civil unrest, assets nationalisation and currency devaluation, just to name a few. In several cases, the Chinese SOE's infrastructural projects macro size and breakneck implementation speed catalyze crisis in already unstable socio-political environments. The solution to political and criminal violence's spillovers along the BRI requests a broader involvement that also encompasses the Chinese insurance and private security sectors.

Along the Maritime Silk Road, **Sarah Y Tong** and **Kong Tuan Yuen** discuss how Singapore could have an indispensable role in the development of BRI, especially in MSR. Singapore could facilitate the closer China-ASEAN economic ties by advocating free trade, widening and deepening regional economic integration. It could also collaborate with partner countries in developing various types of joint projects, given Singapore's experience and competitive advantage in fields of finance, logistics and business management, as well as help strengthen mutual understanding and trust by providing dialogue platforms. However, Singapore also needs to be mindful of the complexities in the region's geopolitical dynamics. For example, given the sensitive nature of the South China Sea issue, Singapore has to try its best to preserve its neutrality and to safeguard ASEAN unity and centrality. Meanwhile, Singapore is also facing growing challenges. On one hand, global trade is decelerating, casting a significant negative shock to Asian countries, especially those that depend heavily on trade. Meanwhile, China is catching up fast in high added-value manufacturing, putting great competitive pressure on more advanced Asian countries and on bilateral economic cooperation. Moreover, Singapore and China may also run into direct competition in third countries as China enhances investment efforts in BRI.

Guanie Lim focuses on the East Coast Rail Link (ECRL), one of China's most prominent construction projects in Malaysia since the inception of the BRI. His chapter offers a balanced perspective on the ECRL by presenting its pros and cons as well as analyzing on-the-ground implementation issues. Despite its promise to alleviate the proverbial 'Malacca Dilemma' and to generate a win-win outcome for both Malaysia and China, the ECRL is hampered by several critical implementation issues, heightening its business and political risks, especially for the Malaysians. There remain significant hurdles to surmount before this undertaking transforms into the 'game changer' that resolves China's over-reliance on the narrow Strait of Malacca and uplifts the living standards of the Malaysians.

Also along the Maritime Silk Road, **Kerry Brown** considers the interaction among China, ASEAN and the United States, and how the issue of regional trust affects Beijing's core strategic interests. The New Silk Road maritime version opened up fresh areas of economic and strategic space around China. It spelled out clearly to the country's maritime neighbours the opportunities and benefits of engaging more with Chinese investment, Chinese trade and Chinese growth just as the land Silk Road had done for the Central Asian partners. In this complex political and diplomatic context, the regional response to BRI has been a mixture of applause and excitement alongside caution.

In the section of Corporate Social Responsibilities (CSR), **Xue Gong** argues that as a centralized state, China is believed to have a strong political and bureaucratic power over CSR implementation, particularly over the SOEs that received enormous national support for overseas investment. However, in recent years, Chinese overseas investments have encountered local resistance and criticism for their non-compliance of local laws and poor implementation of CSR, prominently in Myanmar. This chapter aims to contribute to the understanding of China's political economy in Myanmar's hydropower sector by assessing an often-neglected segment, which regards the evolving roles of the business actors and the externalities of business activities on the state-to-state relations. China's initiative of One Belt, One Road makes the study of Chinese CSR meaningful as it also aims to identify common problems facing Chinese investments and CSR infrastructure development levels of individual host countries. **Tang Zhimin** concludes the CSR section analyzing the effects of Chinese corporate social responsibilities in Thailand. The focus is on why and how CSR can be a tool to mitigate risks for Chinese firms involved in the BRI. CSR is relevant to the BRI risk because the mismanagement of a Chinese firm's responsibility towards environment and society of the Belt and Road countries may directly or indirectly evoke threats to the firm in local political, economic, social and technological systems through its interactions with its stakeholders and local governments. Therefore, CSR programs may give a Chinese firm the local community's acceptance or approval of a company's project or ongoing presence in an area.

From the insurance standpoint, **HaoMing Zhou** underlines the specific importance of the sector in addressing the BRI's challenges. The emphasis on projects construction draws the attention over the Chinese economic international expansion, project contracting and direct investment's requirement for sophisticated risk management tools. The BRI's risk landscape includes countries that are still in the political, social and economic transition phase. The uncertainty in security, inadequate political governance and development direction is commonly prevailing and many multinational risk professionals are reasonably well equipped with knowledge and skills to support Beijing.

Over the Central Asian land mass, **Farkhod Tolipov** argues that the effect of the BRI in Central Asia has economic, transport, geopolitical, cultural, historical and security dimensions and encompasses such vast swaths of Eurasian continent and oceans that it created an impression of global ambitions of China. Central Asia—the epicentre of the ancient Great Silk Road—is once again acquiring a higher profile in the Eurasian and world order, and the five Central Asian countries are facing Chinese 'authoritative and persuasive' presence in the region.

The security of the BRI flagship project in Pakistan, the China–Pakistan Economic Corridor (CPEC) is discussed by **Khuram Iqbal** and **Pinjie Sun** analyzing respectively the CPEC geostrategic implications and the terrorist threat landscape from Xinjiang to Gwadar. Iqbal argues that CPEC is one of the key pillars of the BRI. The peculiar attribute of CEPC is its intersection between over sea 21st Century Maritime Silk Route (MSR) and land-based Economic Silk Road Belt. Its total length is approximately 3000 km spanning from Pakistan's Gwadar port to Kashgar, northwestern China's Xinjiang Uygur Autonomous Region. The macro projects consist of the railway lines, roads, fibre optics, energy pipelines and industrial development zones. Albeit the promises of sustainable development, since the announcement of the CPEC and its ratification the route designated under the Corridor triggered much debate and controversy. The major contentions regard the distribution of economic development and infrastructure projects of this mega venture within the provinces. Besides violent extremism and terrorism, ethno nationalist groups are another daunting challenge for the economic corridor. Also, Sun argues that Southeast Asia constitutes an important transshipment hub for illegal Uyghur migration, some of whom joined local and transnational jihadist extremism. Sun looks at the scope and dimensions of illicit Uyghur movement through Southeast Asia, the implications it holds for local terrorism in this part of the world and the overall effects on the BRI.

James Dorsey's chapter on China's investments in the Arab maelstrom discusses the pitfalls and diverging interests in China's daunting task of promoting investments while avoiding getting entangled in local disputes. China's increasingly significant economic and security interests in the Middle East have several impacts. They affect its energy security but also its regional posture, relations with regional powers as well as the United States and efforts to pacify nationalist and Islamist Uighurs in its northwestern region of Xinjiang. Protecting its mushrooming interests is forcing China to realign its policies and relationships in the region.

Being the terminus of both the overland and the maritime routes envisioned, the European Union faces significant geo-political, economic and geo-strategic consequences from the BRI starting with the China-EU bilateral relation.

Alessia Amighini and **Alica Kizekova** argue the BRI's challenges and opportunities in the European Union, with emphasis on the role of logistics, economic integration and the 16+1. Amighini reviews the state of the art in the scholarly and policy debates as well as in the policy actions and activities taken so far by the European Union as a response to the BRI. The literature has extensively analyzed the determinants of individual countries' access to international markets and bilateral trade flows, and has found support for the hypothesis that trade and infrastructure costs are important, but not the choice of transport modes, let alone the efficiency of the global network of trade routes. While the Chinese way to regional integration tends to be less rule-based and more coalition-based along country-specific interests, the BRI is facing Europe's multilateralism against closed and competing initiatives towards regionalism. Kizekova examines China's activities in Central and Eastern European countries with a specific reference to the 16+1 platform. While in Europe this initiative has been looked upon with suspicion, some countries did not hide their enthusiasm for forging closer partnerships with China and embracing the BRI. The Czech Republic is a case in point, however, it still questions the benefits of opening up to China and what the real outcomes of promised investments domestically and in the wider region are. In response to the criticisms, the Chinese leadership has reassured the Europeans that it's acting peacefully under a win-win premise for all parties involved and that the activities within the 16+1 take into consideration the existing projects, such as China-EU cooperation and the EU infrastructure projects.

The threats to Chinese enterprises and Chinese workers based on foreign soil are poised to increase and there is an urgent need to develop new guidelines for risk assessment, special insurance and crisis management. To face threats, an international cooperation of involved countries must create opportunities to counter all illegal acts. As pointed out by Xi Jinping in the Forum, China is expected to further internationalize the Chinese currency and improve financing channels. China will also turn to syndicated loans coming from international pension funds, insurance companies, sovereign wealth funds, private equity funds and others. Creating the vision for global connectivity requires evidence of concrete accomplishments as people interpret achievements in different ways. Xi's signature economic diplomacy for the BRI has officially taken off. What remains to be done is for China to overcome the hard reality of operational inefficiencies.

Notes

1. Dashuju Kanredian, Yidaiyilu, Gongtong Fanrong Xinyinqin (Looking at Hotspot through Big Data, Belt and Road, New Engine for Mutual Prosperity and Development), People's Daily, March 11, 2015, https://www.yidaiyilu.gov.cn/jcsj/dsjkydyl/1813.htm.
2. Xi Jinping Zai Yidaiyilu Guoji Hezuo Gaofeng Luntan Kaimushi Shang de Yanjiang (Speech by Xi Jinping in Belt and Road Forum For International Cooperation), May 14 2017, http://www.beltandroadforum.org/n100/2017/0514/c24-407.html.

References

Arduino, Alessandro. Belt and Road Initiative – China's Energy Security: Reality Roadblock in Ethiopia. Commentary, Singapore: Rajaratnam School of International Studies, 2015.

Blanchard, Jean-Marc F. "Probing China's Twenty-First-Century Maritime Silk Road Initiative (MSRI): An Examination of MSRI Narratives." Geopolitics 22, no. 2 (2017): 246–268.

Blanchard, Jean-Marc F., and Colin Flint . "The Geopolitics of China's Maritime Silk Road Initiative". Geopolitics 22, no. 2 (2017): 223–245.

Canning, C. Pursuit of the Pariah: Iran, Sudan and Myanmar in China's Energy Security Strategy. Security Challenges. Security Challenges 4, no. 1 (February 2007).

Gong, Xue. A Tale of Two States: Explaining Corporate Social Responsibility Weaknesses of Chinese Investments in Southeast Asia. PhD thesis, Rajaratnam School of International Studies, Singapore: Nanyang Technological University, 2017a.

Gong, Xue. Belt and Road Initiative – China's Belt and Road Forum: What Now? Commentary, Singapore: Rajaratnam School of International Studies, May 2017b.

Li, Mingjiang. China's "One Belt, One Road" Initiative: New Round of Opening Up? Commetary, Rajaratnam School of International Studies, RSIS, 11 March 2015.

Palit, Amitendu. "India's Economic and Strategic Perceptions of China's Maritime Silk Road Initiative". 22, no. 2 (2017): 292–309.

Wang Jisi. "'Xijin': Zhongguo Diyuan Zhanlue de Zai Pingheng ('Look West': ... Wang Jisi)", Huanqiu Shibao (Global Times, Beijing), 26 October 2012.

Zhang, Hongzhou. Building the Silk Road Economic Belt, Problems and Priorites in Central Asia. Policy Report, Singapore: Rajaratnam School of International Studies, May 2015.

PART II

The Belt and Road Security Blueprint

CHAPTER 2

The Uneven Regulation of Private Security in ASEAN Member States

Sebastian Booth and Cindy J. Smith

Introduction

The enormity of the Belt and Road initiative means that its security requirements have the potential to exceed the capacities of both Chinese and partner-state military, security and policing forces (Arduino 2015). Accordingly, the success of the Belt and Road initiative will rely to a large extent on the capabilities of the global private security industry. But whilst these services—ranging from site, property and personal protection to surveillance, cash transportation and associated technologies—can enhance the security of Chinese overseas investments, they also pose significant risks. High levels of competition within the private security industry provides disincentives for companies and individuals to invest in expensive training. This results in low-quality services and poor working conditions, which increase the likelihood of malpractice and risks to both the businesses they protect and the public they face (Button 2008; van Steden and Sarre 2010). Furthermore, those unable to afford private security services are not only excluded from its benefits, but as a consequence face greater

S. Booth (✉)
University of York, York, UK

C. J. Smith
United Nations Interregional Crime and Justice Research Institute, Turin, Italy

A. Arduino, X. Gong (eds.), *Securing the Belt and Road Initiative*,
https://doi.org/10.1007/978-981-10-7116-4_2

insecurity (Bayley and Shearing 1996). Highlighting this dilemma, the United Nations' *Handbook on State Regulation concerning Civilian Private Security Services and their Contribution to Crime Prevention and Community Safety* demonstrates that effective regulatory frameworks allow states, the private sector and communities to benefit from private security services whilst mitigating against the risks they pose to safety (UNODC 2014, p. vii).[1] Yet to date, there has been little systematic research into the operation and governance of private security services in the member states of the Association of Southeast Asian Nations (ASEAN)[2] (on the 'ethnocentrism' of policing research see Manning 2005, p. 32). This stands in stark contrast to two growing research agendas: the first on domestic private security services in other Asian states such as China (Zhong and Grabosky 2009; Arduino 2015), Japan (Yoshida 1999) and South Korea (Button et al. 2006; Nalla and Hwang 2006; Lee 2008; Kim 2015); and the second on private maritime services in the region (Liss 2007; Sciascia 2013).

In light of this, the purpose of this chapter is to provide an overview of domestic private security services operating in ASEAN member states[3] and of existing legal and regulatory frameworks under which they operate. Firstly, this chapter will assess the importance of ASEAN member states within the larger Belt and Road Initiative. We assert that growing overseas investment in the region has and will continue to increase the demand for private security services. Secondly, we provide an overview of the numbers of private security officers and of the corresponding legal and regulatory frameworks in ASEAN member states. Drawing on insights from the security regulation literature, we argue that the unevenness of regulatory frameworks means that overseas investments, companies and communities in some ASEAN member states may be less resilient to the risks posed by private security than in others. Finally, we suggest one potential way forward to create a systematic resolution to the challenges.

ASEAN in the Belt and Road Initiative

The Belt and Road Initiative has been Chinese President Xi Jinping's keynote economic and foreign policy. Evoking the historical imagery of the old Silk Roads, the Belt and Road Initiative seeks to develop and integrate Chinese, Asian and Eurasian economies through infrastructure development, trade liberalisation and economic cooperation along two main axes: the 'Silk Road Economic Belt' and the '21st Century Maritime Road'.

The official blueprint, *Vision and Actions on Jointly Building Silk Road Economic Belt and 21st Century Maritime Silk Road*, indicates that these projects will develop along five 'economic corridors': the New Eurasia Land Bridge Economic Corridor, the China-Mongolia-Russia Economic Corridor, the China-Central Asia-West Asia Economic Corridor, the China-Indochina Peninsula Economic Corridor and the China-Pakistan Economic Corridor (China. State Council 2015). Overall, the planned development spans an area that covers 70 percent of the world's population, 55 percent of global GDP and 75 percent of energy reserves (Lechmacher and Padilla-Taylor 2015). Furthermore, it is estimated that China has invested a total $890 billion in the Belt and Road Initiative (Kynge 2016).

ASEAN member states are set to play a pivotal role in the development of the Belt and Road Initiative. With a combined population of around 620 million and collectively constituting 3.3 percent of the world's GDP, the ASEAN region stands as a lucrative market for Chinese investment, and an established political-economic platform from which to launch the China-Indochina Economic Corridor. The level of proposed Chinese investment in ASEAN is staggering: at the 2014 China-ASEAN Summit, Chinese Premier Li Keqiang announced a $10 billion loan from the China Development Bank for ASEAN regional development and pledged to increase the China-ASEAN Investment Cooperation fund to $4 billion. In June 2016, the Asian Infrastructure Investment Bank granted a loan of $216.5 million, matched by the World Bank, for the National Slum Upgrading Project in Indonesia (AIIB 2016). Moreover, Chinese and ASEAN economies have already begun to undergo a significant degree of integration through the establishment and upgrade of the ASEAN-China Free Trade Area (ACFTA), which has been dubbed as 'one of the world's largest free trade agreements' (UNODC 2016b, p. 10). Significantly, the Belt and Road Initiative overlaps with a wide network of transport, energy and infrastructure developments across the region, including the 'Asian Highway Network', which consists of 141,000 km of roads across thirty-two states (UNODC 2016b, pp. 13–18).

Undoubtedly, growing integration and investment in the region will increase the demand for both public and private security. Chinese overseas investments, sites and workers have been increasingly exposed to political and criminal violence (Arduino 2015, p. 4). Political insurgencies in southern Philippines and Myanmar, political uncertainty in Indonesia and Thailand, as well as inter-state border disputes, raise important questions for the security of overseas investments. In 2011, three private security officers guarding a Japanese-owned nickel mine in southern Philippines were killed by Maoist guerrillas (Financial Times 2011). A further problem is that greater regional integration allows not only for greater mobility for people, goods and money, but enhances flows of drugs, organised crime and trafficking. The illegal trade of people, drugs and wildlife in Southeast Asia is estimated at $100 billion a year. (UNODC 2016b, p. 19).These transnational issues undermine the rule of law within states by contributing to violence, crime and the corruption of government and other law enforcement services (Caballero-Anthony 2005, p. 181). Related, greater economic and political integration raises the importance of developing shared legal and regulatory requirements to prevent loopholes that allow private security companies to act with impunity (Button 2007; Button and Stiernstedt 2016a, b).

Securing the Belt and Road Initiative

The issue of security is absent from the *Visions and Actions on Jointly Building Silk Road Belt and 21st Century Maritime Silk Road.* Until now, Chinese efforts to secure and protect its overseas investments and workers have followed two trends: direct intervention and diplomatic pressure. China's historical commitment to non-interference in the internal affairs of other nations has increasingly been juxtaposed against the need to take a more proactive approach to securing its overseas (mainly commercial) interests. The traditional principle of non-interference has further been contested by public calls for a more proactive and direct approach to the security of its overseas population. On a global scale, China has contributed 8000 soldiers to UN Peacekeeping forces in Africa and has donated $100 million to the African Union. In particular, 700 Chinese soldiers have been deployed to the UN mission in South Sudan, a country where National Petroleum Corp, a Chinese State-Owned Enterprise (SOE) holds 40 percent in a joint venture and sent observers to monitor the independence referendum in 2011. In light of these moves, it seems impossible to disentangle Chinese peacekeeping contributions from interests in oil and mineral extraction. The most obvious iteration of Chinese willingness to directly intervene within other states was in the evacuation of 35,000 Chinese citizens from Libya over an eleven-day period in February and March 2011. These direct interventions have been made under exceptional circumstances in fragile and weak areas, and intervention could prove more problematic in more established states (Swanström 2015, p. 7).

In light of this, the Chinese government has increasingly used diplomatic pressure to ensure the security of their overseas investments and projects. This is exemplified primarily by the issue of protection along the China-Pakistan Economic Corridor, a 3000 km trade route that stems from Kashgar in western China to Gwadar Port on the gulf of Oman. The success of the $46 million project to connect western China to this sea-route is contingent upon the security of projects in the unstable regions of Pakistan-occupied Kashmir and Baluchistan. Gwadar Port and its surrounding military base and energy pipelines routinely come under attack by Baluchistan separatists who accuse the Pakistani government of restricting rights, representation and extracting the regions' resources to develop other parts of Pakistan (Bansal 2008). In 2004, three Chinese engineers were killed in such an attack. The Pakistani government response, apparently driven by Chinese pressure (Bokhari et al. 2016), has been to create a Special Security Division consisting of nine infantry battalions and six civil armed forces increasing the number of security personnel tasked with protecting Chinese investments and workers to 14,000. Included within this new force are 4100 private security guards. Whilst this raises the point that partner states will be responsible for the security of these overseas investments, with the weak policing infrastructure present in most of the ASEAN states (represented by high levels of police corruption and low regard for the rule of law), questions remain as to whether all ASEAN states would be able to follow this example.

Domestic Private Security Services in ASEAN States

The security and success of the Belt and Road Initiative is therefore sure to rest on a range of multilevel, multi-actor security networks. Throughout the world tasks and functions traditionally performed, and to a large extent monopolised,[4] by public police forces are now undertaken by a plurality of actors including private security companies (Johnston and Shearing 2003; Wood and Shearing 2007). Research has demonstrated how private security companies now increasingly operate on a spectrum of public, quasi-public and private spaces, such as airports, shopping centres, gated communities, national infrastructure sites and private businesses (Button 2008; Kempa et al. 2004). Whilst it is important to be mindful of the particular historical, political and cultural contexts in which the private security industry operates (an area that requires further research, see Crawford 2006; White 2010), it would appear that developments in the Southeast Asian policing landscape are mirroring those occurring over the rest of the globe. For example, the responsibility for guarding the national headquarters of the Philippine National Police has recently been contracted out to private security for a fee of 21 million Pesos ($420,000) (Ramos 2014). Multinational private security services also play a significant role in the training of military, police and anti-terrorist units in Cambodia and the Philippines (Singer 2007, p. 13). It is important to note here that Chinese SOEs are increasingly turning to both multinational and Chinese private security companies to secure their overseas assets (Arduino 2015). However, while recognising that the distinction between domestic and international private security contractors are blurred, the use of such companies are usually in the context of weak or failing states in the Middle East and Africa, where there are few or no restrictions on the operation of foreign private security companies. Moreover, there is very little evidence of Chinese private security companies operating in ASEAN member states.

The growth of the private security industry across the region has been remarkable yet uneven. Estimating accurately the numbers of private security officers in ASEAN member states is difficult due to the lack of official statistics, varying definitions of the private security industry (partly due to it being a vast and disparate industry) and the role the industry plays in each country (see Stenning 1989). Furthermore, we recognise that these numbers also represent a snapshot in time and that numbers are constantly fluctuating. With these caveats, Table 2.1 provides an estimate of the number of private security officers as opposed to public police numbers within the ten ASEAN states.[5] Although estimates vary, in some ASEAN member states the private security industry is a significant size. The Philippines has the largest private security force and estimates are between 400,000 and 500,000 (Saha and Rowley 2014, p. 53; Palabrica 2016). Estimates of Thailand vary greatly between 250,000 and 400,000 (Saha and Rowley 2014, p. 52). The wide disparity may be due to recent efforts to legally define and regulate private security services in Thailand. Malaysia is cited as having between 130,000 and 196,000 officers and Indonesia 200,000 (Saha and Rowley 2014, p. 53). The regulated industry in Singapore is estimated to be between 29,000 and 65,000 (Lim and Nalla 2014; Saha and Rowley 2014, p. 54; Sen and Tham 2014). In other states, the private security industry is less established. Reports indicate that there

Table 2.1 Estimates of public police officer and private security officer numbers in ASEAN states

ASEAN member state	*Population*	*Total police*	*Total private security*	*Ratio police to private security*
Brunei	429,000	4,400	3,665	0.83
Cambodia	15,140,000	64,000	30,000	0.47
Indonesia	249,900,000	400,000	200,000	0.5
Laos	6,770,000	No data	No data	–
Malaysia	29,720,000	102,000	196,000	1.9
Myanmar	53,260,000	75,000	No data	–
Philippines	68,390,000	160,000	400,000	2.5
Singapore	5,399,000	40,000	29,000	1.5
Thailand	67,010,000	230,000	250,000	1.09
Vietnam	89,710,000	No data	No data	–

Sources: Interpol (2016)

Notes: Firstly, obtaining accurate data on the number of private security offices is difficult, and where official statistics from state regulatory bodies are unavailable, estimates have been made using news reports and trade association statistics. In the case of Laos, Myanmar and Vietnam there are little data on the size of the public police and private security industry. Secondly in most instances, official estimates usually only refer to the number of licensed individuals or members of trade associations. Thirdly, the definition of public police and private security officers differs from country to country (see Button 2007, p. 111). Thus, these figures should be used as illustrations of the various sizes of public police and the private security industry in each nation

are 3665 licenced private security officers in Brunei (Kamit 2014) and 30,000 in Cambodia (Sen 2014). It is difficult to make an accurate estimate of the number of private security companies and officers in Laos. A 2014 UNICEF Report indicated that seven private security companies operated in the country (UNICEF 2014, p. 16). No data were available for Vietnam and Myanmar.

Legal and Regulatory Frameworks in ASEAN States

The growth and the importance of the private security industry, the growing recognition of the extra-legal powers private security officers hold over citizens, scandals over misconduct[6] and poor standards have driven states to create industry-specific legal and regulatory frameworks (Prenzler and Sarre 2008, p. 265). The purpose of this section is to provide an overview of the patchwork of statutory licensing and training requirements across the ASEAN region. There are no specific legislative, regulatory, voluntary or established positions on private security at the ASEAN regional level. Although private security companies are also subject to general criminal law, civil law, market forces and self-regulation through industry membership, we support the view that these need to be underpinned by specific regulatory frameworks. Furthermore, effective regulatory provisions that sufficiently 'cleanse' the industry—that is, place restrictions on who are able to sell security services—seem to be the first step towards more participatory and deliberative regulatory models (Button and Stiernstedt 2016b, see also Loader and White 2015). It is to the core elements of these frameworks that we now turn.

Responsible Regulatory Authorities

Regulation has been judged to be more efficient and effective in systems where regulatory authority is vested in a single body or organisation as disputes over interpretations and applications of frameworks are minimised (Button and George 2006; Prenzler and Sarre 2008). In most of the ASEAN member states the responsibility for the administration, monitoring and enforcement of regulations and licensing lies with state police forces (as part of Home Ministries; see Table 2.2). In the Philippines, the role of the Security Agencies Guards Supervision Division is 'to provide administrative services and general supervision over the management and operation of all organized private security agencies, private detective agencies and company and guard units throughout the country' (SAGSD 2016, p. 167). According to government sources, Cambodia has recently created a specialised Department of Private Security Management, accountable to the National Police Commissariat General and the Ministry of Interior, which is tasked to address the growing issue of private security in the country (Soleil 2016). Conversely, in April 2012, the Security Industry Regulatory Department and Licensing Division for the Operations Department merged to create a specific Police Licensing and Regulatory Department responsible for regulating: public entertainment, liquor massage establishments, secondhand goods dealers, private lotteries, house-to-house and street collection, arms and explosives and private security in Singapore (Singapore Police n.d.). In other countries, regulatory authority is divided. The Vietnamese Decree Number 52 on the Management of Security Service Businesses outlines the responsibilities of the various tiers of government: whereas the Ministry of Public Security directs police officers to inspect and enforce regulations, the administration of licensing systems are delegated to

Table 2.2 Specific private security legislation, regulation and authorities

ASEAN member state	*Year of entry into ASEAN*	*Specific legislation*	*Year*	*Specific regulatory authority*
Brunei	1997	Security Agencies Act Security Agencies Regulations	2000 2000	Brunei Royal Police Force
Cambodia	1999	Sub-Decree No.289	2013 2016	Ministry of Interior/ General Commissariat of National Police Department of Private Security Management
Indonesia	1967	Regulation of the Head of Police No. 17,18 Regulation of the Head of Police No.24	2006 2007	Indonesia National Police
Laos	1997	None	–	None
Malaysia	1967	Private Agencies Act (Amended)	1971 2006	Ministry for Home Affairs/Royal Malaysian Police
Myanmar	1997	None	–	None
Philippines	1967	Private Security Agency Act No.5487 Presidential Decree No.11 Implementation Order	1969 1972 2005	Philippines Constabulary
Singapore	1967	Private Security Industry Act Private Security Industry Regulations	2007 2009	Singapore Police
Thailand	1967	Security Industry Business Act	2015	Royal Thai Police
Vietnam	1995	Decree on Management of Security Service Business No.52 (Amended)	2008 2010	Ministry of Public Safety

provincial and municipal governments (Decree No.52 2008, ch.3, art.15–17). In Myanmar, private security companies are only required to register in the same manner as any other business. Company directors, supervisors and guards require no criminal background checks or mandatory training. Finally, even in the absence of formal legal and regulatory frameworks, official representatives have confirmed that private security companies in Laos operate with some unspecified oversight from the Ministry of Security (OHCHR 2015).

Coverage

For regulation to be effective, as many sectors of the private security industry must be subject to specific regulation to prevent the emergence of loopholes in the regulatory regime (Button 2012, p. 207–8). Laos has the narrowest regime, with private security companies only having to register for a normal business licence with the Ministry of Commerce. Cambodia and Brunei have general security licences, which are issued to those who 'furnish security guards for the protection of persons of property or to prevent the theft or unlawful taking of property for or in consideration of any payment or other remuneration (whether monetary or otherwise)' (Security Agencies Act 2000 sec.2.2). Most ASEAN states stipulate divisions between particular sectors of the industry. Singaporean regulations distinguish between security officers, private investigators and security service (equipment). Security officers are further distinguished between guards, cash and valuables in transit (CVIT), surveillance, bodyguard, bouncer and traffic regulation roles (Private Security Act 2007, pt.3, s.13 a–e). Philippine law distinguishes between private security agencies, private detective agencies, company guard units and government guard units. In Vietnam, private investigation activities are forbidden (Decree No.52 2008, ch.8, art. 3a). Regulatory regimes are becoming wider. The Malaysian Home Ministry Secretary-General Datuk Seri Alwi Ibrahim recently announced that close protection officers (bodyguards) will have to undergo separate training and licensing by the Royal Malaysian Police from 2017 onwards (Ying 2016).

Licence Requirements and Restrictions

Most ASEAN States—with the exception of Myanmar, Laos and Thailand for which there are no available data—require businesses seeking to sell security services to obtain a licence. Requirements for a private security business licence may range from background checks through to particular educational, financial and insurance criteria (UNODC 2014, pp. 37–8). Regulatory frameworks in Brunei (2000, s.6) and Vietnam stipulate that managers/executive directors must simply undergo background and criminal checks. The Philippine Presidential Decree No.11 (1973) amended the provision of the Security Agencies Act 1969 to place the following restrictions on managers of private security companies, which is representative of frameworks that focus on directors and/or managers:

That the operator or manager of said agency must be at least 25 years of age, a college graduate and/or a commissioned officer in the inactive service of the Armed Forces of the Philippines; of good moral character; having no previous record of any conviction or crime or offense involving moral turpitude and not suffering from any of the following disqualifications:

(1) Having been dishonourably discharged or separated from the Armed Forces of the Philippines
(2) Being a mental incompetent
(3) Being addicted to the use of narcotic drugs or drugs; and;
(4) Being a habitual drunkard

To establish a private security company in Indonesia, one must register with the Department of Industry and Trade, gain a letter of recommendation from the head of the regional police and submit lists of foreign worker checks and specialist licences before they are able to obtain an operational permit. Singapore requires more than basic licensing requirements for private security companies. Beyond background and criminal records tests, directors must have a minimum of two years in security work and demonstrate certain core competencies (as demonstrated by the possession of security management–specific qualifications) (Singapore Police 2013). Furthermore, the Singapore Police also use a grading system for security agencies and private investigation agencies, which assesses companies based on the 'three pillars of operational excellence, namely "operations", "training for operations", and "employment"'. This consists of an assessment of documentation submitted by individual private security companies and on-site audits, and companies are assigned grades from A to D (Singapore Police 2016). Such requirements allow regulators to indicate better quality private security services to buyers, and drive criminality and poor standards out of the industry.

A key concern for states is the distinction between public police forces and the private security industry. In 2015, Interior Minister of Cambodia Sar Kheng encouraged private security companies to employ retired police officers and military personnel, reinforcing the links between public and private forces in the region (Vida and Titthara 2015). These distinctions are further enshrined within uniform regulations. A 2016 Vietnamese Governmental Circular indicated that private security uniforms must be distinct from those worn by the public police and military personnel

(Ministry of Public Security 2016). Moreover, some of the ASEAN nations require private security companies to have more concrete links to the police, military or government. Malaysia, for instance, has specific stipulations regarding the composition of the shareholders/directors of registered private security companies:

> One of the shareholders is at least a former high ranking officer of the Police or army of Malaysia with the least rank of SAC II OR Colonel who owns 30% of company share equity; OR One is at least a former public officer in the management and professional group and has served in security sector for at least five years with the rank grade 52 or has a certificate of security course or at the same level and holds 30% of the company share equity (1971, s.3).

This juxtaposition between the requirements for private security companies to have some formal link with police forces, and the requirement for private security officers to be visually distinct provides an insight into the complex relationship of public and private security forces.

In a similar manner, ASEAN states have put legal restrictions on obtaining an individual private security licence. Throughout the world, stipulations for individual licences typically include: identification checks, criminal background checks, age and height requirements and minimum education and training. Such an example can be found in Section 5 of the Philippine Private Security Agencies Act (1969): 'No person shall be employed as a security guard or watchman or private detective unless he is: (a) a Filipino citizen; (b) a high school graduate; (c) physically and mentally fit; (d) not less than 21 nor more than 50 years of age; (e) at least 5 feet and 4 inches in height'. In some security professions, the stipulations are stricter. For example, in the Philippines, security consultants must have ten years' experience and a master's degree in Criminology, Public Administration or related subjects (Rule 5, Section 5, c,d). There is a shift towards more restrictive competency requirements in order to professionalise the industry and raise standards. For instance, the Thai Security Industry Business Act stipulates that by implementation in 2019, private security officers must have completed all compulsory education, that is up to and including the ninth grade[7] (Securitas n.d.).

Legal and regulatory frameworks also place significant restrictions on both the ability of foreign citizens to establish private security companies and to be employed by them. This limits the extent to which Chinese private security companies are able to operate within these countries as compared to other regions (see Arduino 2015). Chapter 3 Article 5 of the Vietnamese Decree (2008) states that foreigners cannot be employed as security personnel. However, there is a growing openness to foreign security expertise: a 2010 amendment made it possible for joint ventures with foreign private security companies on the condition that the service or technology provided could not be provided totally by Vietnamese parties and that the foreign share is limited to a maximum of 50 percent. Similar arrangements can be found in Thailand. Prior to 2016, Malaysian private security companies could only hire Malay of Nepalese guards, although this dispensation has been extended to two other countries after the imposition of mandatory training requirements have stemmed the flow of guards from Nepal.

Codes of Conducts for private security officers exist in the Philippines and Singapore. These usually go beyond compulsory standards and outline appropriate and ethical behaviour (see UNODC 2014, p. 39). These Codes not only allow private security officers to adequately tackle any ethical dilemmas they may face on the job, but allow tribunals and courts to better judge complaints against officers (Prenzler and Sarre 2008). However, it is interesting to note that these legal frameworks and codes not only direct behaviour but recognise the wider role that private security plays in public safety. An interesting example can be found in the Vietnamese Decree, which states:

> While conducting security service activities, if detecting security- or order-related incidents in the protection areas such as fires, explosions, accidents causing injuries or deaths, public disturbances or other acts with criminal signs, the security personnel performing their tasks in those areas shall rescue the victims, protect the scenes and take necessary measures to minimize damage and simultaneously report such to the nearest police officers for timely handling measures (2008 ch.6 art.4)

Moreover, the Philippine Security Guard Code also states that each private security officer: 'shall keep his allegiance first to the government, then to the agency where he is employed and to the establishment he is assigned to serve with loyalty and utmost dedication' (2006). Developing codes and frameworks that enshrine the flexibility for private security officers to respond to emergencies will enable private security to contribute to public and community safety.

Mandatory Training Requirements

The greatest variance within the ASEAN region concerns the area of minimum compulsory training requirements. Mandatory training standards contribute to public and private safety both by enhancing the quality of security guards and services, as well as encouraging greater professionalism in the industry (Prenzler and Sarre 1998; Button and George 2006; Button 2007; Prenzler and Sarre 2008; UNODC 2014). Companies who wish to engage in security training and certification must be licensed in Singapore, Philippines and Malaysia, however, in other nations such as Vietnam, police forces and government departments are responsible for all certification. The most comprehensive and progressive training system can be found in Indonesia. The minimum training for basic-entry security guards, *Gada Pratama,* is 232 hours. This raises to a cumulative 392 hours for supervisory roles, *Gada Madya,* and 492 hours for security managers or *Major Gada.* Having a rank system that closely mirrors the level of training an officer has undertaken is claimed to provide incentives for security officers to undertake additional training (Button 2008, p. 210). Likewise, in the Philippines the National Certificate I (the mandatory pre-licensing training course for security officers) is 167 hours long. This is waived for ex-police and military personnel. However, on the 2 August 2016, Bill 2471 was introduced into the Philippine Parliament outlining plans to intensify training requirements for security officers. Managers of private security companies must attend a private security executive management seminar to renew their licence. The Basic Supervisory Course is an extra fifty-six hours. In Singapore, there are two basic Security Licensing Units: 'Perform Guard and Patrol Services' (twenty-six hours) and 'Handle Security Incidents and Services' (eighteen hours). However, issues remain with the implementation of training systems. In 2014, it became compulsory for all security guards to attend a 'Certified Security Guards' training programme provided by the Ministry of Home Affairs and Royal Malaysian Police in collaboration with the Security Services Association of Malaysia. However, between May 2014 and December 2015, only 27,000 of 167,000 licensed private security officers in Malaysia had attended the minimum mandatory training. Further, a 2010 circular by the Malaysian Ministry of Home Affairs suggested that many private security companies provide untrained guards far above the legal requirement for 50 percent of security officers to have training (Malaysia 2010, 2006).

Powers of Enforcement

For enforcement to be as effective as possible, regulatory authorities must have recourse to a range of powers and techniques (Button 2012; Loader and White 2015). Having a range of enforcement options—scaled from informal inquiries and written notices through to the power to issue monetary fines and suspend or revoke licences—allows regulators to adopt measured approaches and escalate enforcements if necessary (Ayres and Braithwaite 1992). In Singapore, licensing officers (or warranted police officers) are able to investigate, search and arrest on suspicion those believed to be in breach of the 2007 Act. Similar powers can be found in other ASEAN states, such as Malaysia and Brunei. Brunei Police have recourse to the powers of licence suspension and revocation, as do all police departments across the region, but most sanctions are processed through the wider criminal justice system. For example, the penalty on conviction for supplying unlicensed private security services is $10,000 and two years' imprisonment. There is little evidence of administrative penalties available to any of the regulatory authorities.

Possession and Use of Firearms

The possession of firearms by private security officers is in forbidden in Laos, Malaysia. Myanmar, Thailand and Vietnam. The Brunei code further states that 'any person who in any public place carries or has in his possession or under his control any truncheon, handcuffs, or such other weapon or equipment as may be from time to time specified by the Minister in a notification in the *Gazette*, otherwise than with lawful authority shall be guilty of an offence and shall be liable on conviction to a fine not exceeding $1,000 or to imprisonment for a term not exceeding one month or both' (Brunei Section 16.1). Restrictions on weapons appear to be generally stringent throughout the region, though in countries where possession of firearms is legal, such as the Philippines, they must be effectively enforced.

Employment and Labour Laws

The low quality of the private security industry can be sustained by high workforce turnover, poor pay and poor working conditions. The absence of regulations on minimum standards for working conditions can potentially increase risks to the health and safety of security officers and as a result increase risks to private businesses and the public (UNODC 2014, p. 46).

In the Philippines, probationary periods for security officers are limited to six months after which they are legally entitled to a permanent contract (Philippines DLE 2016). Nominally, there is the existence of minimum wage policies in Malaysia, Singapore and the Philippines. Yet these rights are not necessarily guaranteed. The International Trade Union Confederation has indicated that in Indonesia, Vietnam, Cambodia and the Philippines 'while legislation may spell out certain rights workers have effectively no access to these rights and are therefore exposed to autocratic regimes and unfair labour practice' (2016, p. 20).

Conclusion

This chapter has provided an overview of legislative and regulatory frameworks in ASEAN member states. It is underpinned by the assertion that the Belt and Road Initiative will increasingly rely on domestic private security services, whose quality and effectiveness are improved by the existence of statutory frameworks. It has demonstrated that these frameworks amount to an uneven patchwork of regulatory requirements and restrictions across the region. While it appears that private security is receiving increasing media and governmental attention, significant limitations and problems still exist. Firstly, the unevenness of regulatory requirements may create regulatory loopholes across Southeast Asia, which raises concerns of the safety of Belt and Road projects that cross jurisdictions. Greater economic and political integration require the harmonisation of regulatory frameworks and strengthening of institutional capacities across the regions. Secondly, when state police forces administer, monitor and enforce licensing of private security, this raises concerns of resources, corruption and negative attitudes toward private security services, which may provide barriers to finding an appropriate balance between regulatory compliance and the private security industry's effectiveness (UNODC 2014, p. 24). While this chapter has suggested that compliance with minimum training standards is low, and that enforcement may be hampered by corruption and weakening respect for the rule of law, more research is needed to provide a better picture of the effectiveness of regulatory frameworks.

Given the apparent uneven regulations and implementation of the regulations, lack of training and licensure of private security companies and staff, and the lack of shared data and research on this topic, it is timely to suggest a way forward to support increased security. This lack of systematic and transparent process to ensure private security officers are trained, and to validate the quality of that training that ensures the personnel are well equipped to meet the challenges encountered, should be addressed to improve security. Considering its importance to safety and security, the current situation lends itself to a way forward to create an independent body responsible for developing certifications for private security personnel and companies that adheres to best practices, is evidence based and is from a regional approach. Using a regional approach will ensure that no one country is more or less stringent than its neighbour, resulting in constant pressure to ensure high-quality security.

Acknowledgement Sebastian Booth would like to thank the Economic and Social Research Council (Grant Number: ES/J500215/1) for their financial support during his internship at the United Nations Interregional Criminal Justice Research Institute, during which this research was conducted.

Notes

1. Only two ASEAN member states—Philippines and Thailand—contributed data to the 2011 UNODC Expert Group on Civilian Private Security Services, further demonstrating the lack of data concerning regulation in this region.
2. One notable exception to this is research concerning Singapore, which focuses primarily on the attitudes of private security officers (Nalla and Hoffman 1996; Nalla and Lim 2003; Lim and Nalla 2014).
3. Association of Southeast Asian Nations. ASEAN member states include: Brunei, Cambodia, Indonesia, Laos Malaysia, Myanmar, Philippines, Singapore, Thailand and Vietnam.
4. The proposition that states once maintained a monopoly over the provision of security within their respective territories has stood as the conceptual foundation stone of the governance of security literature. Despite this, it is highly doubtful that any state has held an actual monopoly (Zedner 2006).
5. The ratio is included to give an idea of the size of the private security industry relative to public police forces. We do not intend to make any judgement concerning the extent to which there has been a transformation in policing in Southeast Asia (see White and Gill 2013). This is both beyond the scope of this chapter and would require historical research.
6. Prenzler and Sarre (2008) map out eleven areas of misconduct—fraud, incompetence and poor standards, exploitation of security staff, corruption, information corruption, violence, false arrest, discrimination and harassment, insider crime and misuse of weapons.
7. In Thailand, the ninth grade is known as *Matthayom 3*—the typical age of children in this grade is 15/16 years.

Bibliography

Legal Documents

Security Agencies Act (2000) Ch. 187. Brunei
Security Agencies Regulations (2000) Ch.187. Brunei
Sub Decree No.289 (2013) Cambodia
Regulation of the Head of Police No.17 (2006) Indonesia
Regulation of the Head of the Police No. 18 (2006) Indonesia
Regulation of the Head of the Police No. 24 (2007) Indonesia
Private Agencies Act (2006) Commissioner of Law: Malaysia
Private Security Agency Act No. 5487 (1969) Philippines
Presidential Decree No.11 (1972) Philippines
Rules and Regulations Implementing Act No.5487 (2006). Philippines
Private Security Industry Act (2007) Ch.250A. Singapore
Security Industry Business Act (2015) Thailand
Decree on Management of Security Service Business (2008) Vietnam
Regulations on Security Uniforms for Agencies, Enterprises. No.08/2016/TT-BCA (2016). Vietnam

References

Arduino, A (2015) 'Security Privatisation with Chinese Characteristics: The Role of Chinese Private Security Corporations in Protecting Chinese Outbound Investments and Citizens', RSIS Policy Report, Singapore

Asian Infrastructure Investment Bank (2016) Indonesia: National Slum Upgrading Project. https://aiib.org/en/projects/approved/2016/indonesia-national-slum.html

Ayres, I and Braithwaite, J (1992) *Responsive Regulation: Transcending the Deregulation Debate*. Oxford: Oxford University Press

Bansal, A (2008) 'Factors Leading to Insurgency in Balochistan', *Small Wars and Insurgencies*, 19, 182–200

Bayley, DH and Shearing, C (1996) 'The Future of Policing', *Law and Society*, 30 (3), 585–606

Bokhari, F, Hornby, L and Shepherd, C (2016) 'China Urges Pakistan to Give Army Lead Role in Silk Road Project', *Financial Times*, 21 July 2016. https://www.ft.com/content/5eea66c0-4ef9-11e6-8172-e39ecd3b86fc

Button, M (2007) 'Assessing the Regulation of Private Security Across Europe', *European Journal of Criminology*, 4 (1), 109–128

Button, M (2008) *Doing Security: Critical Reflections and an Agenda for Change*. Basingstoke: Palgrave Macmillan

Button, M (2012) 'Optimizing Security Through Effective Regulation', in T. Prenzler (ed) *Policing and Security in Practice: Challenges and Achievements.* Basingstoke: Palgrave Macmillan, 204–220.

Button, M and George, B (2006) 'Regulation of Private Security: Models for Analysis', in M. Gill (ed) *Handbook of Security.* Basingstoke: Palgrave Macmillan.

Button, M, Park, H and Lee J (2006) 'The Private Security Industry in South Korea: A Familiar Tale of Growth, Gaps and the Need for Better Regulation', *Security Journal,* 19 (3), 167–179

Button, M and Stiernstedt, P (2016a) 'Comparing Private Security Regulation in the European Union', *Policing and Society,* https://doi.org/10.1080/10439463.2016.1161624

Button, M and Stiernstedt, P (2016b) 'The Evolution of Security Industry Regulation in the European Union', *International Journal of Comparative and Applied Criminal Justice,* https://doi.org/10.1080/01924036.2016.1270842

Caballero-Anthony, M. (2005) *Regional Security in Southeast Asia: Beyond the ASEAN Way.* Singapore: Institute of Southeast Asian Studies

China. National Development Reform Commission, Ministry of Foreign Affairs and Ministry of Commerce with State Council (2015) Vision and Actions on Jointly Building Silk Road Economic Belt and 21st Century Maritime Silk Road

Crawford, A (2006) 'Networked Governance and the Post-Regulatory State? Steering, Rowing and Anchoring the Provision of Policing and Security', *Theoretical Criminology,* 10 (4), 449–479

Financial Times (2011) Three Killed as Maoists Attack Philippine Mine. *Financial Times,* 3 October 2011. http://www.ft.com/cms/s/0/421b5710-edca-11e0-acc7-00144feab49a.html?ft_site=falcon&desktop=true

Interpol (2016) Asia and South Pacific – National Central Bureaus in Action. https://www.interpol.int/Member-countries/Asia-South-Pacific

Johnston, L and Shearing, C (2003) *Governing Security: Explorations in Policing and Justice.* London: Routledge

Kamit, R (2014) 'Update Your Security Agency Licences Says Police Commissioner', *BT Archive,* 25 December 2014. https://btarchive.org/news/national/2014/12/25/update-your-security-agency-licences-says-police-commissioner

Kempa, M, Stenning, P and Wood, J (2004) 'Policing Communal Spaces: A Reconfiguration of the 'Mass Private Property' Hypothesis', *British Journal of Criminology,* 44 (4), 562–581

Kim, DW (2015) 'The Development of the Private Security Industry in South Korea: History, Progress and Critical Issues 1950–2014', *Journal of Criminological Research, Policy and Practice,* 1 (3), 143–158

Kynge, J (2016) 'How the Silk Road Plans Will Be Financed', *Financial Times,* 9 May 2016.https://www.ft.com/content/e83ced94-0bd8-11e6-9456-444ab5211a2f

Lechmacher, W and Padilla-Taylor, V (2015) 'Hurdles Ahead Along the "New Silk Road"' Financial Times Blog. http://blogs.ft.com/beyond-brics/2015/09/17/hurdles-ahead-along-the-new-silk-road/

Lee, CM (2008) 'A Comparative Study on the Regulation of Private Security in the United States and South Korea', *Journal of Applied Security Research*, 3 (2), 157–70

Lim, SS and Nalla, MK (2014) 'Attitudes of Private Security Officers in Singapore Towards their Work Environment', *Journal of Applied Security Research* 9 (1), 41–56

Liss, C (2007) 'The Role of Private Security Companies in Securing the Malacca Strait', *Maritime Studies*, 157, 14–22

Loader, I and White, A (2015) 'How Can We Better Align Private Security with the Public Interest? Towards a Civilizing Model of Regulation', *Regulation and Governance*, doi:https://doi.org/10.1111/rego.12109

Manning, PK (2005) 'The Study of Policing', *Police Quarterly*, 8 (1), 23–43

Nalla, MK, and Hoffman, VJ (1996) 'Security Training Needs: A Study of the Perceptions of Security Guards', *Security Journal*, 7 (4), 287–293

Nalla, MK. and Lim, SS (2003) 'Student's Perceptions of Private Police in Singapore', *Asian Policing* 1 (1), 27–47

Nalla, MK and Hwang, E (2006) 'Relations Between Police and Private Security Officers in South Korea', *Policing*, 29 (3), 482–497

Office for the High Commissioner for Human Rights (2015) Committee on the Rights of the Child Considers Reports of Lao People's Democratic Republic on Sale of Children, Children in Armed Conflict. 27 May 2015. http://www.ohchr.org/EN/NewsEvents/Pages/DisplayNews.aspx?NewsID=16016&LangID=E

Palabrica, RJ (2016) 'Rules on Security Guard Services', *Inquirer*, 25 April 2016. http://business.inquirer.net/209774/rules-security-guard-services

Prenzler, T and Sarre, S (1998) 'Regulating Private Security in Australia', *Australian Institute of Criminology: Trends and Issues in Crime and Criminal Justice*, 98, 1–6.

Prenzler, T and Sarre, R (2008) 'Developing a Risk Profile and Model Regulatory System for the Security Industry', *Security Journal*, 21 (4), 264–277.

Ramos, M (2014) 'PNP Hiring Security Guards to Protect Camp Crame', *Inquirer*, 10 January 2014. http://newsinfo.inquirer.net/561245/pnp-hiring-security-guards-to-protect-camp-crame

Saha, J and Rowley, C (2014) *The Changing Role of the Human Resource Profession in the Asia-Pacific Region*. Cambridge: Chandos

Sciascia, A (2013) 'Monitoring the Border: Indonesian Port Security and the Role of Private Actors', *Contemporary Southeast Asia*, 35 (2), 163–187

Securitas (n.d.) New Law for Private Security Companies in Thailand. http://www.securitas.co.th/globalassets/thailand/files/new-law-for-security-companies-in-thailand.pdf

Security Agencies Guards Supervision Division (2016) Citizens Charter. http://www.pnp.gov.ph/images/citizencharter/SOSIA_Services.pdf

Sen, NJ and Tham, C (2014) New Bonuses for New Cops. *The New Paper*, 7 August 2014. http://www.tnp.sg/news/new-bonuses-new-cops

Sen, D (2014) ASEAN Visit Prompts Training. *The Phonm Penh Post*, 22 November 2011. http://www.phnompenhpost.com/national/asean-visit-prompts-training

Singapore Police (n.d.) Private Security Industry. http://www.police.gov.sg/e-services/apply/licenses-and-permits/private-security-industry

Singapore Police (2013) Guidelines On Applying For a Security Agency Licence. https://www.police.gov.sg/e-services/apply/licenses-andpermits/private-security-industry/security-agencies/guidelines

Singapore Police (2016) Security Agency Grading Exercise 2016 Notification Letter. 5 April 2016. https://www.police.gov.sg/~/media/spf/files/e-services/pi/security%20agency%20grading/security_agency_grading_exercise_2016_notification_letter.pdf?la=en

Singer, PW (2007) *Corporate Warriors: The Rise of the Privatized Military Industry*. New York: Cornell University Press

Soleil, MCD (2016) 'New Departments Created to Manage Private Security Service and Gambling Business'. *Agence Kampuchea Press*, 19 December 2016. http://www.akp.gov.kh/?p=92956

Stenning, P (1989) 'Private Policing: Some Recent Myths, Developments and Trends', in D. Biles and J. Vernon (eds) *No 22: Private Sector and Community Involvement in the Criminal Justice System*. Proceedings of a Conference Held 30 November–2 December 1992, Wellington. Canberra: Australian Institute of Criminology.

Swanström, N (2015) 'China's New Silk Road, a Security Deficit?' *Dragon News* 3, 6–7. http://isdp.eu/content/uploads/publications/2015-Swanstrom-China-New-Silk-Road-Commentary.pdf

United Nations International Children's Fund (2014) Annual Report 2014: Lao People's Democratic Republic. UNICEF, Lao PDR. https://www.unicef.org/about/annualreport/files/Lao_PDR_Annual_Report_2014.pdf

United Nations Office on Drugs and Crime (2014) *Handbook on State Regulation Concerning Civilian Private Security Services and their Contribution to Crime Prevention and Community Safety*. Vienna: UNODC.

United Nations Office on Drugs and Crime (2016a) *World Drug Report 2016*. Vienna: UNODC.

United Nations Office on Drugs and Crime (2016b) *Protecting Peace and Prosperity in Southeast Asia: Synchronizing Economic and Security Agendas*. Vienna: UNODC.

Van Steden, R and Sarre, R (2010) 'The Tragic Quality of Contract Guards: A Discussion of the Reach and Theory of Private Security in the World Today', *Journal of Criminal Justice Research*, 1 (1), 1–19

Vida, T and Titthara, M (2015) Security Jobs Mooted for Ex-Cops. *Phnom Penh Post*, 18 May 2015. http://www.phnompenhpost.com/national/security-jobs-mooted-ex-cops

White, A (2010) *The Politics of Private Security*. Basingstoke: Palgrave Macmillan

White, A and Gill, M (2013) 'The Transformation of Policing: From Ratios to Rationalities', *British Journal of Criminology*, 53, 74–93

Wood, J and Shearing, C (2007) *Imagining Security*. Cullompton: Willan Publishing

Ying, TP (2016) All Bodyguards in Country to Undergo Mandatory Training by Police. *New Straits Times*, 10 December 2016. http://nst.com.my/news/2016/12/195856/all-bodyguards-country-undergo-mandatory-training-police

Yoshida, N (1999) 'The Taming of the Japanese Private Security Industry', *Policing and Society*, 9 (3), 241–261

Zedner, L (2006) 'Policing Before and After the Police. The Historical Antecedents of Contemporary Crime Control', *British Journal of Criminology*, 46, 78–96

Zhong, L and Grabosky, P (2009) 'The Pluralization of Policing and the Rise of Private Policing in China', *Crime, Law and Social Change*, 52 (5), 433–455

CHAPTER 3

China's Belt and Road Security: The Increasing Role of Insurance and Private Security Companies

Alessandro Arduino

Introduction

Envisioned by Chinese President Xi Jinping in 2013, the Belt and Road Initiative (BRI), formerly known as One Belt, One Road (OBOR), is intended to promote economic development and exchanges between China and more than sixty countries. The BRI is the spearhead of renewed Chinese overseas foreign direct investment (OFDI) efforts. The initiative encompasses two routes: the Silk Road Economic Belt (SREB), a land route connecting China's western provinces with the European Union via Central Asia and the Middle East; and the 21st Century Maritime Silk Road (MSR), a maritime route that connects Southeast Asia, the Persian Gulf, and the Horn of Africa with the Southern European ports. Both routes stand on five pillars: connectivity, unobstructed trade, financial integration, policy coordination and promotion of cultural proximity. The overall amount of Chinese infrastructural and financial investments along the routes could reach US$4 trillion.

A. Arduino (✉)
Security & Crisis Management Program, Shanghai Academy of Social Sciences (SASS-UNITO), Shanghai, China

A. Arduino, X. Gong (eds.), *Securing the Belt and Road Initiative*,
https://doi.org/10.1007/978-981-10-7116-4_3

Nevertheless, the aim of global connectivity encompasses a wide threat spectrum. Economic returns and risks management in outbound investment activities are two sides of the same coin. In the globalization process, the major risk concerns are no more relegated to a specific country but are evolving across national borders. New technologies and freedom of movement facilitate global trade and development, but at the same time augment the reach of criminal and political violence. The overall BRI's vulnerabilities include political risks that originate from national and international security flashpoints as well as cross-border non-traditional security threats.

While China has remained very cautious in getting involved in the complexities of politics and conflict of other countries, the decade's old principle of non-interference is being adapted to the new realities. Enunciated in 1953 by Prime Minister Zhou Enlai, the non-interference principle is one of the Five Principles of Peaceful Coexistence that constitute the pillars of the Chinese foreign policy. While Chinese academic debate over the actuality of the principle is still open (Duchatel et al. 2014), Beijing has already started to take a pragmatic and proactive stance over the BRI. The new trend under Xi Jinping's BRI is to 'strive for achievement' (fen fa you wei)[1] and it seems that is gradually overtaking Deng Xiaoping's catchphrase 'keeping a low profile while hiding its own ability' (tao guang yang hui),[2] which formed the strategies of generations of Chinese Communist Party officials and the People's Liberation Army (PLA). However, Beijing's implementation of a safe BRI is already facing massive geopolitical challenges. For example, the Southern and Central Asian land route is marred by internal conflicts caused by unresolved regional rivalry and boundaries, water and energy disputes, rising Islamic militancy and internal competition. One of the most serious cases is the Indo-Chinese military standoff in the tri-junction area of Sikkim, Tibet and Bhutan (June 2017). Over the maritime routes, the challenges are equally daunting, ranging from geopolitical and geo-economic concerns towards the disputed South China Sea or piracy along the Somali coast and the Strait of Malacca.

Nevertheless, the recent participation of more than twenty countries' leaders at the Beijing Belt and Road Forum[3] has witnessed the ambivalent role and relevance of the Chinese economic diplomacy. Several countries are eager to be included in the BRI, even downplaying their own national geopolitical agendas in order to advance economic and development priorities.[4]

Among the numerous BRI projects, the China-Pakistan Economic Corridor (CPEC) represents an important security test ground for the overall Belt and Road. The CPEC's flagship development plan amounts to US$63 billion and represents China's enhancement of its own geo-economics statecraft. Failing to fulfil CPEC promises to save Pakistan's dwindling economy could produce far-reaching ripple effects. Also, Pakistan's proximity to Afghanistan, which is also part of the BRI, could be negatively affected by the deterioration of Kabul's grip on the country's internal security (Pantucci 2017) as well as to broader regional disputes involving India, Iran and Saudi Arabia. CPEC aims to connect China's northwest Xinjiang Uygur Autonomous Region to Pakistan's Gwadar's deep water in the southwest via a network of roads, railway and energy interconnected projects. While finance and infrastructure connectivity are the core part of the corridor's blueprint, security issues are still segregated in the fringe of the BRI win-win narrative. While the new commercial routes with China and the macro projects' development are going to benefit the overall Pakistani economic system, local job opportunities in needier areas such as Baluchistan are yet to materialize. Besides the CPEC internal frictions (Bajoria 2009), external suspicion and conflicting dynamics are on the rise. Indian and Saudi distrust over Sino-Pakistani hidden agendas cast doubts on the exclusive economic nature of the BRI. The new energy trade routes that will link the Persian Gulf directly to China are set to generate new power dynamics. From the Indian standpoint, Gwadar's increasing capabilities are a threat to Mumbai support in developing the Iranian port of Chambhar. From the Saudi point of view, the efficiency of the new trade route is going to benefit Iran's growing regional power ambitions. The failed Chinese attempt to develop Sri Lanka's Hambantota port reflects how political turmoil and local grievance could hamper long-term development projects. Also, according to James Dorsey, ethnic and sectarian proxy wars could embroil rivals of China and India in the Saudi-Iranian dispute (Dorsey 2017a). Though the CPEC message is about 'all weather friendship' (Johnson 2015), the cooperation is not based on common cultural or ideological values but pragmatic economic and security necessities.

The Chinese investment footprint in Pakistan started to get traction in 2016 and at the same time, the number of deadly attacks on Chinese workers has increased proportionally.

On May 2017, two Chinese teachers were kidnapped and subsequently executed by self-proclaimed Islamic State (IS) militants who operate in the border area between Pakistan and Afghanistan. According to the IS group's Amaq news agency,[5] the two Chinese nationals, abducted in the Baluchistan capital city of Quetta, were killed as a warning against further Chinese economic expansion. Chinese foreign ministry spokeswoman Hua Chunying admonished that: 'The Chinese side is firmly opposed to the acts of kidnapping civilians in any form, as well as terrorism and extreme violence in any form' (Hua 2017). The incident involving the two Chinese nationals is not isolated, and Beijing's calls to Islamabad for increased security are on the rise.

Also in 2017, the Baluchi independents militants have claimed several major attacks against a perceived menace from the Chinese economic penetration of Pakistan. These include a failed assassination of the deputy chairman of the Baluchistan Senate that cost the lives of 25 bystanders[6] and the savage gunning down of 10 workers[7] along the road to the southern port of Gwadar that connects Central Asia to the Indian Ocean. Threatening Gwadar security is not only an attempt to derail Beijing's efforts to link its western regions with the Indian Ocean and Iran oil sea exports, but also an effort to showcase the BRI vulnerabilities to the world. Similarly, on May 31, 2016 the Sindhudesh Revolutionary Army (SRA), a little-known local group that directly challenges the Pakistani central government's control over the Sindh province, attempted to kill Chinese workers based in the Pakistani city of Karachi.

All Chinese involved in the acts of violence had neither adequate protection nor an appropriate forewarning of the imminent threats in the area. In the case of the Quetta kidnapping, the proximity of several terrorist organizations was easily discounted by the fact that the two teachers operated in an area considered safe for Chinese citizens. Similarly, in the SRA attack, the Chinese workers were considered to be operating in an ordinary business environment, but they suddenly become a target for the terrorists in order to dissuade further Chinese economic support for Pakistan's weakening economy.

Not far from CPEC, the construction of a road by a Chinese enterprise along disputed borders has stirred the ire of India and Bhutan. In the remote mountains of the Himalayas that separate China and India, sudden flashpoints on border disputes lead to costly standoffs that threaten to degenerate into armed confrontation. On June 2017, tensions escalated over a longstanding but mostly overlooked border dispute in the tri-junction area of Sikkim, Tibet and Bhutan. Thousands of troops were summoned after the BRI infrastructure road project raised unexpected antagonisms. To quote the *South China Morning Post*: 'China's building of a road in the Donglang area, also known as Doka La, so quickly turned into the biggest military stand-off between the two armies in years'.[8] While border disputes and the Indian perceived build-up of the Chinese maritime 'string of pearls' attempt at encirclement in the Indian Ocean is a constant hindrance to better bilateral ties; the remote area that is crossed by the new Chinese road was considered a zone 'ready for business'. Reality differs and underlines how the BRI narrative of total inclusiveness is still far from adhering to local realities. In several areas, the Chinese narrative of win-win cooperation is perceived as 'China is going to win twice'. The military standoff highlights once more how the political value that is attached to the BRI's infrastructure development is not to be discounted too easily. The border incident occurred just a few days ahead of the meeting between India President Modi and his American counterpart President Trump. As is already happening from Djibouti to Central Asian countries, the small kingdom of Bhutan, entwined between China and India, is forced to learn the art of multi-vector diplomacy. The Bhutan Ministry of Foreign Affairs issued a démarche to China's diplomatic mission in New Delhi on June 20, 2017, protesting China's intrusive request to 'refrain from unilaterally altering the status quo on the ground' with the excuse of infrastructure building in contested areas. India's deep-rooted suspicion about China's rise and the lack of strategist trust in the development of the BRI exclusive economic interests are going to define the relations in the region for the years to come.

Similarly, in other areas, suspicion and local grievances could derail the overall BRI blueprint. Besides the acts of political violence, the overall BRI footprint has also witnessed several incidents due to a lack of Corporate Social Responsibilities (CSRs), as well as the absence of policies devoted to avoiding environmental degradation, work-related accidents and corruption. These kinds of incidents have fomented tensions that resulted in confrontation between Chinese and local workers. Until 2016, financial risk was the only perceived challenge to the BRI, while criminal and political violence were overlooked. Oversight and management structures need to be set in place. In addition, lessons drawn by the United States from the use of private security companies (PSCs) could be adapted to the Chinese circumstances in order to avoid costly miscalculations.

Belt and Road Initiative Requirements: Special Insurances and Private Security

Confrontations between the local population and Chinese workers are not new in Africa, Central and South Asia as disputes over working conditions and environmental degradation issues are a growing concern over China's OFDI. While the volume of Chinese overseas investment has increased eightfold in the last decade, the amount of Chinese funds dedicated to the BRI is unprecedented.

One oversight that must be addressed is that the BRI requires a wide range of security considerations along both the maritime and land routes. During the 2016 and 2017 attacks, the global reach of the BRI encountered local problems that were not given sufficient attention during the project's economic and security impact analysis. As an example, in the Sindhudesh and Baluchi provinces, the security threats assessment of the local communities and the opposition to the BRI have been missing from the beginning. Furthermore, most of the SOEs and the overall Chinese small and medium-sized enterprises (SMEs) are unaware of the most common threats to intelligence and crisis management practices, which are commonly regarded by Chinese businessmen as a costly overhead.

In order to cope with the problem, China's BRI public diplomacy, utilizing the New Silk Road's metaphor of global connectivity and sustainable development, has attempted to manage or mitigate anxiety over what is characterized as 'China's rise'. At the same time, international and bilateral agreements have paved the way to an overall acceptation of the BRI. Unfortunately, the local population that are directly affected by the macro projects are not always included in a proper stakeholder analysis.

Just after the bombing of the Chinese Embassy in the Kyrgyz capital of Bishkek, Foreign Ministry spokesperson Hua Chunying restated how the safety of personnel abroad is of paramount importance, and that the Ministry of Foreign Affairs (MFA) is taking precautions to ensure the well-being of the Chinese personnel overseas. These first open blows to the BRI urged Beijing to reconsider if the countries that host Chinese investments are able to guarantee Chinese nationals' safety.

While the security problem has not gone unnoticed in Beijing, the solutions could be found elsewhere, namely in international companies that provide: special risk assessment, insurance, private security and perhaps most importantly, crisis mitigation.

Since 2013, the security imperatives of the Chinese BRI opened a new market for PSCs. The shift from a Western-centred market for force to an Asian one has already started. PSCs with 'Chinese characteristics' and Russian *Chastnye Voennie Companiy* (ChVC) are filling the gaps that US or UK counterparts are not able to cover due to the lack of political proximity with the Chinese companies.

While Beijing economic might is without discussion, its own influence in the market for force is just starting to be perceived. Nevertheless, the Chinese insurance sector is realizing the importance of this business niche. Traditional static security, counterterrorism as well as kidnapping for ransom are going to provide important contracts along the BRI. Recently, Chinese insurance experts began to acknowledge the role of prevention in this line of business. Chinese insurance companies that are entering the special insurance market are aware of the need to improve their operational capabilities to levels consistent with international best practices. Special insurance is a lesser-known niche market, but due to the expansion of Chinese OFDI, this is already proving to be a highly profitable sector. Leading Chinese insurance companies such as Ping An and China Taiping groups are already extending feelers that seek cooperation with British insurance experts. With a rising Chinese presence and an increased perception of the Chinese as wealthy individuals, kidnapping for ransom (K&R),[9] is not only an increasing concern but also a new market opportunity.

In this respect, Chinese requirements for private security call for a more complex set of solutions. Chinese SOEs require a set of integrated services in which armed personnel are just one component and not even the most prominent.

Since the 'Going Out' policy, the Chinese government has been encouraging Chinese companies' investment overseas. Thanks to a vast amount of foreign value reserves, Beijing via China Investment Corporation (CIC)—China's sovereign wealth fund—and the state-owned investment banks have penetrated the energy, technology, finance and infrastructure sectors. Chinese preferential loans have found fertile ground in both developed and developing economies.

As the scope and size of Chinese OFDI has been increasing over the years, SOEs have started to acknowledge that the risks associated with outbound investments in emerging economies as well as in developing countries carries a higher failure rate due to intertwined factors such as: economic crises, conflict, civil unrest, assets nationalization and currency devaluation, just to name a few. At the same time, the Chinese SOEs, due to their public nature with commercial capacity, have the tendency to blur the lines between commercial and political factors. Consequently, they tend to rely too optimistically on Beijing's support in case of a crisis. This kind of pattern is well exemplified by decades of Chinese SOEs' investments in Africa that ended with mixed results. Now the narrative is changed.

The Chinese companies, from SOEs to SMEs, that are engaged in overseas contracting, particularly those involved in heavy industry and construction, are first in line to gain from the New Silk Road promises of global connectivity. While the Chinese economy has been slowing down towards a 'new normal',[10] the most hard-hit sectors since 2011 are the ones that are now receiving a lifeblood transfusion with the BRI construction contracts. Beijing's new plans for the BRI are not only going to fuel the recovery for the Chinese heavy industrial sectors, but are already increasing investor confidence in the overall construction sector, ranging from steel mills to concrete factories. After more than five years of falling commodity prices and industrial overcapacity,[11] confidence in the business has returned and the SOEs that are building along the BRI are starting to invest again. For the first time since 2011, there is an increase in heavy machinery sales due to the international, government-led investments. Unfortunately, up to the beginning of 2017 there was not much interest in the overall SOEs' security apparatus upgrade.[12] The SOEs' risk perception as well as willingness to pay for professional security services is still low. Thus, more than half of the BRI projects are related to infrastructure building and several Chinese SMEs that are SOE subcontractors run their businesses on limited profit margins that do not allow for high security expenses.

The BRI encompasses more than 60 countries, differentiating broadly in local conditions. In this respect, the tasks of Chinese corporations that operate along the BRI share only one commonality: high complexity.

Each project from the Sino-Pakistan Economic Corridor (US$63 billion) to the Poly-GCL natural gas pipeline in Ethiopia (US$5 billion) or the Mes Aynak copper mine in Afghanistan (US$3 billion) includes several layers of complexity ranging from financial, technical, operational, political and physical security risks. Greater complexity entails greater risks.

While the energy sector has reached a certain degree of maturity in risk management and mitigation, the majority of the Chinese SOEs and private corporations that are interested in becoming active stakeholders along the BRI are still unaware of the complexity of the task. Moreover, the BRI approach to crisis management is rooted in the government-to-government (G2G) agreements. This bilateral approach provides a risk assessment that is legally binding between China and the countries involved in the BRI. Nevertheless, the G2G approach is encumbered by several limitations. The most obvious is the separatist's antagonism towards their central government. Other limitations include weak links between central and provincial governments, cultural and religious barriers as well as historically rooted unresolved disputes. Due to these challenges, the ability of Chinese private security companies to provide accurate, on-going security assessments, scenario planning, crisis prevention and mitigation is going to be a key requirement for success in a long-term international economic cooperation and sustainable development that is at the core of the BRI.

As already mentioned, the security threats to the Chinese workers in Pakistan are increasingly known in Beijing.[13] Islamabad has pledged to deploy a considerable military force to protect Chinese nationals in that region and promised 15,000 uniformed personnel in support of the CPEC. The previous attack in Karachi against Chinese workers and the recent violence in the coastal city of Gwadar[14] reflects the lack of a comprehensive, on-going risk assessment as the projects rolled out. While an initial risk analysis is mandatory during the pre-project assessment by the National Development Research Commission (NDRC), it is also imperative to monitor how the on-going project is affecting local communities. Security is dynamic and the Chinese infrastructural projects' size and speed of implementation add stress to already unstable socio-political environments. Understanding and managing this stress is a challenge that cannot be ignored if the benefits of these projects are to be realized.[15] Furthermore, CPEC's internal problems are augmented by a complex web of international friction points that involve ethnic and sectarian proxy wars. Abundant examples range from the Indo-Pakistan to the Saudi-Iranian disputes that could entangle Chinese economic assertiveness into undesirable political confrontations (Dorsey 2017b).

Separatism and insurgency are primary variables in the risk assessment equation, not only in Pakistan but also over several countries that are connected by the BRI. More often than not, their value is overestimated without taking into account local problems that are ignited by the influx of Chinese capital and workers. The impact of Chinese infrastructure projects in local communities disrupts the internal dynamics of power and wealth, creating a new breed of winners and losers as well as provoking the danger of anti-Chinese sentiments. Several cases, from Central Asia (Putz 2015) to Africa and from Vietnam to Indonesia, have already showcased how changes stimulated in local communities by Chinese investments have ended in violent confrontations.

Private Security Corporations with 'Chinese Characteristics'

The post–Cold War security vacuum is characterized by an increasing demand for private military and security services. Currently, the rise of the BRI in 2013, spearheaded by the Chinese SOEs, induces novel demands for a new market for force. New actors include a spectrum of contractors that range from international PSCs with a corporate structure, more similar to a multinational corporation than to the private militaries before the 1990s, and an increasing number of Chinese PSCs with global ambitions. The growth of the Chinese PSCs resonates with the controversial role played by international PSCs in US-led conflicts. Compared to the United States, China is not engaged in large-scale conflicts and does not have at present a necessity to outsource logistical and infrastructural services in war zones.[16] Nevertheless, the necessity for security protection and emergency evacuation in different areas of the globe is driving Beijing to formally privatize various security roles (Arduino 2017).

Several Chinese PSCs emerged onto the international arena, employing a mix of local and foreign resources. The mix changes with respect to each specific requirement and depends heavily on foreign expertise in risk assessment and the use of armed personnel. Chinese PSCs—with some rare exceptions related to maritime security—are barred by the MFA to employ Chinese armed contractors.[17]

Nevertheless, one key point is already clear. While Chinese government officials are still debating the use of Chinese PSCs, the business opportunity for reaping high profits is already being perceived by a rising number of local security service providers. Also, the growing need for protective services by Chinese enterprises has attracted a large number of international players looking for cooperation with the emergent local PSCs (Arduino 2015).

Since the 2010[18] amendment of the obsolete 1993 law that regulates the Chinese PSCs, several Chinese firms have evolved their business model from a local security provider—so-called bodyguards for wealthy clients—to international operations with liaison offices in Beijing. The number of local Chinese security corporations that offer close personnel protection and unarmed guards total more than 5000 registered entities that account for roughly three million security officers. Among these companies, less than a dozen have the capabilities and the experience to provide stand-alone international services. At the same time, the growing need for protective services by Chinese enterprises has attracted a large number of international players looking for cooperation with the emergent local PSCs. (e.g., Control Risks, G4S, FSG).

Among the international cooperation, the presence of Frontier Service Group HK[19] Company in Beijing attracted most of the media attention due to the fact that the FSG chairman is Eric Prince, founder of the US private military corporation Blackwater. In stark contrast to Western perceptions, due to the killing of innocent civilians in Iraq (Schaill 2007), a significant section of the Chinese security apparatus and PSCs' management perceive the Blackwater model as efficient.[20] Prince's sales pitch for his former company Blackwater, which was 'no client died during Backwater's watch' (Prince 2013), has found fertile ground in China.

Blackwater's aggressive tactics have earned critique and scorn; yet at the same time have been praised by the government officers and civilians they were escorting. At the same time, several Chinese academics in Beijing's security circles are already underlining the incompatibility of the previous Blackwater model with China's security needs.[21]

Thus, the Chinese PSC capabilities in providing overseas security services are not comparable to those provided by their top foreign counterparts. Chinese SOEs, however, still prefer to employ Chinese contractors. The cooperation with international PSCs is deemed a 'necessary evil' until the Chinese PSCs acquire the skillsets required to reach high-level operational capabilities. The desire to employ only Chinese PSCs is rooted not only in the required language and cultural sensitivity, but also in the opinion that only Chinese security corporations will be able to preserve the SOEs' confidential information. PSCs with 'Chinese characteristics' employ former PLA personnel, People's Armed Police (PAP) or Chinese security officers with links to the national security apparatus. Hence, the perception that only local PSCs are able to protect the integrity of the SOEs' business data. Also, local PSCs like RWY are well known in the civilian and military circles in Beijing as their increasing recruitment absorbs most of the military personnel that has been dismissed since the restructuring of the armed forces.

According to the research published by the Chinese think tank Phoenix (Phoenix 2017) in cooperation with Qinghua University in Beijing, the ranking of the top 10 Chinese security firms is as follows:

1. G4S
2. Control Risks
3. Beijing DeWe Security Services Co., Ltd.
4. Zhongguo Anbao China Security Industry Co., Ltd.
5. Hua Xin Zhong An (Beijing) Security Service Co., Ltd.
6. Shanghai Zhongchenwei Security Service Group Co., Ltd.
7. Beijing Dingtai Anyuan Guard & Technology Research Institute
8. Shengzhen Zhongzhou Tewei Security Consultant Co., Ltd.
9. Beijing Guanan Security & Technology Co., Ltd.
10. Shandong Huawei Security Group Co., Ltd.

The service provided by these companies comprises the protection of the workers' compound during large-scale energy and infrastructure projects, the security of the Chinese shipping companies' vessels and logistic hubs as well as the safety of corporate officials and high-value individuals travelling abroad. The ample spectrum of services is summarized as follows:

- Risk assessment, providing security reports in order to allow the company business feasibility study and mandatory government security assessment
- Risk management, monitoring the evolution of the Chinese footprint and the reaction of the local stakeholders, adapting with the daily risks and threats
- Risk mitigation, coping with ongoing crisis, providing medical extraction for injured personnel and evacuation of Chinese nationals in cooperation with the Chinese MFA
- Risk transfer, supporting the insurance companies to find suitable partners to share the risk burdens
- Security compliance audit reports on the Chinese company overseas offices
- Training security personnel and company officials

Whereas the PLA's local involvement in the Chinese business environment has been tamed in the last decade, the role of SOEs in shaping foreign policies has been increasing. With the latest purge of corrupted officials in the PLA (The Economist 2015), President Xi Jinping has accomplished a long-standing reform to detach the PLA (Grossman and Chase 2016) from the entrepreneurial side of the Chinese development. At the same time, the privatization reform of the state assets has been hijacked towards the more efficient public sector where the SOEs still benefit from government support and a favourable line of credit from the state's banks.

At the same time, the PSCs' new role is poised to foster innovation and adaptation of new technologies in the field (Strachan 2013). Drone recognizance capabilities, matched with satellite data gathering provided by specialized PSCs, could foster the SOEs' risk assessments and strategy building. In addition, it is going to provide affordable specialized services to other PSCs that do not have the need to train and maintain dedicated hardware and personnel. Additionally, Chinese PSCs providing this kind of specialized support to Chinese enterprises do not need to overcome the language and cultural barriers where 'lost in translation' could compromise an entire operation. In this respect, individual Singaporean citizens with previous military or police backgrounds are employed by Chinese PSCs mainly for their Chinese languages skills.[22] Along the overall BRI, several mergers and acquisitions will oblige the Chinese SOEs to share their IT network, which is going to generate cyber security risks. In the energy sector, for example, the acquisition of local power grid companies by their Chinese counterparts is forcing cyber security compromises that could affect the SOEs' reliance on their closed and almost 'air gap' IT networks in the mainland. In this respect, President Xi himself called for a closer public-private sectors partnership in shaping an efficient, modern and competitive national security sector. The newly formed Central Commission for Integrated Military and Civilian Development is not only in charge of promoting the integration of the public Military Industry Complex with the private one but also overseeing the PSCs' training functions and integration with the public security apparatus.[23]

Belt and Road Security: Who Is in Charge?

One of the several perception gaps that affect the BRI is a clear statement of who is in charge of the overall initiative. If, in the financial sector, the lack of clear understanding of the decision mechanism can produce inefficiencies and missed opportunities, then, in the security sector, a late reply or the lack of coordination during a crisis could end in tragedy. The MFA and the Ministry of Defense (MOD) are both committed to the

BRI. Also, the Chinese NDRC defines in detail the conditions for overseas investment in the document, 'Interim Authorization Criteria for Overseas Investments', but the security threats that the Chinese SOEs are going to face outside Mainland China are still discounted. Beijing exercises supervisory rights over the SOEs through the State-owned Assets Supervision and Administration Commission of the State Council (SASAC), which in 2011 produced new risk control measures.[24] Although the SASAC maintains a supervisory role, most of the decision-making power it is still vested in the SOEs' internal structure and several layers of byzantine bureaucracy, shielding the management from an effective supervision by the government's controlling bodies. Therefore, the SOEs are able to develop independent overseas investment strategies with the only requirement being to include a summary in their annual investment plans. The mandatory regulatory approvals include not only the NDRC but also the Ministry of Commerce (MOFCOM); there is increasing uncertainty about which is the leading controlling government body. All these government bodies have a say on the matter, but none has definitive veto power.

The contemporary role of PSCs with 'Chinese characteristics' is entirely different from the role played by private military security companies (PMSCs) that were employed during the two Iraqi conflicts and the Afghan stabilization campaign. Nevertheless, Chinese SOEs that employ private security still struggle with several perception gaps with regard to present security threats as well as how best to utilize security contractors.

The methods and information in producing the type of risk assessment and threat intelligence required for contemporary Chinese SOE operations abroad include the following. First, there is the need to understand the impact of a project in the region where the SOEs will operate. This assessment is a critical part of the overall country risk scenario. Most of the time, disease, local disputes and car crashes generate more victims than the average terrorist attack. The root of the problem is not only related to the lack of security and risk managers inside the SOEs but also to the different risk perceptions that Chinese companies have compared to their Western counterparts. The political risk and the possible social media fallout that a kidnapped or killed Chinese citizen can generate back home are finally increasing the level of awareness.

The first characteristic related to Chinese OFDI is that most of the time it is of a greater scale compared to the other projects run in the host country. Chinese SOEs are prone to move swiftly from one project to the next, engaging in a steep learning curve each time as they attempt to adapt to local necessities and habits. At the same time, sole reliance on Chinese workers who are segregated in gated compounds near to the work site produces anti-Chinese sentiment. The perception of local jobs loss or the suspicion of environmental degradation is common. Typically, the small segment of the local community that provides goods and service to the Chinese companies increases the bitterness in the other part of the community that is cut out from the sudden influx of yuan.

Most of the time, the Chinese management, which is duly focused on project delivery while preparing to jump into the next financing opportunity, fails to read the local community before and during the project implementation. The managers typically rely heavily on the illusion that the central government of the host country will preserve their safety and intervene to protect their businesses.

Regarding human resource management, the Chinese security sectors are still promoting a culture of a 'race to the bottom' in order to cut costs and improve profitability relying on competition that focuses on the lowest price.[25] A business culture of high-level service provision must be substituted for the current approach that tends to favour the lower bidder. The role of training and nurturing of qualified and well-paid security officials must replace human resource procedures that up to now have failed miserably to attract talent.

The Chinese central government, which is the driving force to develop China PSCs' efficiency and accountability, is in the process of promoting changes not only in the overseas deployment but also in the local security arena. Present dangers to the Chinese workers and infrastructures have demonstrated to Beijing that just 'throwing money at the problem' is not always the most viable solution.

Albeit the market for force renaissance in China and abroad, the role of PSCs is in dire need of clarification. The lack of checks and balances allows the PSCs to operate in a grey area easily exploited. Also, the market for force benefits is constrained by ineffective oversight and control.

In Search of a Safe Chinese Dream

The effect of China's activities on the international system is already inducing changes and reactions from the current rules-based status quo. The existing rules made and enforced by conservative powers are dwindling from including China as rule-maker and opposing the Chinese rise.

Nevertheless, the BRI has the potential to challenge the patterns of the world's most important sea and land routes trade channel. Beside the mercantilist narrative of the New Silk Road the BRI could also become a channel for the distribution of ideas that could challenge US-European cultural predominance. Several of the markets that will receive the impulse from the BRI investment and new infrastructures are going to create new markets that are geographically out of the US-European reach. The initiative, if successful, is going to provide to China a solid platform in maintaining the status quo as an economic superpower. Therefore, the question of the creation of a RMB zone, that will rival the US dollar 'is not an if but a when'. As soon as the People's Bank of China shifts from yuan-denominated credit swaps to a full convertibility of the yuan expanding the money supply, the BRI is going to reach its peak. At the same time, Beijing actions in protecting Chinese national and investments abroad are already affecting local and international security equilibriums. If Beijing is successful in establishing the BRI, it is creating an infrastructure with no equivalent whose primary purpose is to transfer natural resources to China. In addition, Beijing is creating a platform for broader security agreements and cooperation that is not linked to ideology but is deeply entangled in economic interests. While the US administration under President Trump's leadership is showing interest in withdrawing from a rules-based international order, China's BRI could fill that vacuum.

A first glance at today's private security market, as compared to the involvement of PSCs in the Iraq and Afghanistan conflicts (Singer 2003), could lead one to believe a scaling back in quality and quantity of private security services is in order; however, this is not the case. The BRI 'global' need for security in today's global marketplace will supply lucrative contracts, and demand sophisticated insurance groups and PSCs capable of intelligence acquisition, risk analysis and crisis management across several countries. PSCs with Chinese characteristics are not at the forefront of the next battlefield, but will rather occupy a niche market between state provision of security and the preservation of Chinese economic interests overseas. The contemporary market for force's main driver, as in all business, is profit, and Chinese PSCs are well aware of the potential.

Chinese SOEs without the proper security market knowledge and economical evaluation of risk are prone to choose the cheapest available option. The asymmetry in the pricing information is a problem that most of the Chinese SOEs are still unable to appreciate. Focusing solely on the price of security services and not on the quality of the output is still a common mistake among SOE managers that are already fighting narrow profit margins. This situation is also encouraged by a current lack of detailed regulations and a performance monitoring system. While the role of private security could have improved the chances of the Chinese victims in Quetta and Karachi, it is not foreseeable that a private force could have avoided a military impasse by the tri-junction area of Sikkim, Tibet and Bhutan border dispute.

Private soldiering in the new millennium has left unanswered centuries-old questions on how the use of force by non-state actors is appropriate. The BRI security narrative will experience the same problems when the increase of violent threats to Chinese assets is going to blur the line between defensive security and pre-emptive strikes. At the same time, the various stakeholders that are involved in the BRI could deviate or cause deviations from Beijing's blueprint. SOEs with different agendas and Chinese PSCs not aligned with the central government's long-term strategy could ignite unexpected crisis. The lack of transparency, accountability and separation from the established chain of command structure is a current fixture of the private market for force. While it is not a question whether Chinese PSCs will have a foreign policy of their own, their undisputed allegiance to Beijing should not be taken for granted.

The never-ending story over the legitimacy of the PSCs is not going to end with the involvement of China. Nevertheless, the debate over the market for force must strive to impose a strict regulatory and auditing framework that includes multilateral cooperation and enforcement mechanisms. The Chinese 'socialist market' model could promote a top-down approach fostering efficiency and effectiveness in the provision of security through a rule-based PSCs' code of conduct. Therefore, Beijing efforts along the BRI need to be focused on the creation of a 'one-stop shop' able to attract and lead all the security stakeholders, enforcing at the same time a proper monitoring and control system.

Notes

1. Fen Fa You Wei: 'The key difference between the KLP and the SFA is that the former focuses on economic gains and the latter seeks to strengthen political support'. Yan Xuetong 'From Keeping a Low Profile to Striving for Achievement' The Chinese Journal of International Politics 2014.
2. Tao Guang Yang Hui: 'Xiaoping's proposal, which he reads as meaning "observe calmly, secure our position, cope with affairs calmly, hide our

capacities and bide our time, be good at maintaining a low profile, and never claim leadership." Global Times June 15, 2011 http://www.globaltimes.cn/content/661734.shtml.
3. China Daily 'Xi vows Belt, Road support', May 15, 2017 http://www.chinadaily.com.cn/china/2017-05/15/content_29343505.htm.
4. China Daily 'List of Deliverables of the Belt and Road Forum for International Cooperation', May 16, 2017 http://www.chinadaily.com.cn/china/2017-05/16/content_29359377.htm.
5. Reuters 'Islamic State says it killed two Chinese teachers kidnapped in Pakistan', June 8, 2017 http://www.reuters.com/article/us-pakistan-china-islamic-state-idUSKBN18Z20O.
6. Aljazeera 'Bomb attack kills at least 25 in Pakistan's Balochistan' May 13, 2017 http://www.aljazeera.com/news/2017/05/blast-kills-pakistan-balochistan-170512095736342.html.
7. Pakistan Forward B'aloch Liberation Army guns down 10 construction workers in Gwadar' May 15, 2017 http://pakistan.asia-news.com/en_GB/articles/cnmi_pf/newsbriefs/2017/05/15/newsbrief-02.
8. *South China Morning Post* 'China, India border dispute bubbles over once more, but no one is quite sure why. Experts unsure why Chinese road construction project at tri-junction with Bhutan sparks huge military stand-off, but incident shows tensions remain high', July 3, 2017 http://www.scmp.com/news/china/diplomacy-defence/article/2100871/china-india-border-dispute-bubbles-over-once-more-no.
9. 'K&R… a market worth about $250m in 2006 doubled in size by 2011…' from *The Economist*; Schumpeter Business and Management 'Kidnap and Ransom Insurance. I'm a client … get me out of here.' June 27, 2013 http://www.economist.com/blogs/schumpeter/2013/06/kidnap-and-ransom-insurance?fsrc=rss.
10. China's 'New Normal' defines the transition from accelerated economic development of two-digit GDP increase in the last three decades and a slower but steady economic development focused on 6–7% GDP growth per year.
11. After 54 consecutive months of year-on-year falls, the producer price index (PPI) rose 0.1% year-on-year in the month, according to the National Bureau of Statistics (NBS) October 14, 2016.
12. Author interview with the Chinese Contractors Association managers, Beijing September 2016.
13. *China Daily* 'Key part of Pakistan economic corridor opens up' November 15, 2016.
14. 'Soon we'll start hiring 700–800 police to be part of a separate security unit dedicated to Chinese security, and at a later stage a new security division would be formed', Jafer Khan, regional police officer in Gwadar told Reuters.

Syed Raza Hassan 'To protect Chinese investment, Pakistan military leaves little to chance' Reuters January 26, 2016 http://www.reuters.com/article/pakistan-china-security-gwadar-idUSKCN0VH06F.

15. Interview with Control Risks Partner Michael Humphreys, November 2016 Shanghai.
16. United States Central Command reported in January 2015 that 54,700 private contractors worked for the Defense Department in its areas of responsibility. http://www.acq.osd.mil/log/PS/reports/CENTCOM%20Census%20Reports/5A_January2015.pdf.
17. Regulation on the Administration of Use of Guns by Full-time Guards and Escorts Decree adopted in 2002 via No.356 of the State Council of the People's Republic of China, English translation http://www.lawinfochina.com/Display.aspx?lib=law&Cgid=40814.
18. Regulation on the Administration of Security and Guarding Services, adopted in 2009 via State Council Order No. 564, Article 1. English translation http://www.lawinfochina.com/display.aspx?lib=law&id=7779.
19. Frontier Services Group Limited, previously known as DVN (Holdings) Limited (HKSE: 00500), China investment bank CITIC Group is one of the major shareholders. 'Security and logistics services in frontier markets. We help businesses operating in frontier markets overcome complex security, logistics and operational challenges. From Asia to Africa, FSG delivers reliable, bespoke and fully integrated project logistics solutions that cover air, sea and ground transport.'
20. Author interview with Chinese PSC managers in Beijing during the preparation of 'Security Privatisation with Chinese Characteristics: The Role of Chinese Private Security Corporations in Protecting Chinese Outbound Investments and Citizens' IDSS/RSIS China Programme 30 June 2015 https://www.rsis.edu.sg/rsis-publication/idss/security-privatisation/#.WRZrXBOGNAY.
21. Interview with Dr. Jianming Mei, Director Research Center for Counterterrorism, People's Public Security University of China in Beijing, February 2017.
22. Author's interviews with retired Singapore Military attaché and former Singapore police force expert in K&R.
23. *China Daily* 'Xi: Integrate military and civil sectors' June 21, 2017 http://www.chinadaily.com.cn/china/2017-06/21/content_29822602.htm.
24. Circular n16 (2006) Circular n225 (2008), Circular n16 '*Interim measures for the supervision and* administration *of overseas State-owned assets of central State-owned Enterprises*' (2011).
25. Author's interview with Western security companies top management in Shanghai and Singapore.

References

Arduino Alessandro (2017), 'China's Belt and Road Initiative Security Needs. The Evolution of Chinese Private Security Companies' RSIS 29 August 2017 https://www.rsis.edu.sg/wp-content/uploads/2017/08/WP306.pdf

Arduino Alessandro (2015) 'Security Privatisation with Chinese Characteristics: The Role of Chinese Private Security Corporations in Protecting Chinese Outbound Investments and Citizens' IDSS / RSIS / Non-Traditional Security / Policy Reports, 30 June 2015 https://www.rsis.edu.sg/rsis-publication/idss/security privatisation/#.WS489BOGPOQ

Bajoria Jayshree (2009) 'Pakistan's Fragile Foundations' Council on Foreign Relations' March 11, 2009 https://www.cfr.org/backgrounder/pakistans-fragile-foundations

Dorsey James (2017a) 'Pakistan Caught in the Middle as China's OBOR Becomes Saudi-Iranian-Indian Battleground' The Huffington Post, May 05,2017 'The Deep-Sea Port of Gwadar in Balochistan is a Lynchpin of China's One Belt, One Road Initiative, and a Mere 70 Kilometres from the Indian-Backed Port of Chabahar in Iran, Viewed by Saudi Arabia as a Potential Threat to One of the Most Important Sea Routes Facilitating the Flow of Oil from the Gulf to Asia.'

Dorsey James M (2017b) 'Conflict in the Middle East Threatens Pakistan and Lynchpin of China's One Belt, One Road' South Asia Journal, May 14 2017. http://southasiajournal.net/conflict-in-the-middle-east-threatens-pakistan-and-lynchpin-of-chinas-one-belt-one-road/

Duchatel Mathieu, Brauner Oliver and Zhou Hang (2014) ' Protecting China's Overseas Interests'. The Slow Shift Away from Non-Interference' (June 2014) SIPRI Policy Paper 41 Cap.2

Grossman Derek, Chase Michael (2016) 'Xi's Purge of the Military Prepares the Chinese Army for Confrontation'; RAND Blog 2016 http://www.rand.org/blog/2016/04/xis-purge-of-the-military-prepares-the-chinese-army.html

Hua Chunying 'Remarks on the Two Chinese Killed in Pakistan' Ministry of Foreign Affairs June 9, 2017 http://www.fmprc.gov.cn/mfa_eng/xwfw_665399/s2510_665401/t1468973.shtml

Hua Chunying 'Remarks on Chinese Embassy in Kyrgyzstan Hit by Terrorist Attack. China Strongly Condemns the Horrific Terrorist Attack Against the Chinese Embassy in Kyrgyzstan. Terrorism Is the Common Enemy for the International Community, Posing the Gravest Threat on Regional Countries. China also Falls Victim to Terrorism. We Will Strengthen Anti-terrorism Cooperation with Regional Countries Including Kyrgyzstan Under Bilateral and the Shanghai Cooperation Organization (SCO) Frameworks, Clamp Down on All Forms of Terrorism, and Take Tangible Efforts to Ensure the Safety of Chinese Institutions and People in Relevant Countries and Uphold Regional Peace and Stability.' http://www.fmprc.gov.cn/mfa_eng/xwfw_665399/s2510_665401/t1393115.shtml

Johnson Keith (2015) 'China Invests Billions in Its 'All-Weather Friendship' with Pakistan' Foreign Policy http://foreignpolicy.com/2015/04/16/china-invests-billions-in-its-all-weather-friendship-with-pakistan-silk-road-gwadar-indian-ocean/

Pantucci Raffaello (2017) 'China Expanding Security Role in Afghanistan' Reuters March 1, 2017 http://www.reuters.com/article/china-afghanistan-securityrole-idUSKBN1683QY

Phoenix (2017) International Think Tank official Website: Haiwai Anquan Guangli Baogao (Overseas Secuirty Management Report) http://pit.ifeng.com/event/special/haiwaianquanguanlibaogao

Prince Eric (2013) 'Civilian Warriors: The Inside Story of Blackwater and the Unsung Heroes of the War on Terror' Penguin 18 November 2013

Putz Chaterine (2015) 'China-Kazakhstan Copper Mine Brawl: Food for Thought? Authorities Stress that the Fight Was Just a Fight, Not a Pending Geopolitical Flash Point.' The Diplomat, July 14, 2015. http://thediplomat.com/2015/07/china-kazakhstan-copper-mine-brawl-food-for-thought/

Scahill Jeremy (2007) 'Blackwater: The Rise of the World's Most Powerful Mercenary Army' Nation Books

Singer Peter Warren (2003) 'Corporate Warriors: The Rise of the Private Military Industry; Ithaca, NY London; Cornell University Press

South China Morning Post 'China, India Border Dispute Bubbles Over Once More, But No One Is Quite Sure Why. Experts Unsure Why Chinese Road Construction Project at Tri-junction with Bhutan Sparks Huge Military Stand-Off, But Incident Shows Tensions Remain High' July 3, 2017 http://www.scmp.com/news/china/diplomacy-defence/article/2100871/china-india-border-dispute-bubbles-over-once-more-no

Strachan Hew (2013) The Direction of War. Contemporary Strategy in Historical Perspective. Cambridge University Press

The Economist 'Xi Jinping's Fight Against Corruption in the Military Continues', 31 July 2015 http://www.economist.com/news/china/21660257-china-nets-its-most-senior-army-general-yet-xi-jinpings-fight-against-corruption-military

Yan Xuetong (2014) Fen Fa You Wei: "The Key Difference Between the KLP and the SFA is that the Former Focuses on Economic Gains and the Latter Seeks to Strengthen Political Support." "From Keeping a Low Profile to Striving for Achievement" The Chinese Journal of International Politics

PART III

Maritime Political and Security Risks

CHAPTER 4

Singapore's Role in the Belt and Road Initiative

Sarah Y. Tong and Tuan Yuen Kong

Introduction: The Belt and Road Initiative and Its Significance

Promulgated by China's President Xi Jinping, the Belt and Road Initiative (BRI) has two arms, one over land and the other maritime. The one over land, the Silk Road Economic Belt (SREB), links China with the countries to its west such as Kazakhstan, Uzbekistan and Turkey located along the original Silk Road. The other, the 21st Century Maritime Silk Road (MSR), includes countries along the South China Sea, Pacific Ocean, Indian Ocean and Mediterranean Sea. In 2013, Chinese President Xi Jinping gave an address at Kazakhstan's Nazarbayev University to promote the idea of SREB for strengthening the countries' connectivity along the old Silk Road. In October of the same year, Chinese leaders introduced a similar idea in Indonesia's parliament to cover the countries along the maritime routes by the concept of MSR.

Sarah Y. TONG is senior research fellow at East Asian Institute of National University of Singapore. KONG Tuan Yuen is visiting research fellow at same institute.

S. Y. Tong (✉) • T. Y. Kong
East Asian Institute, National University, Singapore, Singapore

A. Arduino, X. Gong (eds.), *Securing the Belt and Road Initiative*,
https://doi.org/10.1007/978-981-10-7116-4_4

The BRI will likely prove to be an important, development-oriented initiative. Started by China, the world's most populous country and the second largest economy, BRI involves many partner countries and broad coverage with ambitious goals. BRI to date covers about sixty countries with more than 50% of the world's population, 75% of the energy resources and 40% of gross domestic product (GDP) around the world.[1] Most significantly, it aims to promote economic ties among partner countries by shortening the transporting distance between China and other countries along the Belt Road through building up transportation infrastructure such as high-speed railway and port construction. It not only broadens the scope of trade among these countries, but also reduces the transportation cost compared to the current route. For example, China has launched the China-United Kingdom route, which connects sixteen cities in China with fifteen cities in Europe that cross through Kazakhstan, Belarus and the European Union. This route is one of the constructive developments of the China Railway Express to Europe, which is targeted to spread all over major European cities in 2020.

Moreover, the routes of the MSR, which firstly linked to most of the countries in the Association of Southeast Asian Nations (ASEAN), are apparently more promising and fruitful to China. First, the growing ASEAN-China economic relations have been simultaneously developed when China become the 'world factory'. The role of ASEAN countries in the global supply chain for the products of final assembly in China is significant. Second, most of the ASEAN countries are developing countries that need to implement the infrastructure improvement that China is pushing up the project through BRI. Third, ASEAN as a whole is geographically closer to China with strong historical linkages and close economic collaborations. Within the broad BRI framework, China has proposed projects in the Southeast Asia region, such as the construction of the Kunming-Singapore railway. It will cross through mainland Southeast Asia countries in Southeast Asia and help strengthen regional cooperation among maritime countries in Southeast Asia along the South China Sea and Strait of Malacca.

The implementation of the BRI is significant to observing and understanding China's outward behaviour especially toward neighbour countries by deepening economic collaboration, but it may face many challenges. The rising anti-globalization tendencies worldwide make the future of free trade increasingly uncertain. The United States President Donald Trump and his 'Buy American, Hire American' policies pose risks to the existing global trading system. Potential geopolitical confrontation is another concern that will impact and determine the scope and scale of countries' willingness to participate in BRI, particularly in the sovereignty issue of the South China Sea.

Singapore could serve an indispensable role in the development of BRI, especially in MSR. Singapore could facilitate closer China-ASEAN economic ties by advocating free trade, widening and deepening regional economic integration. It could also collaborate with partner countries in developing various types of joint projects, given Singapore's experience and competitive advantage in the fields of finance, logistics and business management, as well as help strengthen mutual understanding and trust by providing dialogue platforms.

However, Singapore also needs to be mindful of the complexities in the region's geopolitical dynamics. For example, given the sensitive nature of the South China Sea issue, Singapore has to try its best to preserve its neutrality and to safeguard ASEAN unity and centrality. Meanwhile, Singapore is also facing growing challenges. On one hand, global trade is decelerating, casting a significant negative shock to Asian countries especially those that depend heavily on trade. Meanwhile, China is catching up quickly in high added-value manufacturing, putting great competitive pressure on more advanced Asian countries and on bilateral economic cooperation. Moreover, Singapore and China may also run into direct competition in third countries as China enhances investment efforts in BRI.

Rationale Behind China's BRI

The BRI may have multiple underlying considerations. First, it could support China's more prominent outward stance. Second, it helps to cultivate closer ties with a large number of developing countries. And third, it is a useful tool to promote China's domestic economic rebalancing. Indeed, China has become increasingly influential regionally and globally, due to its remarkable economic growth and integration with the world economy. The country has now become a major trading partner and key investor with most of countries in the world, especially the Southeast and East Asian countries. The BRI will help enhance China's strong economic ties with its partner countries. In addition, Chinese companies could provide a lot of cost-competitive infrastructure solutions to developing countries for construction, such as power stations and highways, creating a win-win outcome.

From China's official narratives, the key principles of BRI are promoting joint development among countries along the routes, advocating open and cooperative models, establishing harmonious and inclusive regional relationships, enhancing market-oriented policies, and providing mutual benefit to participants in the BRI. In particular, Chinese government has set up five targets of connectivity in terms of policy communication, infrastructure connectivity, trade link, capital flow and understanding among peoples through bilateral and multilateral cooperation as well as regional and sub-regional coordination.

For more than the last three decades, China's development has been highly associated with economic liberalization and opening up to the outside world. Since the mid-1990s, China has been the largest recipient of foreign direct investment (FDI) among developing countries. According to China's Ministry of Commerce, China received US$489.42 billion in foreign capital from 2013 to 2016. In particular, FDI in high-tech industries increased by 11.7% year-on-year on average during this period.[2] Since the early 2000s, China has also been encouraging outward FDI by Chinese firms, including both State-Owned Enterprises (SOEs) and non-state firms. In the 2000s, Chinese government encouraged SOEs to invest abroad to explore international markets through its Going Out campaign. The Chinese outward FDI has tremendously increased from US$2.9 billion in 2003 to US$170.1 billion in 2016.[3] The BRI is another step to enhance the country's outreach. Chinese government took the opportunities to introduce the BRI so as to create more room for the growth of outward FDI.

Through BRI, China also aims to intensify economic ties with its neighbours, rekindle its historical linkages, and strengthen relations with developing countries. One part of BRI—the Silk Road Economic Belt—made a clear reference to the historical route on which China sent delegations from Changan to Central Asia and Persia for trading ties in 200 BC of the Han Dynasty. Chinese businessmen mainly sell silk and pottery to the people along the route to trade back Arabian glassware, Persian carpet, Indian spices and so on. Another part of BRI—the 21st Century Maritime Silk Road—always recalled the history of the seven expeditions of Zheng He in 14th century AD of the Ming Dynasty to visit Southeast Asia and trade back local ivory, bird nests, spices and so on. Moreover, the BRI not only includes the neighbour countries that China has historically established economic relations with along the routes, but Chinese government also expanded it to developing countries located in the proximity and keen on taking part in the connectivity.

With a strong focus on trade and investment, the BRI complements several domestic development objectives for China, such as reducing excessive production capacity in certain sectors and developing China's inland regions. In the last decade, cutting down industrial overcapacity, for example, to eliminate Zombie companies, has become an important objective for the Chinese government. In the country's 13th Five-Year Plan (2016–2020), the Chinese central government highlighted that the problem of excessive production capacity could hinder economic restructuring and urged local authorities to come up with solutions. Some policy makers had already proposed to shift the industries with production overcapacity, such as iron and steel, to certain neighbouring countries for their industrial upgrading.

For the Xi Jinping leadership, the BRI also serves to signify China's rise, with a stronger external posture and perceived favourable image. Chinese government has promised to build China into a moderately prosperous society and a strong manufacturing power by 2020. To reach the destination, China has to sustain medium to high levels of economic growth in the next few years. Meanwhile, as a large country, China should maintain good relations with the outside world as it aspires to a peaceful rise. This is especially important with respect to its neighbouring countries, to alleviate their anxieties from both political and security considerations.

The BRI Has Significant Implications for Southeast Asia

Bilateral economic relations between China and ASEAN have developed strongly since the early 2000s and continued to strengthen after 2008. In particular, trade and the type of investment have varied significantly. BRI is an auxiliary force to advance China's economic relations with ASEAN member states through particular and substantive plans.

As China's close neighbour and key economic partner, ASEAN stands to gain from the BRI through greater trade and investment flows, infrastructure construction, and industrial parks and other joint development projects. China is already the largest or second largest trade partner for ASEAN countries and has become an increasingly important investor in

Southeast Asia. Besides, most ASEAN countries are looking for infrastructure investment funding that could help to drive their domestic industrial upgrading and economic growth. Chinese investment under the BRI has a strong focus on infrastructure and thus provides more opportunities for both China-ASEAN closer economic cooperation and ASEAN countries' future development.

Therefore, ASEAN's involvement in BRI is based primarily on their economic rationale, such as the size of the economy, the level of industrial development and the current economic relation with China. Nonetheless, it is apparent that infrastructure investment is the most attractive for most ASEAN countries, even though the BRI has a much broader coverage.

China has proposed to build the Kunming-Singapore railway system to facilitate economic exchange among the countries in the Indochina region. Three planned routes start from Kunming in China's Yunnan province via Myanmar, Laos and Vietnam respectively, which then join together in Bangkok, Thailand and across Malaysia, and finally reach Singapore. At present, only parts of the second route (via Laos) have been launched for construction. Chinese companies had successfully obtained the construction contract of the China-Laos section and the Laos-Thailand section, although the latter was suspended because the Thailand government requested redrafting of the contract. China has also been active in bidding for the Kuala Lumpur-Singapore High Speed Railway—the Malaysia-Singapore section—and will compete with Japanese companies again for the potential Bangkok-Kuala Lumpur section. Apart from the Kunming-Singapore railway project, China has also taken part in a joint venture agreement on October 2015 to build the Jakarta-Bandung High Speed Railway in Indonesia.

In addition to exploring infrastructure collaboration in railway construction projects in ASEAN, China also developed other cooperative engineering projects such as the construction of dams and ports. For dam building, China had help in the Bakun Dam project in Malaysia, Myitsone Dam project in Myanmar, and Kamchay Dam project in Cambodia. For port construction, Chinese-invested port projects in ASEAN included the expansion of Kuantan Port and Malacca gateway in Malaysia, Tanjung Sauh Port on Batam Island in Indonesia, and deep-sea port on Madae Island in Myanmar. In 2017, China signed an agreement with the Philippines government to provide assistance for 40 infrastructure projects, including 15 for financing and 25 for feasibility studies.[4] Among them, the Subic-Clark Railway project, Davao Coastline and Port

Development project, Cebu International and Bulk Terminal project, and the bus rapid transit system for the Philippines' NAIA Airport project received the most attention.

China also promoted industrial capacity cooperation with ASEAN countries. Among ASEAN member states, Myanmar, Cambodia, and Laos have greater need to improve infrastructure. At present, their collaborations with China are mainly in agricultural and light manufacturing industries. Vietnam has deeper industrial capacity cooperation with China, such as in the export processing industry, after Vietnam initiated economic reforms in the late 1980s. In comparison, Malaysia, Thailand, the Philippines and Indonesia have broader industrial coordination. China-Malaysia even mutually set up 'Two Countries, Twin Parks' to develop complementary industries. Indonesia invited Chinese companies to invest in natural resources industries and Thailand welcomes Chinese SOEs to set up factories of automobile manufacturing and green-energy production.

However, the future of free trade is unclear when the sound of anti-globalization is gradually amplified. US President Donald Trump, withdrew from the Trans-Pacific Partnership (TPP) Agreement on his first day in office and vows to renegotiate the North American Free Trade Agreement (NAFTA). It signals that the United States is reviewing the implication of globalization and free trade to its domestically political and economic development. The Trump administration indicated its preference for bilateral economic agreement rather than multilateral trade packs. Protectionism and an anti-globalization sentiment have proliferated in other regions, such as the European Union. These new developments place serious constraints on the future of global trade and economic development, especially to trade-dependent regions such as East and Southeast Asia.

Territorial disputes in the region may also obstruct the participation and cooperation of countries in the BRI, such as those involved in the South China Sea issue. Even though bilateral relations between the Philippines and between Vietnam and China have improved significantly, the issue remains a thorny one and there is no easy solution. In addition, other factors will also affect the regional geopolitical dynamics, such as the repeated assertion for freedom of navigation by the United States. Thus, bilateral economic ties between China and ASEAN have to operate under a more complex and dynamic trilateral China-US-ASEAN relationship.

Singapore Can Play an Important Role

Among ASEAN member states, Singapore could play a significant role in facilitating closer China-ASEAN economic ties through the BRI. When China's Foreign Minister Wang Yi met with Singapore's Foreign Minister Vivian Balakrishnan in February 2017, it was expected that Singapore would play a substantively coordinative role to strengthen China-ASEAN relations for regional economic development. Despite Singapore's small population, it is the most advanced and open economy with the highest GDP per capita (US$53 thousand in 2016) in ASEAN.

More importantly, Singapore's investment in its ASEAN neighbours has been substantial and its share in ASEAN's total rose further in recent years from 17% in 2012 to 27% and 25% in 2014 and 2015, respectively (Fig. 4.1). This suggests that Singapore has deepened its integration into ASEAN economic cooperation in recent years. According to ASEAN's official statistics, the top three economic sectors that Singapore invested in in the regions include manufacturing (US$3.8 billion), agriculture, forestry, and fishing (US$3.6 billion) and finance and insurance (US$2.8 billion) in 2015.[5] Meanwhile, the three sectors that saw the fastest growth in investment from Singapore in ASEAN between 2012 and 2015 are agriculture, forestry, and fishing (56.6% a year), information and

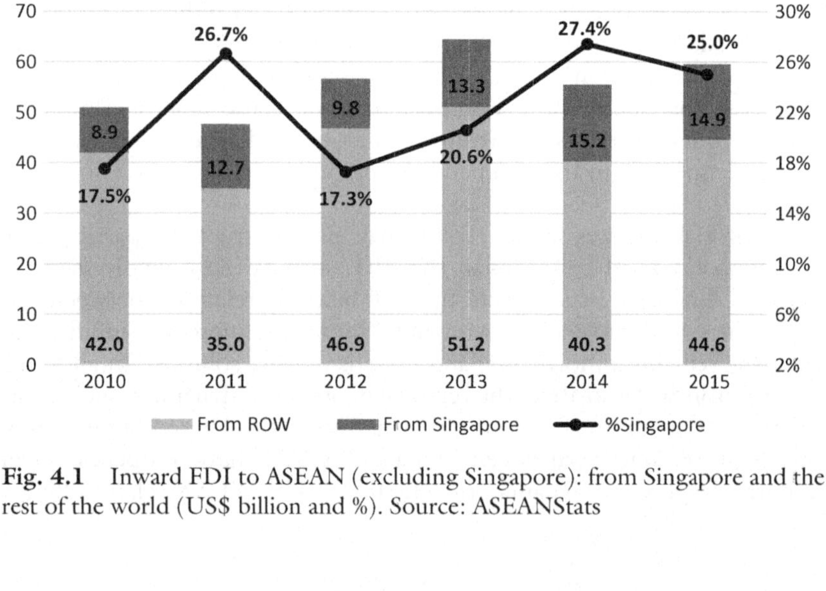

Fig. 4.1 Inward FDI to ASEAN (excluding Singapore): from Singapore and the rest of the world (US$ billion and %). Source: ASEANStats

communication (46.4% a year), and wholesale and retail trade (44.2% a year) (Table 4.1). It is apparent that Singapore not only has rich experience investing in ASEAN in traditional industries such as manufacturing and agricultural, but has also expanded investment into various modern service sectors.

Singapore's economic success is highly correlated with its opening-up strategy. As free trade is a fundamental policy in Singapore for development, the country naturally strongly supports the establishment of the ASEAN Economic Community (AEC). It is also keen on signing up free trade agreements (FTAs) with its trading partners, both bilateral and multilateral. As shown in Table 4.2, Singapore has an extensive network of 20 effective FTAs, including the China-ASEAN Free Trade Agreement (CAFTA), as well as a number that are still under negotiation.[6] It demonstrates Singapore's inclination to promote bilateral, regional and multilateral trade deals, including, for example, the TPP and the Regional Comprehensive Economic Partnership (RCEP). Despite the recent change in the US government's stance on free trade in general and on TPP in particular, Singapore continues to advocate free trade and deeper regional economic integration, which largely coincides with China's policies.

Besides, Singapore has been a key investor in China since the 1980s, and since 2013, it has been China's largest foreign investor. In particular, the two governments have cooperated closely to carry out Government-to-Government (G2G) projects with China, including the Suzhou Industrial Park (SIP), the Tianjin Eco-city (TEC) and the Chongqing Connectivity Initiative (CCI). The SIP started more than 20 years ago and has become an important pillar for growth and industrial upgrading in Suzhou. The TEC started in 2007, focusing mainly on ecological development in terms of energy-saving and environmentally friendly projects.

Table 4.1 Singapore's investment to other ASEAN states by sectors, 2015 (US$ million)

Sectors	*2012*	*2015*	*Average annual growth (%)*
Manufacturing	2,514	3,784	14.6
Agriculture, forestry and fishing	929	3,565	56.6
Finance and insurance	3,521	2,799	–7.4
Wholesale and retail trade	453	1,359	44.2
Information and communication	269	844	46.4

Source: ASEANstats

Table 4.2 Singapore's free trade agreements

Bilateral FTAs	*Regional/multilateral FTAs*
	Implemented FTAs
China	ASEAN-Australia-New Zealand
India	ASEAN-China
Japan	ASEAN-India
Korea	ASEAN-Japan
New-Zealand	ASEAN-Korea
Panama	ASEAN Free Trade Area
Peru	EFTA-Singapore
Australia	GCC-Singapore
Costa Rica	Trans-Pacific Strategic Economic Partnership
Jordan	
United States	
	Concluded/signed FTAs
European Union	Trans-Pacific Partnership
Turkey	
	FTAs undergoing negotiation
Canada	ASEAN-India (Service and Investment)
Mexico	ASEAN-India (Service and Investment)
Pakistan	Regional Comprehensive Economic Partnership
Ukraine	

Source: IE Singapore

In line with the development of the BRI, the CCI project was announced in 2016 and has been considered a prominent demonstration under the BRI, China's 'Go West' development strategy and the Yangtze River Economic Belt strategies.[7] According to the latest meeting of the Singapore-China Joint Council of Bilateral Cooperation (JCBC), held in Beijing on 27 February 2017, both countries have committed to broaden cooperation through existing G2G projects in the fields of biomedical industries, logistics, property development and certain high-tech industries. The Singapore-China G2G projects have not only strengthened bilateral countries' economic ties, but also serve as examples for how governments could work jointly to promote local development, such as establishing industrial parks, export-processing zones and so on.

Beyond the three G2G projects, China and Singapore have also developed strong economic ties through non-government projects, not only in China but also in other parts of Asia. For example, the Singapore-based Ascendas-Singbridge Group has set up the Knowledge City in Guangzhou, the IT Park in Dalian, and the Science and Technology Park in Hangzhou. The company also cooperated with a Chinese company, the China Machinery Engineering Corporation, to build up other industrial parks in other Asian countries.[8] Such Business-to-Business (B2B) cooperation could also play a significant role in the development of BRI in ASEAN member countries.

Indeed, there have already many joint efforts between Chinese and Singapore businesses to extend their business interests regionally and globally. Another example is Pacific Shipping Lines (PSI) Ltd. In addition to entering a joint venture agreement with Singapore's PSA International (PSA) and China's Guangxi Beibu Gulf International Port Group to operate a new container terminal in China's Qinzhou City, PIL also has a project with the China Shipping Container Lines (CSCL) to extend shipping services in order to enhance Singapore-China-Africa networks. Such B2B joint efforts toward third countries will likely be a key focus of future development for Singapore-China bilateral economic cooperation through the BRI. This is particularly true in areas where Singapore has strong competitive advantages such as logistics and modern services.

Singapore has the potential to be a key logistical hub to facilitate the BRI. According to SPRING Singapore, Singapore was ranked second in the World Bank Logistic Performance Index 2010, the best among Asian countries.[9] Its seaport is connected to 600 ports of 123 countries by 200 shipping lines and its airport has 4500 linkages with 200 cities of 60 countries. Also, the Quality of Living survey of 2017 ranked Singapore the best place to live in Asia for expatriates.[10] Singapore has a well-developed logistics industry with an innovative supply-chain management system, highly skilled personnel, niche capabilities and customized solutions and an international-standard legal system. The country's strong legal and regulatory framework, especially in intellectual property right (IPR) protection, and rich experience in corporate social responsibility implementation, also makes it highly attractive to multinational companies for setting up regional or global headquarters.

The rapid advancement of various modern service sectors in Singapore enables the country to play an essential role in helping to facilitate the BRI in many aspects. Singapore could utilize its advanced and well-regulated financial sector to promote bilateral investment, to develop an offshore RMB centre, to provide direct financing through its capital market, and to facilitate cooperation among Singapore and Chinese banking institutions for infrastructure investment financing. Already, the International

Enterprise (IE) Singapore has respectively signed memorandums of understanding (MOUs) with the Industrial and Commercial Bank of China (ICBC), the China Construction Bank (CCB) and the Bank of China to provide assistance in commodities trading, financing and related professional financial services to Singapore companies in infrastructure projects under the BRI. In addition, the Bank of China also launched the global energy commodity business centre and global commodity repo centre in Singapore in November 2015.[11]

It is worth noting that, according to the latest survey report by the Startup Genome project, a US-based organization, Singapore ranked number one in the world for start-up talent in 2017, overtaking Silicon Valley.[12] The report highlighted that Singapore's innovative policies have been essential to the attractiveness of its start-up ecosystem. It remarked that there are about 1600–2400 tech start-ups in Singapore receiving government subsidies, such as the US$13.2 billion research and development initiative, and schemes of early-stage venture capital funds. In addition, Singapore's geographical location, with easy access to the world market and relative cost of hiring engineers, attracts start-ups to set up companies in Singapore. Accordingly, the average salary of a software engineer in Singapore is around US$35 thousand, still much lower than the global average (US$49 thousand). Such an outstanding performance of Singapore in recruiting talented persons could not only strengthen Singapore-China economic relations in advancing industrial specialization and product customization, but also boost the People-to-People (P2P) exchange between the two in sharing patents, knowledge, and start-up management.

Alongside bilateral economic cooperation, Singapore could play an important role to enhance mutual understanding and trust between China and countries in Southeast Asia by providing dialogue platforms and facilitating direct and indirect communications. As of now, multiple platforms already exist for bilateral dialogue between China and ASEAN countries for various issues, including the ASEAN Regional Forum (ARF), the ASEAN Plus Three (APT) Summit, the East Asia Summit (EAS) and the ASEAN Defence Ministers Meeting (ADMM-Plus). Non-traditional security issues such as international economic crime are also discussed in these dialogues.

Singapore has already had to be active in initiating the various discussion platforms. In addition, it has also provided numerous unofficial channels to coordinate among countries that have various geopolitical concerns in the region. For example, the Singapore Institute of International Affairs

(SIIA) hosts ASEAN and Asia Forum (AAF) every year to gather political and security perspectives from experts, leaders, business professionals, government officials and academia. To enhance mutual trust, the Shangri-La Dialogue, held in Singapore, serves as another important venue for defence professionals to exchange views and understanding on regional security issues from countries in the Asia-Pacific region. Recently, it has become an outstanding platform for China, the United States and Southeast Asia to express their views on the sovereignty issue of the South China Sea.

There are various MOUs between ASEAN and China, including those for Information and Communication Technologies (ICT); Transport; Sanitary and Phytosanitary Cooperation Standards; Technical Regulations and Conformity Assessment (TBT); Health Cooperation; Science and Technology Partnership (STEP) Programme; and Disaster Management Cooperation. As an advanced economy, Singapore could help others in the region by sharing its experiences not only in economic growth, but also in promoting socio-cultural development. It could lead others extending these MOUs toward deeper cooperation. By expanding and deepening connectivity and integration between China and ASEAN, and among ASEAN countries, such broad and comprehensive cooperation will provide a stronger foundation for the development of BRI. Indeed, such broad-based cooperation underlines the general concept of connectivity, which was highlighted in the BRI and reaffirmed as fundamental in promoting ASEAN connectivity at the 15th ASEAN-China Summit in 2012.[13]

Challenges Lie Ahead

There are numerous challenges to improving Sino-Singapore relations, which will also affect Singapore's role in the BRI. One concerns the geopolitical tension arising from the South China Sea disputes. Since 2016, misperceptions toward each other on the issue seem to have eroded mutual trust and hindered the development of bilateral relations. From Singapore's standpoint, it maintains that the disputes be resolved based on international law and peaceful settlement. Singapore also reiterated that freedom of navigation in the South China Sea and a united ASEAN are the country's national interest. From China's perspective, although Chinese government did not respond directly to Singapore's assertion, certain incidents hinted at its displeasure toward Singapore. One example is the seizure of nine of Singapore's Terrex Infantry Carrier Vehicles (ICVs) at the Port of

Hong Kong in November 2016 that were held for more than two months. Meanwhile, the 2016 annual meeting of the JCBC was delayed, and later held in January 2017. Although the two cases were eventually resolved without being proliferated into other areas, these may have a lasting impact by arousing a real sense of hurt between the people and by deepening distrust between the governments.

The second challenge comes from the global economic slowdown and China's economic restructuring. As global economic growth decelerated, protectionist sentiment strengthened and growth in world trade slowed down sharply. Asia suffered more, having been a highly trade-dependent region. In 2014 and 2015, world merchandise exports grew by 2.7% and 3.0% in volume, only slightly higher than those in world GDP, at 2.5% and 2.4%, respectively. Meanwhile, Asia's contribution to global trade growth declined, from about two percentage points in 2011 to about one percentage point for export and less than half a percentage point for import in 2015 (Fig. 4.2). Difficulties in trade development globally and regionally will inevitably pose challenges to export-oriented countries such as China and Singapore, to both their bilateral trade and their trade relations with other economies.

In addition to merchandise trade, trade in services has also suffered setbacks in recent years. In 2015, world export in commercial services declined by 6%, most seriously in transport, which contracted by nearly

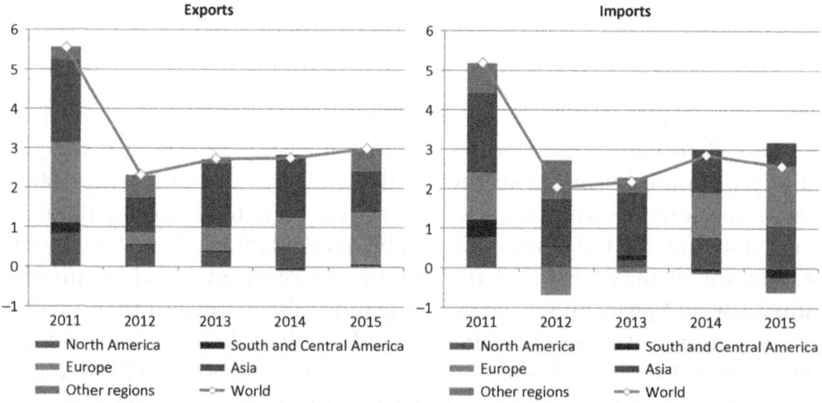

Fig. 4.2 Contributions to growth in world merchandise trade in volume, by regions, 2011–2015 (Annual % change). Source: WTO Secretariat

10% (Fig. 4.3). This dealt a serious blow to Singapore, having strong comparative advantages in the sector and ranked the world's tenth largest exporter in commercial services in 2015. At the same time, it also highlights the importance of bilateral cooperation. China was the world's second largest importer in commercial services in 2015, following the United States, accounting for more than 10% of the world total.

On the other hand, China's efforts to restructure its economy and to upgrade its industry will also have important implications for bilateral economic relations. By introducing the Made in China 2025 strategy, China aims to move its industries upward along the value chain, through the promotion of high added-value and high-tech industries. Such restructuring efforts will likely narrow technology gaps between Chinese and Singapore businesses and intensify competition, reducing room for business cooperation.

The third challenge arises from Chinese investment in third countries. In recent years, for example, China has made a tremendous amount of investment in Malaysia. The latest projects, including China-funded ports and the East Coast Rail Line (ECRL), were launched in late 2016 and expected to be completed in five to 10 years. The ECRL, which connects the Klang Port on the west coast of Peninsular Malaysia with the Kuantan Port in its east coast could have a significant impact on Singapore's business interest, as shipping through the Pacific Ocean to the Indian Ocean

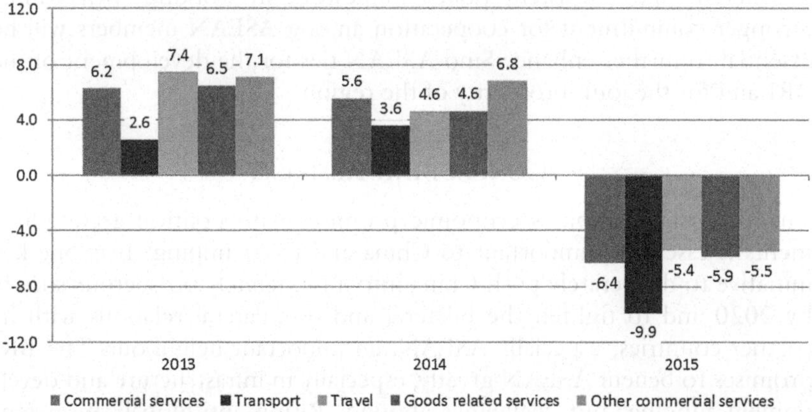

Fig. 4.3 Value growth of commercial services exports by category, 2013–2015 (%). Source: WTO Secretariat

or vice versa could then bypass the port of Singapore via ECRL. Similarly, in the previous decade, China had reached an agreement with the authorities of Myanmar to build a pipeline across the country to the southwest region of China. This pipeline could provide about 260 thousand barrels-per-day refinery capacity from the port of Kyauk Pyu in Myanmar to China's Yunnan province 770 kilometres away,[14] an alternative and perhaps eminent oil trading route from the Middle East to China, significantly weakening the strategic importance of the Port of Singapore. Such potentially damaging impacts on Singapore's business interest from Chinese investment may also include that from the Gwadar Port of Pakistan, which provides China with a much shorter maritime access to Europe, Africa and the Middle East, diminishing the importance of the Strait of the Malacca and the Port of Singapore.

Finally, the diversity and diverging interests among ASEAN countries could be another serious challenge for Singapore to play an important role in the development of the BRI. Since the early 2000s, China's influence on the global economy has grown stronger. In ASEAN, in particular, China has become the region's most important economic partner in trade, investment, tourism and personnel exchange. The increasingly direct and deep linkages between China and ASEAN member states have gradually but considerably weakened Singapore's role as a coordinator between the two. More essentially, the fragility and vulnerability of ASEAN unity also makes it difficult for ASEAN, and for Singapore in particular, to maintain a coherent and consistent policy framework in working with China. Stronger commitment for cooperation among ASEAN members will be essential to further enhance Sino-ASEAN ties for the development of the BRI and for the joint prosperity of the region.

Concluding Remarks

The BRI that combines economic promises with political accomplishments is essentially important to China and to Xi Jinping. It is one key initiative to deliberately push China into a moderately prosperous society by 2020 and to tighten the bilateral and multilateral relations with its partner countries, especially ASEAN, an important neighbour. The BRI promises to benefit ASEAN greatly, especially in infrastructure and development funding, but challenges abound. Rising anti-globalization tendencies and potential sovereignty conflict concerning the South China Sea are two of the major stumbling blocks for advancing ASEAN-China relations through BRI.

Although there has been much political rhetoric, there is a greater need for the Chinese government to better articulate its plans and approaches to enhance cooperation with ASEAN via BRI. Meanwhile, there is a significant role for Singapore to play in BRI for closer regional economic ties and integration and joint project implementation between ASEAN and China. Anyhow, greater mutual trust and stronger bilateral relations would be essential for developing BRI. In particular, the changing geopolitics in the South China Sea may lead to irrational quarrels among ASEAN countries due to divisiveness and the misperception among countries in the region, including those between Singapore and China. More efforts are needed from both sides to enhance mutual understanding and cooperation for their long-term interest. In seeking long-term growth opportunities, Singapore also has to monitor closely Chinese industrial development and investment activities both domestically and in third countries so as to identify key areas of cooperation and avoid direct competition.

Notes

1. 'China's one belt, one road plan covers more than half of the population, 75% of energy resources and 40% of world's GDP'. *South China Morning Post*, 21 June 2016. http://www.scmp.com/business/china-business/article/1978396/chinas-one-belt-one-road-plan-covers-more-half-population-75 (accessed on 15 March 2017).
2. 'FDI to get boost, new commerce chief vows', *The China Post*, 1 March 2017.
3. 'China outbound investment retreats as capital controls bite', *The Strait Times*, 16 February 2017. http://www.straitstimes.com/business/economy/china-outbound-investment-retreats-as-capital-controls-bite (accessed on 18 February 2017); the statistics is from Ministry of Commerce of People's Republic of China http://fec.mofcom.gov.cn/article/tjsj/tjgb/ (accessed on 18 February 2017).
4. Recto Mercene, 'Manila, Beijing to sign more investment deals', *Business Mirror*, 15 Mar 2017. http://www.businessmirror.com.ph/manila-beijing-to-sign-more-investment-deals/ (accessed on 16 March 2017).
5. ASEANstats Database: http://data.aseanstats.org/ (accessed on 15 March 2017).
6. 'Singapore Free Trade Agreements', *IE Singapore*, https://www.iesingapore.gov.sg/Trade-From-Singapore/International-Agreements/free-trade-agreements/Singapore-FTA (accessed on 20 March 2017).

7. 'Singapore has consistently abided by "One China policy": DPM Teo', *Channel NewsAsia*, 26 Feb, 2017. http://www.channelnewsasia.com/news/singapore/singapore-has-consistently-abided-by-one-china-policy-dpm-teo/3551408.html (accessed on 9 March 2017).
8. 'Why China's plan to build a new Silk Road runs through Singapore', *Today*, 15 Aug, 2016. http://www.todayonline.com/chinaindia/china/why-chinas-plan-build-new-silk-road-runs-through-singapore (accessed on 10 March 2017).
9. 'Singapore -The Global Logistic Hub', *the Industrial Brochure of Logistics*, SPRING Singapore. https://www.spring.gov.sg/Developing-Industries/LOG/Documents/Industry_Brochures_Logistics.pdf (accessed on 14 March 2017).
10. 'Singapore ranked best place to live in Asia for expats: Mercer's survey', *Channel NewsAsia*, 14 March 2017. http://www.channelnewsasia.com/news/singapore/singapore-ranked-best-place-to-live-in-asia-for-expats-mercer-s/3593172.html?cid=fbcna (accessed on 14 March 2017).
11. IE Singapore's website: MOUs with China https://www.iesingapore.gov.sg/Venture-Overseas/Browse-By-Market/Asia-Pacific/China/MOUs (accessed on 12 March 2017).
12. 'Singapore overtakes tech mecca Silicon Valley as No. 1 for global start-up talent', *The Strait Times*, 21 March 2017. http://www.straitstimes.com/business/economy/singapore-overtakes-tech-mecca-silicon-valley-as-no-1-for-global-startup-talent (accessed on 22 March 2017).
13. 'Overview of ASEAN-China Dialogue Relations', Association of Southeast Asian Nations. http://asean.org/?static_post=overview-asean-china-dialogue-relations (accessed on 21 February 2017).
14. 'Beset by delays, Myanmar-China oil pipeline nears start-up', *Reuters*, 21 March 2017.

CHAPTER 5

Resolving the Malacca Dilemma: Malaysia's Role in the Belt and Road Initiative

Guanie Lim

Introduction

Since its 2013 announcement by Chinese President Xi Jinping, the Belt and Road Initiative (BRI) has become arguably China's most crucial engagement tool with the rest of the world. While there are numerous interpretations on how the BRI is to be realized, scholars generally agree that infrastructure investment is one of the most prominent vehicles undergirding Chinese expansion (Arase 2015; Ferdinand 2016; Summers 2016). For China, the construction of land- and ocean-based infrastructure networks is crucial to promote its trade and investment linkages with other foreign markets. Securing infrastructure projects is also crucial for China's infrastructure and engineering firms, many of which are suffering from overcapacity and a stuttering domestic business environment as a result of the recent deceleration of the Chinese economy following years of rapid growth.

China's spending spree, like most other initiatives of similar stature, is bound to have a profound impact on the recipient countries, especially those deemed strategic in the context of the BRI. Take Pakistan for instance; its stature as a staunch Chinese ally in South Asia and proximity to China's occasionally restive westernmost province of Xinjiang has

G. Lim (✉)
Nanyang Technological University, Singapore, Singapore

A. Arduino, X. Gong (eds.), *Securing the Belt and Road Initiative*,
https://doi.org/10.1007/978-981-10-7116-4_5

allowed it to attract considerable political and economic support from Beijing. To this end, Chinese funding has been the major impetus fuelling the construction of large-scale infrastructure projects such as the economic corridor interlinking Pakistan's Gwadar Port and Xinjiang (see Brewster 2014; Mackerras 2015). Over in Southeast Asia, Malaysia, a major regional economy as well as China's largest trading partner in this subcontinent, has tapped into the longstanding China-Malaysia bilateral relationship and resilient ethnic Chinese business networks that straddle both countries to advance its ambitions. It has been tipped to benefit greatly from the influx of Chinese capital associated with the BRI, particularly by Malaysia's political and business elites (e.g., Free Malaysia Today 2016a; Malay Mail Online 2015; The Star 2017; Zhang and Zhao 2016). One of the primary reasons undergirding their optimism is solid Chinese support in the construction of big-ticket public projects such as the East Coast Rail Link (ECRL) (Straits Times 2016; TODAY 2016). Touted as a 'game changer' that could alter existing trade routes, which currently ply between the busy Strait of Malacca and the South China Sea via Singapore, the ECRL is one of the largest public projects enthusiastically endorsed by Prime Minister Najib Razak during his week-long visit to Beijing in November 2016 (Lopez 2016). With state-owned China Communications Construction Company (CCCC) as the main contractor, it is poised to connect Kuala Lumpur, the country's commercial capital, to the states on the east coast of Peninsular Malaysia, namely Pahang, Terengganu, and Kelantan. The ECRL is broadly expected to benefit both Malaysia and China, as the next two sections will explain.

Notwithstanding such optimism, one must take into account on-the-ground implementation and state-society relations. This chapter attempts to address this issue, presenting a more balanced perspective on the ECRL. It is hoped that a clearer reading of such a pivotal Chinese project can bolster our understanding on how the BRI actually takes shape in Malaysia. It unearths the ECRL by analyzing its pros and cons, shedding light on some issues not commonly covered by mainstream analysts. The chapter ultimately argues that the ECRL, while appearing grandiose, is likely to add little to the growth of Malaysia. There remain significant hurdles to surmount before one can claim that this undertaking is truly beneficial to Malaysia.

This chapter begins with an examination on the political economy of Malaysia. In particular, it links the bottleneck facing Malaysia in its drive to become a high-income nation with the growing importance of Chinese inward foreign direct investment (FDI). It also illustrates some of the more prominent Chinese projects in recent years, highlighting the business and political risk that have hitherto limited their impact. The subsequent section details the ECRL. It focuses first on the project's background information before three key points of contention are discussed. The chapter concludes with a summary of the main arguments and research findings, along with an analysis of their policy implications.

China's Emergent Role in the Malaysian Economy

Since its independence in 1957, Malaysia has maintained a fairly liberal stance towards international trade and capital to drive its economy. This outward-oriented strategy has yielded some degree of success as the Southeast Asian country became part of a second tier of newly industrializing economies (NIEs), following close on the heels of the first-tier NIEs (i.e., Korea, Taiwan, Singapore, and Hong Kong) (Felker 2009; Hill et al. 2012; Lim 2016b; Suehiro 2008; Wong and Cheong 2014). Yet, Malaysia's strategy is predicated on the ability to continually uplift its productive capability and secure foreign capital and markets. Both avenues have been severely curtailed since the 1997 Asian Financial Crisis (AFC). The crisis unveiled that FDI mainly entered the non-productive economic sectors such as real estate and speculative finance (see Jomo 2003; Sheng 2009). Although Malaysia has tried to redirect FDI to the more productive economic sectors, such as manufacturing, since the AFC, the country's technological capability remains relatively modest (e.g., Brooker 2013; Lim 2014; van Grunsven and Hutchinson 2016; Wad 2009). For the latter, Menon (2014) shows that Malaysia has not succeeded in regaining the confidence of international investors in the years following the AFC, although it has maintained an edge in international trade (especially in agricultural commodities).[1] It has also been challenged by a newer group of NIEs (e.g., Laos and Kenya) who offer companies lower business costs. Put together, weaknesses on both fronts have bogged the country down in a middle-income trap (Hutchinson 2015). It now struggles to transition towards higher value-added activities that require increasingly more sophisticated technologies and higher-quality human capital. It is also worth mentioning that Prime Minister Najib has devoted significant attention to lifting the country out of the middle-income trap since assuming office in 2009 (see Prime Minister's Department 2015). In the international development circle, there is just as much research conducted on this topic (see Flaaen et al. 2013; Hasanov and Cherif 2015; Larson et al. 2016; Yusuf and Nabeshima 2009).

The path dependence of the above strategy, coupled with the need to break out of the middle-income trap, has forced the Malaysian leadership to target FDI providers outside its 'traditional' group (i.e., Western Bloc, Singapore, and Japan). In other words, 'non-traditional' FDI providers such as China and Saudi Arabia are becoming attractive economic partners. In the case of China, it has emerged as an attractive FDI contributor, particularly since the formulation of the BRI (Kong 2016). According to the Malaysian Investment Development Authority, China became Malaysia's largest investor in 2016, contributing an investment totalling USD 1.6 billion (MYR 4.8 billion; equivalent to 17.5% of total FDI inflow) (MIDA 2016). Chinese FDI has eclipsed those from the Netherlands (USD 1.1 billion; MYR 3.2 billion; 11.7%), Germany (USD 860.9 million; MYR 2.6 billion; 9.5%), United Kingdom (USD 860.9 million; MYR 2.6 billion; 9.5%), Korea (USD 728.5 million; MYR 2.2 billion; 8.0%), and Singapore (USD 695.4 million; MYR 2.1 billion; 7.7%). Despite its increasing importance to the Malaysian economy, Chinese investment has not always fulfilled its oft-touted potential. More specifically, such investment does not exist in a vacuum and is influenced by business and political risks, many of which are not easily grasped by the Chinese firms. For the Chinese firms that only recently internationalized, the risk inherent in a distant, emerging market like Malaysia can prove particularly challenging.

One needs only to look at some of the more prominent Chinese projects in the country. Officially launched in 2013, the Malaysia-China Kuantan Industrial Park (MCKIP) in the state of Pahang was born out of the suggestion of Prime Minister Najib. It is also the sister park of China-Malaysia Qinzhou Industrial Park (CMQIP) in Guangxi province. Both industrial parks are critical for they are often earmarked as flagship BRI projects in the region and more generally, the ideal demonstrative case studies for other Southeast Asian countries (Kong 2016). While the CMQIP is moving full steam ahead, the MCKIP has been hampered by a series of niggling issues, ranging from poor land conditions, withdrawal of key investors, and disagreement between the federal government and the Pahang state government (Nanyang Siang Pau 2014). It is only in recent years that the MCKIP has seemingly turned the corner following a series of restructuring and negotiation between key stakeholders. According to the chairman of its new master developer, it secured a total investment of

USD 1.9 billion (MYR 5.6 billion) in 2016 and is aiming to garner another USD 3.3 billion (MYR 10.0 billion) in 2017 (Rafee 2017).

In the automotive industry, low-cost carmaker Chery Group has cooperated with Alado Corporation (a Malaysian ethnic Chinese firm) to both assemble completely-knocked-down (CKD) automobile kits into completely-built-up (CBU) units and to distribute the latter in the domestic market (Lim 2015). In assembling the CKD kits, Alado Corporation has entered into an agreement with an independent contract assembler, meaning that Chery does not need to expend resources to set up its own manufacturing facility in Malaysia. For the distribution of the CBU units, Alado Corporation has established a trilateral joint venture between itself, Chery, and the Lembaga Tabung Angkatan Tentera (LTAT) (or the Armed Forces Fund Board). The strong local knowledge of Alado Corporation and the LTAT makes them worthy allies of Chery in its aim to penetrate the Malaysian market. Nevertheless, Chery's market share remains marginal. According to multiyear statistics published by the Malaysian Automotive Association (MAA), a trade and lobby group representing the interest of the automotive firms in the country, Chery has not been able to garner more than 1% (per annum basis) of the domestic market share from 2008 to 2016 (MAA 2011, 2013, 2017). Chery's strategy of producing vehicles for the masses has not yielded much success as this market has traditionally been held captive by Proton and Perodua, two domestic firms that were already in business since the 1980s and early 1990s respectively. More crucially, Chery is not able to market cheaper vehicles to compete against Proton and Perodua chiefly because the latter enjoy a more favourable duty and tax regime (see Lim 2017b). To overcome such bottlenecks, Chery has devoted significant efforts to re-strategize its business plan in the domestic market. For a time, a partnership with Proton was mulled. However, in May 2017 this avenue was closed when the Geely Automotive Holding Group, another Chinese carmaker, announced that it had agreed to acquire a 49.9% stake in Proton (Zhang et al. 2017).

These two examples reflect the difficulties involved in the internationalization of Chinese firms. The Chinese firms often are impacted by regulatory and non-regulatory barriers as well as political economic factors not commonly experienced in China. Even in the event that they have faced such challenges in China, the means to solve them are usually rather different in a foreign market like Malaysia. The broader implication of the cases of MCKIP and Chery suggest that Chinese investors need to be wary of the different commercial setting of Malaysia (at least in relation to China) and devise better mechanisms to manage the risk involved in their ventures into Malaysia. If handled inappropriately, their ventures could get bogged down for a relatively long period, depressing returns to the stakeholders.

Understanding the East Coast Rail Link

In his November 2016 visit to Beijing, Prime Minister Najib declared that the ECRL, along with several government-led initiatives, would take China-Malaysia ties to 'new heights' (Straits Times 2016). In other words, one is to expect a win-win solution out of the ECRL. For Malaysia, the ECRL is particularly helpful to boost its economy. Firstly, the project is expected to better connect the relatively backward east coast (Pahang, Terengganu, and Kelantan) to the more prosperous west coast (primarily Selangor and Kuala Lumpur). The 600 km mega project is scheduled to connect passengers and freight from Port Klang in Selangor to Tumpat in Kelantan, stringing along smaller towns such as Mentakab (Pahang) and Dungun (Terengganu). According to Tee (2017), the ECRL will cut travel time from 12 hours (by road) to about four hours. The improved connectivity is expected to bridge the longstanding economic divide between the east and west coasts of Peninsular Malaysia. According to the prime minister, the economy of Pahang, Terengganu, and Kelantan would experience an additional annual growth of 1.5% when the ECRL is completed as high value-added economic activities in sectors such as agriculture and tourism are stimulated (Jalil 2017; New Straits Times 2016). It will also breathe new life into the relatively more marginal Kuantan Port by linking it via railway to the bustling Port Klang, an issue further explored in the subsequent paragraphs.

Secondly, the ECRL will provide a major boost and a new source of contracts for the local construction sector, especially as subcontractors to CCCC (Tee 2017). Valued at a gigantic sum of USD 18.2 billion (MYR 55.0 billion), it represents one of Malaysia's 'last push' public projects in order to escape the middle-income trap and graduate into a high-income country by 2020. Indeed, it has been fast-tracked by the government to commence construction in July 2017 rather than in late 2017 as initially expected (Tee 2017). This is a significant development as public projects of this kind usually involve a relatively long period of bureaucratic deliberation and technical evaluation.

Thirdly, in terms of financing, 85% of the project is to be financed with soft loans from Beijing, a boon to Malaysia's increasingly strained public coffers (see Lopez 2016). Like many of China's major overseas infrastructure projects, the state-owned Export-Import Bank of China plays the role of financier while another state-owned enterprise (SOE) (i.e., CCCC) comes in as the project's main contractor, handling engineering, procurement, construction, and commissioning (EPCC) matters (Straits Times 2016). According to the Malaysian Ministry of Finance, China's financing terms are favourable as the interest rate is lower than what the ministry can obtain from the international markets. Furthermore, the repayment period of 20 years is relatively generous, helping Malaysia spread its financial outlay over a longer than usually permissible period (Channel NewsAsia 2016).

For China, the ECRL represents another landmark BRI project with a key Southeast Asian partner. The project highlights Malaysia's special relationship with China when, under Prime Minister Tun Abdul Razak, it became the first Southeast Asian country to establish diplomatic ties with the Chinese in 1974. The bilateral tie has blossomed under successive Prime Ministers, especially under the leadership of Prime Minister Najib (the son of Tun Abdul Razak) (Free Malaysia Today 2016a; Ngeow 2017). Moreover, the ECRL has a geopolitical dimension for it connects the aforementioned Kuantan Port (jointly owned by a Malaysian conglomerate and a Chinese SOE) on the east coast of Peninsular Malaysia to Port Klang on the west coast (Lopez 2016). This potential land bridge could provide a 'significant resolution' to China's over-reliance on the Strait of Malacca, what it calls the 'Malacca Dilemma'. About 80% of current Chinese energy needs pass through this narrow waterway. This new network will create alternative trade routes, but with significant Chinese involvement as China, through its SOEs, now has a direct interest in both the Kuantan Port and the ECRL itself (see Fig. 5.1). While a combined sea and land route via Kuantan Port and the ECRL is estimated to cost more (in bulk cargo per tonne) than the existing sea route via Singapore, the travel time can be shortened by a sizeable 30 hours (18% reduction from current levels). The shorter travel time is useful for the movement of time-sensitive goods such as exotic food and biomedical products. However, these new routes, if they come to fruition, could bypass Singapore (Southeast Asia's de facto shipping and commercial hub) and offer exporters new options to reach markets in wealthy Northeast Asia. Likewise, exports from Northeast Asia could also get to the Strait of Malacca without going through Singapore.

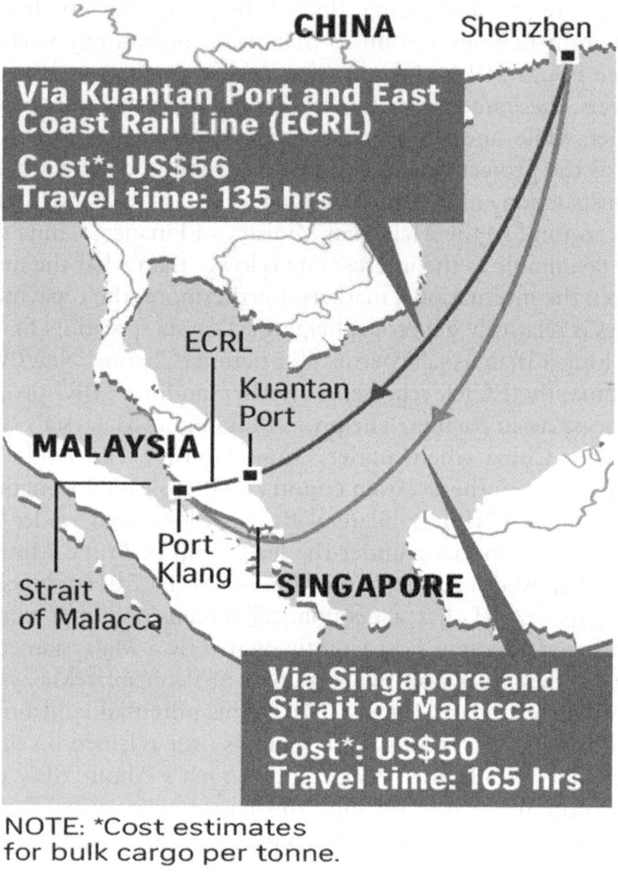

Fig. 5.1 Potential trade routes opened up by the East Coast Rail Link. Source: Lopez 2016; Note: *Cost estimates for bulk cargo per tonne

Looking Beyond Grand Strategy and Great Vision

Notwithstanding the hype surrounding the ECRL, there are several uncertainties that could just as well undermine it. Firstly, it is not especially relevant to the needs of the Malaysian economy. To this end, one needs to carefully consider the opportunity cost of the much touted USD 18.2 billion (MYR 55.0 billion). While USD 18.2 billion (MYR 55.0 billion)—roughly equivalent to the gross domestic product (GDP) of Perak (a mid-sized

Malaysian state)—represents a huge stimulus, it can arguably be disbursed in a manner that better fits the current and future needs of the economy. As illustrated in the earlier sections, one of the main causes behind Malaysia's middle-income trap is its inability to transition towards higher value-added activities that require increasingly more sophisticated technologies and better-quality human capital. According to international development experts, the most immediate forms of government action to rectify this issue involve deepening Malaysia's domestic industrial and innovation capabilities (Hasanov and Cherif 2015; Yusuf and Nabeshima 2009), expanding technical and vocational education and training, and attracting highly productive foreign firms to locate production in Malaysia (Flaaen et al. 2013). All of these policy measures require sustained public funding and the Malaysian government would do well to allocate and disburse resources for them. While it is unfair (and even counterfactual) to suggest that the Malaysian government could secure an amount equivalent to USD 18.2 billion (MYR 55.0 billion) to fund these three broad policies, the crux of the matter is that such policies are more meaningful to the Malaysian economy than a big-ticket public project stretching mostly through a remote part of Peninsular Malaysia. The conduct of some contemporary Chinese-led projects in Malaysia has also weakened the thesis that projects of this nature help in providing business and employment opportunities to the locals. Indeed, the Forest City project (driven by Country Garden of Guangdong province) in the southern state of Johor has drawn the ire of Mahathir Mohamad, Malaysia's longest-serving Prime Minister (1981 to 2003). He particularly harps on two interrelated issues: the outflow of capital and jobs to Chinese firms and the influx of Chinese immigrants. In his widely read blog, Mahathir (2017) had claimed that: '[W]e cannot allow thousands of acres to be owned, developed and settled by foreigners. If we do that literally they would become foreign enclaves... We are going to see large chunks of Malaysia being developed by the foreign buyers and being occupied by them'.

In addition, there seems to be some confusion regarding the nature in which China has chosen to finance the ECRL. To this end, some media outlets have mistakenly classified the ECRL as part of a larger state-led investment package announced during Prime Minister Najib's high-profile visit to China in November 2016 (see Free Malaysia Today 2016b; Malay Mail Online 2016a; The Star 2016). For instance, The Star (2016) wrote: 'Najib... witnessed the exchange of 14 business arrangements with *proposed investments* [emphasis added] estimated at RM143.64bil held at the Malaysia-China Business Forum...' (). Yet, the reality about the ECRL is that, as illustrated in the previous section, it is essentially a loan provided by a Chinese bank (in this case, the state-owned Export-Import Bank of China) to a Chinese main contractor (in this case, it is CCCC), which in turn carries out most of the construction. There is no investment in the form of a controlling ownership in a business in the recipient country (in this case, Malaysia) by an entity based in another country (in this case, CCCC), directly contrasting the conventional definitions of FDI. Put another way, CCCC is only contractually obligated to carry out all EPCC matters before turning it over to the Malaysians upon its completion. This is also the norm in most of the BRI projects across the word as the Chinese construction firms (such as CCCC) have no long-term interest in the projects, apart from the usual legal responsibilities related to the performance and safety of the end product. In summary, the eventual owners of the ECRL are the Malaysians, either through a SOE or a private firm. In any case, the Malaysian citizenry will be the ultimate payers for it. More prosaically, the ECRL can be interpreted as primarily a China-China transaction, with Malaysia capturing a relatively small share of the benefit.

Secondly, there are concerns that the cost of the ECRL is too steep, which is likely to reduce its sustainability. While no two railway projects are ever the same because the exact costing depends on factors as varied as terrain, train technology, length of rail, and financing conditions, it is still possible to draw on the experience of recent developments to gain a broader perspective. To this end, Table 5.1 provides a comparison of relatively recent prominent railway projects both in Malaysia and abroad. Overall, the ECRL is more expensive, almost exclusively to a significant degree, compared to the projects listed in Table 5.1.

On the domestic front, the 179 km Gemas-Johor Bahru route costs only USD 2.4 billion. This translates to a cost of USD 13.2 million per

Table 5.1 A comparison of the East Coast Rail Link against recent railway projects

Railway projects	*Construction cost (USD)*	*Parameters*
East Coast Rail Link (Malaysia)	18.2 billion; 30.4 million per km	600 km
Gemas-Johor Bahru (Malaysia)	2.4 billion; 13.2 million per km	179 km
Padma Railway (Bangladesh)	4.9 billion; 22.5 million per km	215 km
Phase 2A of Mombasa to Malaba (Kenya)	2.4 billion; 20.3 million per km	120 km

Source: Yeo (2017), Barrock (2016), Kable (2017)

Note: USD 1: MYR 3.02

km, less than half the equivalent cost of the ECRL. An interesting note is that this project's main contractor is another Chinese SOE, China Railway Engineering Corporation (CREC). Moreover, an initial study conducted in 2009 by HSS Integrated Sdn Bhd priced a railway project that broadly utilizes the same route as the ECRL (but with a shorter railway of 545 km) at USD 9.6 billion (MYR 29.0 billion).[2] This translates to an average cost of about USD 17.6 million (MYR 53.2 million) per km, slightly more than half the price of the ECRL's price of USD 30.4 (MYR 91.7 million) per km. It is rather puzzling why a 10% increase in length to 600 km can result in such a drastic hike in construction cost. An executive from a construction firm concurs and was quoted as saying: 'It could be the most expensive rail infrastructure project in the world in its class ... It's a good project but not at this ridiculous price' (Barrock 2016). The executive estimates the construction cost of the railway at only USD 11.9 billion (MYR 35.9 billion). He further claims that his construction industry colleague, who is from a European outfit, believes that the figure should be about USD 10.6 billion (MYR 32.0 billion) for the entire stretch. Both estimates provision the need to tunnel through the Titiwangsa mountain range, a major cost component of the ECRL. If their analysis is proven correct, then they represent a substantial overpricing of USD 6.3 billion (MYR 19.1 billion) to USD 7.6 billion (MYR 23.0 billion).

Comparing the ECRL to other recent international projects, one observes a similar tendency of potential overpricing of the former. In Bangladesh, China Railway Construction Corporation (CRCC), a Chinese SOE, signed a USD 4.9 billion (MYR 14.7 billion) contract in August 2016 to build the 215 km Padma railway linking Dhaka to Jessore, which includes the construction of 66 major bridges, 244 minor bridges, 14 new stations and the procurement of 100 passenger coaches. This project works out to USD 22.5 million (MYR 68.1 million) per km, a 26% discount vis-à-vis the ECRL. In Kenya, the government in October 2016 launched the construction of the 120 km Phase 2A (of the 489 km standard-gauge railway line) that will link Mombasa to the Ugandan border at a cost of USD 2.4 billion (MYR 7.3 billion). On a per km basis, this Kenyan project will cost about USD 20.3 million (MYR 61.4 million). While there is no indication of the number of bridges that will be built or if there will be any tunnelling works involved, this project's cost of USD 20.3 million (MYR 61.4 million per km) is still cheaper than the ECRL by a noticeable 33%. More interestingly, this project has been awarded to CCCC, the same main contractor involved in the ECRL.

The viability of the ECRL takes on a more negative tone if one also considers the operating cost. While transporting a container by rail can be 20 times less expensive than by air, it is still more costly than shipping by sea. In the case of the ECRL, moving bulk cargo via the combined sea and land route of Port Klang, the ECRL, and the Kuantan Port is about USD 6 per tonne more expensive than the existing sea route via the Strait of Malacca (Woo 2017). In addition, the purported shorter transit time of the ECRL of 135 hours (compared to 165 hours via Singapore and the Strait of Malacca; an 18% reduction of the travelling time) is only advantageous for the movement of high-value and/or time-sensitive goods (see Lopez 2016). Shippers of general merchandise goods are not usually interested in paying more (in the form of multiple port and rail handling fees instead of a singular shipping fee) for the combined sea and land route opened up by the ECRL. There is also the issue of practicality as merchants generally want to minimize the parties handling their goods. After hypothetically unloading sea freight at Port Klang and transferring them onto train carriages, one still has to haul the freight over to Kuantan Port before eventually loading them to another merchant ship. Even accounting for the advantages opened up by the shorter travel time, this represents an increase in handling parties (public seminar, Singapore, 20 March 2017). While this chapter recognizes that shipping technology might yet evolve in the future to facilitate the utility of the ECRL, it must be stated that contemporary business practice does not promote this kind of freight movement. More prosaically, moving freight by block trains is not a perfect substitute for container vessels because of the limited capacity that block trains offer. According to Woo (2017), the latest crop of London-bound trains departing from China can only carry about 200 20-foot equivalent units (TEUs) of goods, while a large container vessel can carry as many as 20,000 TEUs.

Thirdly, the ECRL is hampered by its lack of clarity and transparency. According to Yeo Bee Yin, an opposition lawmaker, the project has been awarded to CCCC without an open tender. Without an open tender, there is a high possibility that the project will be overpriced and/or even overdesigned as there is a lack of competition (see Yeo 2017). More generally, the opposition bloc has long argued for the need to open up the tender process for public procurement to make the bidding process more competitive and to ensure better value-for-money. It also helps to reduce rent-seeking, a longstanding issue plaguing public projects in Malaysia (see Pua 2011). In addition, the federal government has not made available the

ECRL's feasibility study to the public. When queried on the subject in November 2016, Transport Minister Liow Tiong Lai promised that the feasibility study on the ECRL will be released once it is finalized. However, no specific date was given by Liow (Malay Mail Online 2016b). As of June 2017 (a month before the construction of the ECRL is scheduled to kick off in July 2017), the feasibility study has still not been realized by the transport minister. Without publicly releasing a detailed engineering and economic feasibility study, both the practicality and cost of the ECRL will always be in doubt. The Malaysian public stands to lose even more if the ECRL does not generate enough passenger and freight volume, leading to underutilization and an exorbitant undertaking, a point raised in the earlier paragraphs.

There also appears to be a lack of information on the last stretch of railway (at least 60 km) linking Gombak to Port Klang. Unlike the rest of the railway, this 'missing link' has been omitted from public display, leading to some confusion. To complicate matters further, this last stretch of railway is situated in Selangor, a key opposition state. Moreover, the passage between Gombak to Port Klang cuts through dense urban areas, which makes acquisition of land and its redevelopment even more expensive than a comparable passage in the relatively sparse east coast. Yeo (2017) questions whether this omission is a ploy from the federal government to exclude the opposition Selangor state government from the ECRL's decision-making process. As of April 2017, the federal government only had one meeting with the Selangor state government regarding the ECRL (Yeo 2017). In view of the ECRL's importance to the national economy and the decision to fast-track it from late 2017 to July 2017, Yeo's scepticism is understandable.

Conclusion

This chapter has illustrated China's increasing influence in Malaysia. It has also shown how the ECRL is a manifestation of the BRI. As one of Malaysia's most ambitious government-to-government infrastructure projects in recent years, it has the potential of improving both the welfare of Malaysia as well as extending the geopolitical goals of China. In particular, the new routes opened up by the ECRL not only alleviate China's over-reliance on the Strait of Malacca, but also foster closer trade connectivity with other economies. In addition, massive and long-term foreign projects such as the ECRL can help eat up China's overcapacity and reduce unemployment within the country, two of the more pressing concerns occupying the thoughts of Chinese policymakers. Malaysia, as a recipient state on the other side of the BRI, stands to benefit too if it manages to secure enough Chinese support in bridging its developmental gaps, especially those related to infrastructure provision. Nevertheless, the ECRL raises several points of concern. To this end, its lack of relevance to Malaysia's broader industrialization goals, exorbitant cost, and informational gap have cast doubt on the ECRL. All of these are business risks that cannot be ignored if the project is to come into fruition. While the Malaysians, as the eventual 'owners' of the ECRL, have to be mindful of such issues, CCCC and the Chinese government need to understand that projects that do not add value to the recipient state (in this case, Malaysia) are bound to reinforce the perception that Chinese-led initiatives are self-serving in nature. Coupled with other broader geopolitical issues such as the ongoing dispute between China and several Southeast Asian countries on the demarcation of the South China Sea, lopsided projects such as the ECRL could jeopardize China's reputation, undermining the intended goals of the BRI.

More broadly, the ECRL's implementation thus far offers some useful lessons to both China and other smaller countries involved in the BRI. Firstly, Chinese-funded projects have to match the needs of the recipient countries as much as possible. It is self-defeating if one were to carry out exorbitant public sector projects that are only marginally beneficial to the local populace. Therefore, it is advisable to seek the advice of stakeholders representing the interest of the local community rather than relying solely on government-to-government dealings. By roping in more stakeholders, the projects should more closely reflect on-the-ground reality, generating goodwill for the Chinese. The lack of goodwill at the level of the citizenry has complicated similar Chinese projects, judging from recent events in Vietnam, a regional economy that also relies heavily on Chinese investment and trade. In 2014, a series of anti-China protests occurred in Vietnam, but they soon evolved into violent riots across major industrial hubs in the country. While the event was triggered by China's deployment of an oil rig in a disputed region of the South China Sea, the rapid escalation from largely peaceful protests in isolated locations to the rest of Vietnam suggests that there is an already significant level of unhappiness towards the Chinese amongst the domestic populace.

Secondly, the construction cost and feasibility of projects such as the ECRL must be revealed to the public. This is to prevent project overdesigning as well as overcharging, a perception that unfortunately has plagued the ECRL. While Chinese engineering firms (such as CCCC) are renowned for their value-for-money and fast turnaround, these benefits are unlikely to trickle down to the local populace if there are leakages surrounding big-ticket purchases such as railway networks. Moreover, one also has to take into consideration the operating cost of public projects. As far as the ECRL is concerned, the operating cost is a worrisome issue for it does not seem capable of surmounting the technical and commercial limits of the existing period. While it might still bear fruit in the long run, the ECRL risks becoming a 'white elephant' project if such limits are not overcome soon enough.

Thirdly, and related to the previous point, the recipient states themselves have to practice good governance standards. In the case of the ECRL, it appears that some of the issues raised in the previous section can be prevented, or at least softened, had the Malaysian government taken more robust measures to enforce positive spillover for its citizenry. While a detailed list of policy prescription goes beyond the remit of this chapter, one of the simplest measures available to the BRI recipient states is to make open as much as possible information on the projects. A more transparent approach will not only minimize incidences of misunderstanding, but also allow better feedback from the bottom up.

Notes

1. Exacerbating the inability to lure foreign investors is the growing trend of Malaysian firms investing abroad. Some of the reasons include diminishing returns in the domestic marketplace as well as potentially better opportunities (perceived or otherwise) outside of the country (see Lim 2016a, 2017a; Sim and Pandian 2007; Tham et al. 2015).
2. This study was commissioned by the East Coast Economic Region Development Council in December 2009 for a proposed 545 km route from Kuala Lumpur to Tumpat, passing through Mentakab, Kuantan, Kuala Terengganu, and Kota Bharu. Broadly speaking, this route mirrors that of the ECRL (Malay Mail Online 2016b).

References

Arase, D. (2015). China's Two Silk Roads Initiative: What It Means for Southeast Asia. In D. Singh (Ed.), *Southeast Asian Affairs 2015* (pp. 25–45). Singapore: Institute of Southeast Asian Studies.

Barrock, J. (2016, 8 November). Malaysia's East Coast Rail Line Could Be World's Costliest. *The Edge*. Retrieved from http://www.theedgemarkets.com.sg/article/malaysias-east-coast-rail-line-could-be-world%E2%80%99s-costliest

Brewster, D. (2014). Beyond the 'String of Pearls': Is There Really a Sino-Indian Security Dilemma in the Indian Ocean? *Journal of the Indian Ocean Region, 10*(2), 133–149.

Brooker, D. (2013). From 'Wannabe' Silicon Valley to Global Back Office? Examining the Socio-Spatial Consequences of Technopole Planning Practices in Malaysia. *Asia Pacific Viewpoint, 54*(1), 1–14.

Channel NewsAsia. (2016, 31 October). China Set to Build, Finance Malaysia's East Coast Rail Line Project. *Channel NewsAsia*. Retrieved from http://www.channelnewsasia.com/news/asiapacific/china-set-to-build-finance-malaysia-s-east-coast-rail-line-proje-7766916

Felker, G. (2009). The Political Economy of Southeast Asia's Techno-Glocalism. *Cambridge Review of International Affairs, 22*(3), 469–491.

Ferdinand, P. (2016). Westward Ho – The China Dream and 'One Belt, One Road': Chinese Foreign Policy under Xi Jinping. *International Affairs, 92*(4), 941–957.

Flaaen, A., Ghani, E., & Mishra, S. (2013). *How to Avoid Middle Income Traps? Evidence from Malaysia*. Washington: World Bank.

Free Malaysia Today. (2016a, 31 October). China a True Friend and Strategic Partner, Says Najib. *Free Malaysia Today*. Retrieved from http://www.freemalaysiatoday.com/category/nation/2016/10/31/china-a-true-friend-and-strategic-partner-says-najib/

Free Malaysia Today. (2016b, 1 November). M'sia-China Sign Historic 14 Agreements Worth RM144b. *Free Malaysia Today*. Retrieved from http://www.freemalaysiatoday.com/category/nation/2016/11/01/msia-china-sign-historic-14-agreements-worth-rm144b/

Hasanov, F., & Cherif, R. (2015). *The Leap of the Tiger: How Malaysia Can Escape the Middle-Income Trap*. Washington: World Bank.

Hill, H., Tham, S. Y., & Zin, R. H. M. (2012). Malaysia: A Success Story Stuck in the Middle? *The World Economy, 35*(12), 1687–1711.

Hutchinson, F. (2015). *Mirror Images in Different Frames? Johor, the Riau Islands, and Competition for Investment from Singapore*. Singapore: Institute of Southeast Asian Studies.

Jalil, H. (2017, 17 June). ECRL Is a Game-Changer and Mindset Changer: Najib. *The Sun Daily*. Retrieved from http://www.thesundaily.my/news/2017/06/15/ecrl-game-changer-and-mindset-changer-najib

Jomo, K. S. (Ed.) (2003). *Southeast Asian Paper Tigers? From Miracle to Debacle and Beyond*. London: Routledge.

Kable. (2017). *Mombasa-Nairobi Standard Gauge Railway Project, Kenya*. Retrieved from http://www.railway-technology.com/projects/mombasa-nairobi-standard-gauge-railway-project/

Kong, T. Y. (2016). China's 21st Century Maritime Silk Road: Malaysian Perspectives. In T. W. Lim, H. Chan, K. Tseng, & W. X. Lim (Eds.), *China's One Belt One Road Initiative* (pp. 289–306). London: Imperial College Press.

Larson, G., Loayza, N., & Woolcock, M. (2016). *The Middle-Income Trap : Myth or Reality?* Washington: World Bank.

Lim, G. (2014). The Internationalisation of Mainland Chinese Firms into Malaysia: From Obligated Embeddedness to Active Embeddedness. *Journal of Current Southeast Asian Affairs, 33*(2), 59–90.

Lim, G. (2015). China's Investments in Malaysia: Choosing the 'Right' Partners. *International Journal of China Studies, 6*(1), 1–30.

Lim, G. (2016a). Firm Entry Modes and Chinese Business Networks: Malaysian Investments in Vietnam. *Singapore Journal of Tropical Geography, 37*(2), 176–194.

Lim, G. (2016b). Managing Technological Development: A Study of Vietnam's Telecommunication Goods Industry. *Journal of Comparative Asian Development, 15*(2), 276–299.

Lim, G. (2017a). What Do Malaysian Firms Seek in Vietnam? *Journal of Asia-Pacific Business, 18*(2), 131–150.

Lim, G. (2017b). China's 'Going Out' Strategy in Southeast Asia: Case Studies of the Automobile and Electronics Sectors. *China: An International Journal, 15*(4), 157–178.

Lopez, L. (2016, 22 December). Malaysia's East Coast Rail Line Touted as a Game Changer. *Straits Times.* Retrieved from http://www.straitstimes.com/asia/se-asia/malaysias-east-coast-rail-line-touted-as-a-game-changer

MAA. (2011). *Market Review for 2010 and Outlook for 2011.* Retrieved from Petaling Jaya: Malaysian Automotive Association.

MAA. (2013). *Market Review for 2012 and Outlook for 2013.* Retrieved from Petaling Jaya: Malaysian Automotive Association.

MAA. (2017). *Market Review for 2016 and Outlook for 2017.* Retrieved from Petaling Jaya: Malaysian Automotive Association.

Mackerras, C. (2015). Xinjiang in China's Foreign Relations: Part of a New Silk Road or Central Asian Zone of Conflict? *East Asia, 32*(1), 25–42.

Mahathir. (2017, 6 January). FDI. Retrieved from http://chedet.cc/?p=2394

Malay Mail Online. (2015, 18 March). Johor Sultan Says Forest City Property Project will Boost State Economy. *Malay Mail Online.* Retrieved from http://www.themalaymailonline.com/malaysia/article/johor-sultan-says-forest-city-property-project-will-boost-state-economy

Malay Mail Online. (2016a, 1 November). Malaysian, Chinese Companies Make History with Signing of 14 Agreements Worth RM144b. *Malay Mail Online.* Retrieved from http://www.themalaymailonline.com/malaysia/article/malaysian-chinese-companies-make-history-with-signing-of-14-agreements-wort

Malay Mail Online. (2016b, 16 November). Release All ECRL Studies to End Our Questions, DAP MP Tells Transport Minister. *Malay Mail Online.* Retrieved from http://www.themalaymailonline.com/malaysia/article/release-all-ecrl-studies-to-end-our-questions-dap-mp-tells-transport-minist

Menon, J. (2014). Growth Without Private Investment: What Happened in Malaysia and Can It Be Fixed? *Journal of the Asia Pacific Economy, 19*(2), 247–271.

MIDA. (2016). *Malaysia Investment Performance Report: Strengthening the Growth Momentum*. Kuala Lumpur: Malaysian Investment Development Authority.

Nanyang Siang Pau. (2014, 12 December). Slow Development Causes MCKIP to Be Way Behind CMQIP. *Nanyang Siang Pau*. Retrieved from http://www.malaysianchinesenews.com/2014/12/slow-development-causes-mckip-to-be-way-behind-cmqip/

New Straits Times. (2016, 9 November). (Statement) ECRL Project Not Hastily Decided; Proposed Since 2007. *New Straits Times*. Retrieved from https://www.nst.com.my/news/2016/11/187009/statement-ecrl-project-not-hastily-decided-proposed-2007

Ngeow, C. B. (2017). Barisan Nasional and the Chinese Communist Party: A Case Study in China's Party-Based Diplomacy. *The China Review: An Interdisciplinary Journal on Greater China, 17*(1), 53–82.

Prime Minister's Department. (2015). *Economic Transformation Programme: Annual Report 2014*. Putrajaya: Prime Minister's Department.

Pua, T. (2011). *The Tiger that Lost Its Roar: A Tale of Malaysia's Political Economy*. Kuala Lumpur: Democratic Action Party.

Rafee, H. (2017, 24 January). MCKIP Secures RM19b in Investments, Targets Another RM10b this Year. *The Edge*. Retrieved from http://www.theedgeproperty.com.my/content/1041295/mckip-secures-rm19b-investments-targets-another-rm10b-year

Sheng, A. (2009). *From Asian to Global Financial Crisis: An Asian Regulator's View of Unfettered Finance in the 1990s and 2000s*. New York: Cambridge University Press.

Sim, A. B., & Pandian, J. R. (2007). An Exploratory Study of Internationalization Strategies of Malaysian and Taiwanese Firms. *International Journal of Emerging Markets, 2*(3), 252–273.

Straits Times. (2016, 1 November). Malaysia to Award $18.3b KL-Kelantan Rail Project to China. *Straits Times*. Retrieved from http://www.straitstimes.com/asia/malaysia-to-award-183b-kl-kelantan-rail-project-to-china

Suehiro, A. (2008). *Catch-Up Industrialization: The Trajectory and Prospects of East Asian Economies*. Singapore: NUS Press.

Summers, T. (2016). China's 'New Silk Roads': Sub-National Regions and Networks of Global Political Economy. *Third World Quarterly, 37*(9), 1628–1643.

Tee, L. S. (2017, 11 March). Flushed with Construction Jobs. *The Star*. Retrieved from http://www.thestar.com.my/business/business-news/2017/03/11/flushed-with-construction-jobs/

Tham, S. Y., Teo, Y. N., & Kam, A. J. Y. (2015). Outward Foreign Direct Investment from Malaysia. *Journal of Southeast Asian Economies, 32*(3), 358–374.

The Star. (2016, 1 November). M'sian, Chinese Firms Sign Agreements Worth RM144bil. *The Star*. Retrieved from http://www.thestar.com.my/business/business-news/2016/11/01/malaysian-and-chinese-firms-sign-14-agreements-worth-rm144bil/

The Star. (2017, 2 June). M'sia and China Share the Same Views. *The Star*. Retrieved from http://www.thestar.com.my/news/nation/2017/06/02/mutual-interests-in-security-issues-msia-and-china-share-the-same-views/

Today. (2016, 1 November). China to Build and Finance M'sia's S$18.3b East Coast Rail Link Project. *Today*. Retrieved from http://www.todayonline.com/world/asia/china-build-and-finance-msias-s183b-east-coast-rail-link-project

van Grunsven, L., & Hutchinson, F. (2016). The Evolution of the Electronics Industry in Johor (Malaysia): Strategic Coupling, Adaptiveness, Adaptation, and the Role of Agency. *Geoforum, 74*, 74–87.

Wad, P. (2009). The Automobile Industry of Southeast Asia: Malaysia and Thailand. *Journal of the Asia Pacific Economy, 14*(2), 172–193.

Wong, C.-Y., & Cheong, K.-C. (2014). Diffusion of Catching-Up Industrialization Strategies: The Dynamics of East Asia's Policy Learning Process. *Journal of Comparative Asian Development, 13*(3), 369–404.

Woo, J. (2017, 7 January). New Silk Road's Impact on Shipping Will Be Limited. *Straits Times*. Retrieved from http://www.straitstimes.com/business/new-silk-roads-impact-on-shipping-limited

Yeo, B. Y. (2017, 2 April). *Three Questionable Areas of East Coast Rail Line (ECRL)*. Retrieved from http://www.yeobeeyin.com/2017/04/three-questionable-areas-of-east-coast.html

Yusuf, S., & Nabeshima, K. (2009). *Tiger Economies under Threat: A Comparative Analysis of Malaysia's Industrial Prospects and Policy Options*. Washington: World Bank.

Zhang, M., Rasiah, R., & Lee, K. Y. J. (2017). Navigating a Highly Protected Market: China's Chery Automobile in Malaysia. *Journal of Contemporary Asia*, 1–18.

Zhang, M., & Zhao, S. (2016, 19 November). Malaixiyacheng: Zhongmaqiye 'Yidaiyilu' Hezuo Xindianfan [Bandar Malaysia: A 'One Belt, One Road' Role Model]. *China News Service*. Retrieved from http://www.chinanews.com/cj/2016/11-19/8068498.shtml

CHAPTER 6

The PRC's Maritime Silk Road Initiative, Southeast Asia, and the United States

Kerry Brown

This chapter considers the interaction among China, the Association of Southeast Asian Nations (ASEAN), and the United States and how the issue of regional trust affects Beijing's core strategic interests. The New Silk Road maritime version opened up fresh areas of economic and strategic space around China. It spelled out clearly to the country's maritime neighbours the opportunities and benefits of engaging more with Chinese investment, Chinese trade, and Chinese growth just as the land Silk Road had done for the Central Asian partners. In this complex political and diplomatic context, the regional response to the Belt and Road Initiative (BRI) has been a mixture of applause and excitement alongside caution.

PRC: A History as a Land Power and Its Implications for South East Asia

The history of the People's Republic of China (PRC) regarding itself as a sea power as opposed to a land one is relatively short. According to scholars like Robert S. Ross, the default of states preceding the PRC has been to view themselves almost wholly as land powers—something that prevailed

K. Brown (✉)
King's College, London, UK

A. Arduino, X. Gong (eds.), *Securing the Belt and Road Initiative*,
https://doi.org/10.1007/978-981-10-7116-4_6

in the first two decades after the creation of the PRC in 1949. This is understandable. It is predominantly from Chinese land borders, wherever they have been in recent centuries, that problems have come. In Ross's words: 'Two thousand years of continental expansion and threats from land powers have created a Chinese bias towards the development of land power, just as secure land borders and extensive oceanic frontiers have fostered an American "insular perspective" on international politics'.[1] Sea security only figured from the nineteenth century and the era of British adventurism. Before this, the Ming and Qing needed to secure borders to the west and north against hostile neighbouring powers.

Even in the Maoist era, from 1949, there seemed little role for a modernised navy. The People's Liberation Army (PLA), and the PRC's ballistics and nuclear ambitions, all figured as part of the great project to reconstruct the nation. Perhaps the dominant motif for the sea in the eyes of Chinese leadership up to the 1980s was a place useful for logistics and trade. It did not seem to figure as one that carried a profound security dimension. That only started in the first decade of the post-1978 reform era under Deng Xiaoping and his colleagues when the concept of modernising and building better naval capacity reared its head.

The construction of decent naval capacity also went hand in hand with renewed interest in the issue of maritime borders and the sovereignty of the South China Sea constellation of islands and island features.[2] The PRC's naval strategy also seemed to create for the country a whole new set of ambitions and interests that it had never had before. Since the 1980s, these have intensified, creating the capacity to take a view on interests thousands of kilometres from its land shores. The PRC now has at least one aircraft carrier (against 10 for the United States). But its list of serviceable smaller vessels seems to increase each year. As of 2015, there were 496 ships listed in the assets of PLAN. These included nuclear and conventions submarines, amphibious war ships, frigates, destroyers, and corvettes.[3] Despite the huge expansion, while, in gross numbers this now amounts to more than the US figure, the quality, capacity, and technological capacity of Chinese ships is still far behind that of the American ones.

What is not in dispute is that the PRC is now far closer to being able to credibly defend its interests in the seas around its coasts than ever before. All of this has created a new set of geopolitical issues for China's closest maritime neighbours, who until the 1980s, and particularly in the last decade, have had to shift from handling a China that was more inward looking and confined to its own territorial space both economically and diplomatically from 1949 to the 1980s, to a China now that in almost every dimension, from naval power to direct investment, is an active and increasingly important player in the region, and one that frequently offers a counter-narrative to regional development to that provided by the United States and it alliance system and Asian presence.

Staking Out a Benign Narrative: The Maritime Silk Road

It is in the midst of this complex, new regional situation that the concept of a Maritime Silk Road Initiative needs to be primarily understood, for the Belt Road Initiative (BRI) (which the Maritime Silk Road is a part of) is predominantly a *regional* initiative, despite its wide, global dimensions. It is widely appreciated that the PRC is now articulating grand, unilateral diplomatic ideas and that is a striking development. But under President Xi Jinping and the leaders around him, there has been an attempt to 'tell the China story' as he reportedly asked Politburo colleagues to do in the early part of his tenure. Part of this is to move away from the almost silent posture under the Hu Jintao leadership from 2002 to 2012 of keeping tight-lipped about everything, and attempting to speak more clearly to the outside world about the country's intentions—most of which were, according to domestic discourse, benign. And of course, the most immediate impact of a China story with greater ambition and reach will be felt directly in China's own region. China's Asian story, therefore, what was called at the Boao Regional Forum in 2015 a story of 'common Asian destiny', will be of immediate and intimate interest to China's Southeast Asian neighbours. The question is whether the region shares these ideas of a common destiny, and if not, where the points of disagreement and dissent are.

Xi Jinping's original idea issued in 2013 when he was touring Central Asia of a new Silk Road of course fits the narrative outlined previously of China as a land power, interested in reenergising and reinvigorating its western border theatre of interest in order to gain benefits for its west region domestically. Investment and trade figures from the PRC into this region had rocketed in the previous few years giving a natural backbone to this idea.[4] Soon after the New Silk Road Initiative was announced, however, a maritime version appeared. This too opened up fresh areas of economic and strategic space around the PRC, completing the circle. It spelled out clearly to the country's maritime neighbours the opportunities and benefits of engaging more with Chinese investment, Chinese trade, and Chinese growth just as the land Silk Road had done for the Central Asian partners.

Both sides of the initiative were, and remain, remorselessly economic at least in their public face, as will be shown later. But underneath that objective there is a sense in which they also, in very different ways, aim to create a zone of greater security commonality and interest. For the Central Asia states, the predominant security issues are maintaining good resource and energy routes, guarding against Islamic extremism and its impact in China's western Xinjiang autonomous region, and to some extent countering the involvement and influence of Russia. For the Southeast Asian region, resource and supply routes are similarly important, but there is the added complexity of dealing with America's interests in this region. The calculation for both land and sea routes is a simple one: a country with deep trade and business links into the PRC is less likely to see any benefit in antagonising and opposing it. Trade might not bring love—but it does bring a certain level of pragmatic, albeit grudging loyalty. Even setting the bar low, this was something the PRC had never had before.

The New Silk Road became, in 2014, the One Belt, One Road initiative. This at least spelled out more clearly the maritime dimension—belt for sea channels, road for the land ones. By 2016, this settled into the current terminology—the Belt and Road Initiative, or BRI.

Institutional and Policy Framework

One thing to get clear is the domestic understanding of the BRI's parameters as it is presented within the PRC. There is surprisingly little official guidance on what the BRI actually is, either in its sea or land manifestation. Perhaps the most useful outline was produced in early 2015, when the National Development and Reform Commission (NDRC) with the Ministry of Commerce, with the authority of the State Council, issue an official White Paper, with the grand title: 'Vision and Actions on Jointly Building Silk Road Economic Belt and 21st-Century Maritime Silk Road'.[5] The aim of BRI, it states in the paper's preamble is:

> ...to promote the connectivity of Asian, European and African continents and their adjacent seas, establish and strengthen partnerships among the countries along the Belt and Road, set up all-dimensional, multi-tiered and composite connectivity networks, and realize diversified, independent, balanced and sustainable development in these countries.

This shows ambitious scope. For those looking for greater granularity however, the paper offered little specifics. Repeating the mantra that the aim was for 'win-win co-operation' and for civilisational contact and connectivity (a word that is repeated several times in the paper), it lays out the five broad objectives that the initiative needs to attend to:

1. Policy co-ordination: to 'fully coordinate their economic development strategies and policies, work out plans and measures for regional cooperation, negotiate to solve cooperation-related issues, and jointly provide policy support for the implementation of practical cooperation and large-scale projects'.
2. Facilities connectivity: to 'improve the connectivity of their infrastructure construction plans and technical standard systems, jointly push forward the construction of international trunk passageways, and form an infrastructure network connecting all sub-regions in Asia, and between Asia, Europe and Africa'. In terms of maritime links, the aim was to 'build smooth land-water transportation channels, and advance port cooperation; increase sea routes and the number of voyages, and enhance information technology cooperation in maritime logistics'. Connectivity also embraces energy infrastructure such as oil and gas pipelines, and the construction of cross-border optical cables and other communications trunk line networks, creating what is called 'an Information Silk Road'.
3. Unimpeded trade: for this area, the aim is to boost investment and trade cooperation by removing investment and trade barriers, enhancing customs cooperation, and working together on law enforcement. In particular, what is labeled as 'trade structure' in the paper is singled out for improvement, with e-commerce expanded, promoting trade through investment, and balancing out trade levels. For the marine road, cooperation in marine-product farming, deep-sea fishing, aquatic product processing, seawater desalination, marine biopharmacy, ocean engineering technology, environmental protection industries, marine tourism, and other fields is referenced. Attention will be paid to research and development and to building up service industries.
4. Financial integration: the 2015 paper states that 'financial integration is an important underpinning for implementing the Belt and Road Initiative'. This maps the PRC's policy in the previous ten years to incrementally, and in a controlled way internationalised,

RMB. So bilateral currency swap and settlement arrangements are proposed, and the development of bond markets in Asia. 'Chinese financial institutions and companies are encouraged to issue bonds in both RMB and foreign currencies outside China, and use the funds thus collected in countries along the Belt and Road', the paper states.

5. People-to-people links: this involves the exchange of students, cultural and soft power dialogue, and tourism.
6. This at least gives some idea of the Chinese understanding of what the BRI is driving to achieve. The question is whether these are ideas, and ambitions, shared by the Southeast Asian regional partners. The rest of the chapter will offer examples, and then map them against the five key objectives outlined previously to see how much commonality there actually is.

The Rationale Behind the Maritime Road in the Southeast Asian Region

As already stated, the Southeast Asian Region, and in particular the countries within the Association of Southeast Asian Nations (ASEAN) through geographical and economic proximity to China are the set of countries likely to be most affected by the maritime aspects of the BRI, and the ones that figure most in its initial stages. For them, the need to conceptualise its overall purpose is perhaps more pressing than anywhere else. With the demise of President Obama's Trans-Pacific Partnership (TPP) after the election of his successor Donald Trump in November 2016, there is the possibility that the BRI will map out a new kind of alternative trade zone, geared more towards Chinese interests.

BRI in the Southeast Asian region does have other dimensions though, some of which carry overt political meanings. One interpretation of the idea is simply that while it carves out a large economic zone linked to the PRC's interests and centred on it across Asia, it is also aimed at creating more strategic and diplomatic space for itself. A more dominant role in Asia, clearing the United States in particular from its zone of influence and allowing it more freedom to act is a natural objective, particularly as China aims to incrementally resolve the outstanding maritime border issues, and to control as much as it can, in fact or at least by stealth, of the area covered by the notorious Nine-Dash Line, the vast stretch of water reaching down as far as the coast of Malaysia that the PRC lays claim to.

The value of China's economy and trade strength as a means of incentivising its neighbours and making them question their more traditional alliances with the United States has been a feature of the last decade, and has only intensified under President Jinping. The most recent example of this has been the case of the Philippines, whose recently elected President Dutarte, on a visit to Beijing in October 2016 stated that the United States was no longer a key ally and that relations with China were more important—a comment that he was subsequently to qualify. Attempting to turn the region to a position more favourable to being acceptable to China's aims to be dominant and have greater strategic space through use of its economic assets is unsurprising. The question is whether the BRI will achieve this with its current core elements.

The Issue of Regional Trust Towards the PRC's Core Strategic Interests

What the maritime does need to do is address the very clear undercurrent of distrust and suspicion about PRC's intentions among some of China's neighbours. Close to China, they are the ones who have most familiarity with its aims, and feel its intentions most intensely. Recent evidence of bad feelings and relations has been plentiful. For Vietnam, there is the issue of the two countries having armed conflict as recently as 1979. Over 2014 and into 2015 a massive Chinese oil platform, the *Haiyang Shiyou 981*, which was accused of invasively going into disputed waters by the Vietnamese, caused even further bad feelings. The PRC in turn accused Vietnam of building permanent features to create island-like entities in the South China Sea. Japanese relations with the PRC are even more complex, with the continuation of profound bad feelings from the Second World War referred to once more during the convening of a massive military parade in Beijing to mark the seventieth anniversary of the ending of the war in September 2015. Unsurprisingly, Japanese Prime Minister Abe did not attend. Nor, for that matter, has either he or President Jinping exchanged high-level visits bilaterally, despite their very active global travel schedules elsewhere in the world. The Philippines proved nervous enough of Chinese intentions in the maritime area to make the first moves in going to the International Court of Arbitration, referred to previoulsy, even though since then President Dutarte has been far more conciliatory. The mysterious disappearance of the Air Malaysia Flight MH370 in 2014 on the way from Kuala Lumpur to Beijing with many Chinese nationals on board exacerbated an already strained relationship, with protests outside the Malaysian embassy in Beijing over the handling of the incident and the paucity of information being given about what was happening.

Alongside the issue of the South China sea claims with all their complexity sits the unresolved issue of Taiwan island, something that could have immense impact on the Southeast Asian region should it be mishandled. Taiwan has enjoyed de facto independence from the PRC, and has existed as the Republic of China on Taiwan from 1949. Despite having its own currency, army, flag, and, most importantly, democratic political system and identity, Taiwan is still regarded by Beijing as a province of the mainland, and its 24 million citizens have to travel around a world where they enjoy visa-free access to almost 150 countries, but where their 'country' only has diplomatic recognition from 22 states. Taiwan is clearly the major strategic interest for the PRC. Under Mao Zedong and Deng Xiaoping, the attitude towards final reunification was pushed far into the distance. As historian John Garver writes in a recent history of the PRC's diplomacy after 1949, the most opportune moment to have taken Taiwan into its sovereign territory was just after its victory in the civil war in 1949. The Korean War, however, provoked by North Korean leader Kim Il-sung's decision to invade the south caused the PRC to be distracted, facing the United States directly in a conflict on its northeast border. As Garver states, 'Loss of a golden opportunity to secure Taiwan was the first cost to the PRC of Mao's green light to Kim Il-sung's war'.[6]

Under President Jinping, the focus on Taiwan has grown more intense. Speaking to a visitor from Taiwan in late 2013, he reportedly stated that 'increasing mutual political trust across the Taiwan Straits and jointly building up political foundations are crucial for ensuring the peaceful development of relations'. He went on to state somewhat ominously: 'Looking further ahead, the issue of political disagreements that exist between the two sides must reach a final resolution, step by step, and these issues cannot be passed on from generation to generation'.[7] Momentum seemed to be maintained during the twilight era of Taiwanese President Ma Ying-jeou's period in office, culminating in the remarkable meeting between the two leaders in Singapore in November 2015. Despite this revolutionary diplomacy, however, the election of Tsai Ing-wen in January 2016 from the opposition Democratic Progressive Party in Taiwan, with their harder line on cross-strait relations, meant that the PRC's attitude towards how it could best promote its reunification strategy once more became unclear.

In many ways, the very clear strategic intent that Beijing has made towards Taiwan over the last six decades, never relinquishing the use of force to deal with the island, provides one of the great sources of instability. It is a fundamental pillar of the regime's legitimacy in Beijing to defend Chinese territorial integrity. Unilateral declarations of independence by the island would be 'cassus belli', with an anti-secession bill passed in Beijing in 2005 to ensure this commitment to immediate military response is enshrined in law. Even without a specific law, no Chinese leader is likely to be able to tolerate this particularly with the ratcheting up of nationalism in recent years, and the ways in which with falling GDP growth the regime needs to seek legitimacy in other areas beyond the creation of material prosperity. For Jinping's China, the country does not want to just be rich—it wants to feel rich, and see the impact of this wealth on its status elsewhere in the world. Taiwan walking away from it would be a disaster for national face and prestige. This is a quandary the leadership has created from themselves because, in many ways, Taiwan is not that important for the PRC economically these days—and perhaps not that significant strategically, as long as Taipei is less committed to its relations with the United States. However, commitment to unification has now been embedded in the whole narrative of the Party State and has become part of its identity.

There is a larger context within which to understand Taiwan's meaning for China, and one that directly links to its relations with other Southeast Asian countries around it. When the PRC looks across the Pacific, it sees a line of treaty alliances that link with America. This more than anything else constricts its space. From Japan to South Korea, Philippines, Malaysia, down to Australia and New Zealand—all these countries have longstanding security links with the United States that commit each to self-protection and mutual defence. An attack on one, under the treaties, is an attack on the United States. The most problematic of these security deals is the informal one with Taiwan, the 1979 Taiwan Relations Act. Established in 1979 when the United States shifted its formal diplomatic relations from Taipei to Beijing, it acts as a guarantee of Washington's continuing support for the Taiwanese. While subject to interpretation, the act does commit the United States to consider supporting Taiwan in its quest for security, largely through the sale of high-technology weapons systems. Beijing always has to consider this when thinking through options on

Taiwan. In effect, any direct move while this act is in place would be a move against the United States. That places Taiwan policy within the network of treaty alliances with the United States at their heart, which China faces in its own region.

In some respects, the whole story of the PRC's moves in the South and East China Sea over the last decade or so can be interpreted as expanding the area around its most significant outstanding claim and strategic interest—Taiwan island. The Republic of China through its role as a signatory of the Treaty of San Francisco signed between Japan and 48 other countries in 1951 to signal the resolution of outstanding issues from its defeat in the Second World War is also a claimant on some of the islands and territory in the local seas. In that sense, its interests sometimes elide with that of the PRC. Beijing has been able therefore to assert that it is defending all Chinese interests, not just its own, in the disputed area. The controversial Nine-Dash Line, for instance, is inherited from the Republic of China in the pre-1949 era. The PRC is insistent that it is asserting legitimate 'Chinese' claims over the whole territory being argued over. But this also expands the scope of what is on one level simply a dispute over the sovereignty of one island (Taiwan) and its limited number of satellites, to the far larger one of the PRC's strategic freedom in an immense territory stretching down to the coast of Indonesia and Malaysia. Unsurprisingly, therefore, the larger claim gets more attention than the smaller one—even though the smaller one is the most crucial and important for the PRC's core interests.

Regional Response to BRI

In this complex political and diplomatic context, the regional response to BRI has been a mixture of applause and excitement alongside caution. As of November 2016, the BRI has resulted in very few tangible projects that carry its badge. So there is very little record to go from. But there has been rising Chinese interest in foreign direct investment across the Asian region, which has only intensified over the last decade. This gives a menu of some of the opportunities, and the issues, that the BRI will need to embrace to be successful and have wider meaning.

One of the most important potential partners for the BRI is Singapore. The seven million-strong city-state has one of the longest running investment relations with China, dating back to the very start of the reform process in the early 1980s. It invested, contentiously (largely because the local authorities set up a competing zone right next to it almost immediately after it was established), in the Suzhou Industrial Park, one of the earliest such projects, in the China, and maintains an interest there to this day. It also works with the Tianjin Ecological Park and the Chongqing Science Park. These give it already extant intellectual and investment exchange interlinks with China. Singapore carries other attractions for China as it seeks a stronger role through BRI. It figures as a major finance centre, with a RMB centre agreed in the early 2010s, and as a huge port and logistics centre. It also has a strong legal system and robust rule of law. So the opportunities of working with Singaporean companies and partners gives China advantages in looking to work elsewhere in ASEAN countries.

Singapore's role as a facilitator of dialogue was underlined by its unique ability to host former President of Taiwan Ma Ying-jeou and PRC President Xi Jinping in November 2015 for the first ever summit between the two leaders since 1949. In the BRI, therefore, Singapore continues to see its role as a facilitator and partner for China with others in terms of projects and investments. The main risks it faces, however, are the increased competition that China will offer its own services sector industries as it continues to shift from a manufacturing and export based model to a high value-added one. Singapore has to prepare perpetually for the day when China shifts from being a partner to a direct competitor. Maintaining its advantages will becoming increasingly hard in the face of the real problems of asymmetry in size between the two.

For Indonesia, there are separate issues. Indonesia has already figured as one of the potential recipients of a joint Asia Investment Infrastructure Bank (AIIB) and World Bank grant.[8] Its critical need for infrastructure means that it should be a natural partner for the BRI and the kind of co-operation it outlines. Under President Joko Widodo, there have been concerted attempts to attract more PRC foreign direct investment. Even so, Chinese investment, according to the Indonesia Investment Co-ordinating Board, still ranks below that of the United Kingdom, Japan, and the United States. Between 2008 and 2015, there were 2526 projects, with a committed investment in 2015 of USD 2.4 billion. These created jobs for an estimated 89,000 people—a figure far less than the 1.1 million associated with Singaporean investment.

The profile of investment from China into Indonesia too is striking—with a fifth going into machinery, a fifth into electricity and gas, and then mining. The problems associated with this kind of investment are ones that the BRI, if it sees an uplift in co-operation, will need to address: demands that, for Chinese investment, Chinese companies bring unskilled labour into the country (a common feature of Chinese companies' demands throughout the region), and the lack of experience that Chinese investors have in the country. According to the Confederation of Indonesia Trade Unions, Chinese direct investors often fail in their projects to comply with wage, health, and retirement insurance regulations, and are poor at corporate social responsibility. This is particularly the case in the mining sector. The evidence from extant Chinese investments so far is mixed. For one by Petrochina, the state-owned Chinese energy company, it has invested in local schools, and involved the local community where it is active in job creation, and so on, but it has not been good at technology sharing or environmental compliance—something shared by other relatively large Chinese companies. This track record therefore needs to be explicitly addressed in any future BRI opportunities.

The case of Vietnam is even more problematic. A country bordering China with a long history of conflict and disagreement with China, it has been one of the most aggressive contenders in the South China Sea issue. Chinese FDI in Vietnam has increased in the last ten years, from 72 projects with a committed capital of USD 81.2 million in 2004 to 175 with USD 175 million in 2015. More than 90 per cent of this is in manufacturing and mining. But according to Vietnamese research, the Chinese investments have suffered from the same issues as those in Indonesia. The Tan Nguyen Bauxite Mine, as an example, has been criticised for lack of compliance with environmental regulations, insensitivity in dealing with local communities, and failure to observe minimum wage requirements. A hydropower project from China has been berated for poor occupational safety regulations and work practices. On top of this, other Chinese investments have lacked technology transference, and have suffered from labour issues. A China Railway project in Hanoi from 2014 has been associated with a number of accidents leading to several fatalities.

In Thailand, once more, while Chinese investment has increased it again only figures as 2.1 per cent of the overall figure for FDI. Once more, it is in mining and resources, and construction. And once more, it has been criticised for failure to transfer technology, lack of environmental compliance, poor observance of local rules and regulations, and general lack of cultural and local knowledge when dealing with staff and communities.

There are of course other countries in the region—from Cambodia to Myanmar, to Laos and Malaysia—that also have deepened engagement with China and figure in the BRI maritime concept. But for these, the set of challenges and issues outlined in the case of Singapore, Indonesia, Vietnam, and Thailand are similar.

The Opportunity of Sharing: BRI and Investment, Finance and Politics

It is clear that there is a vast potential for infrastructure provision across the Asian region, and particularly in Southeast Asia, something exemplified by the case of Indonesia given previously. It was in order to service this that the Asian Infrastructure Investment Bank (AIIB) was set up, on China's instigation, in 2014. Many of its 56 founding parties are from the region, including countries like Indonesia, Malaysia, Thailand, Myanmar, and the Philippines. The AIIB is one of the most tangible outcomes of the BRI, providing a financial backbone to the idea of China taking a greater role in the development of the region. Despite initial American reservations, the AIIB has been joined by a number of European countries, and, eventually, despite initial refusal, by Australia.

The AIIB operates as a potential financer for projects, though the current committed capital is only USD 200 billion, which is miniscule compared to projects funded by the Asian Development Bank and the World Bank. What the AIIB does do, however, is to operate as a means by which China can share ideas about its own experience of building infrastructure, and developing its economy, beyond its borders.

This willingness to share has to confront, however, some of the perennial challenges that Chinese investment and involvement have faced, outlined by the case studies in this chapter. These broadly fall into the following categories, and are married to the five objectives outlined in the NDRC Belt Road Initiative announcement from the Chinese government referred to previously:

1. Policy co-ordination: Chinese involvement is feared to be geared too much to its own self-interest, to be asymmetrical, creating a zone around it favourable to its own economic and security priorities. Chinese companies are accused of being ignorant, or heedless, of local laws and regulations. For deeper policy co-ordination, China

will need to offer much more detailed ideas about its plans, and its implementation strategy, to regional partners.

2. Facilities connectivity: China is seen as having the capital and some of the technological ability to achieve this for the rest of the region. However, it is accused of being unwilling to share or transfer technology. It is also distrusted as a supplier of some telecom technology through espionage reasons. There is a trust deficit in many countries in the region, meaning that being reliant on China for such connectivity will carry a high security price.
3. Unimpeded trade: With the demise of the TPP, China does stand to create its own free trade zone across the region. Its investment and trade figures have increased hugely in the last two decades, giving it a strong advantage in this area. But there are complaints that its trade is often geared against the employment of countries it trades with, that its investments suffer from poor local knowledge, rule of law, compliance, environmental standards, and cultural understanding, and that they are still relatively small players.
4. Financial integration: The AIIB and the rise of the use of Chinese RMB trading offer a good foundation here, though the USD, Euro, and Japanese Yen are still more widely traded. This area also depends on China opening its current account and its currency to the outside world, rather than maintaining its protected status. China has more to gain than lose in this area through partnership with Singapore and other more developed economies.
5. People-to-people links: These links are growing through tourism and trade throughout Southeast Asia. But as the demonstrations against Chinese investment in Vietnam in 2015 after issues over the South China Sea, and protests in China against Malaysia after the MH70 disappearing aircraft the same year showed, relations that on the surface can seem harmonious can quickly deteriorate. China through its size and the scope of its ambition in ideas like the BRI can create as much distrust as warmth.

Responses: Pivoting Versus 'The Big Deal'

With its dense network of different kinds of treaty alliances, and because of its immense strategic and economic importance, it is unsurprising that many fear the situation in the Asia Pacific region, broadly covered by the maritime BRI, is delicate, and becoming more dangerous. Japanese Prime

Minister Shinzo Abe was not alone in musing over whether the situation in 2014 in his region was much like that which prevailed in Europe before the First World War, where commitments between nations led to a domino effect and the start of a huge, destructive, and needless war once an issue provoked their collapse.[9] Such thinking continued the anxieties over the previous decade, inside and outside the PRC, over how to avoid conflict when a power was rising and, slowly, replacing a dominant one. Some international relations experts like Christopher Coker wrote on the very possibility of war in the Asian region between China and the United States being the best possible defence against it ever happening.[10] Others like Belgian academic Jonathan Holslag painted a picture of a region where the possibility of war was much more imminent than people thought.[11]

Within the region, the spectrum of opinion on how to respond to China's increasing role is captured by the arguments between, on the one hand, Australian academic Hugh White, and on the other hand, former US Undersecretary of State Kurt Campbell. For White, the onus is on the United States to articulate a new role in Asia, and one that cedes more space to China. 'Essentially, America has three options', White argues:

> It can resist China's challenge and try to preserve the status quo in Asia. It can step back from its dominant role in Asia, leaving China to attempt to establish hegemony. Or it can remain in Asia on a new basis, allowing China a larger role but also maintaining a strong presence of its own. Most Americans assume that the first of these options is the only choice. Only a few take the second option seriously, although that could change. Most don't even consider the third.[12]

For Campbell, however, things are more complicated. The United States and China have a relationship that is defined by a 'careful, calibrated mixture of cooperation, competition, and interdependence developed over decades'. Both countries need to 'coexist in an increasingly interconnected Asia and to work together for the betterment of both countries and the region'. Fundamental to this is a rules-based order, which the United States had taken the lead in, and which China has profoundly benefited from. They, in turn, are built on what Campbell calls 'time tested principles': 'freedom of navigation, sovereign equality, transparency, peaceful dispute resolution, sanctity of contracts, free trade, and cooperation on transnational challenges'. The pivot to Asia exists to defend these principles, which, in turn, will avoid hegemony by any one power in the region.[13]

Either side of this argument, there is the issue of just how a vision like the BRI, particularly its maritime dimension, might help to satisfy those like Campbell in the United States, or figures like White in Australia, who seem to be coming from different directions in arguing over what China's role in the region in the future should best be like. For the five core dimensions of Chinese intention mapped out in the BRI, on the surface at least all seem to spell out relatively benign intentions. Policy co-ordination, trade harmonisation, people-to-people links, greater connectivity, and financial co-operation are all good things. But it is clear too that policy makers in Washington have remained somewhat unconvinced that this is the full story from Beijing's point of view. For them, there is often a disjoint between the actions and the rhetoric of the PRC leadership. And the BRI, while stepping some way towards filling in some of the gaps around Chinese intentions, still leaves a lot unstated or simply avoided.

With the Trump presidency starting from early 2017, even more uncertainty is introduced. Trump has a contradictory and wholly inconsistent position on the region, one characterised by hawkishness in terms of the economy (a desire to have tougher trade deals with China and more emphasis on job creation back in the United States) along with a willingness to relax some of the United States' security interest in the region and ask it to look after itself. Trump, for instance, has questioned the need for the United States to commit so much financially to the security role it plays throughout the Southeast Asian and Asian region. If implemented, this would cause a major shift in the power dynamics around China, creating a potential vacuum that it would be able to fill were it to fill this advantageously. There are many other areas, however, where China might find this new responsibility unwelcome. It has made it clear it has no desire to be a regional, let alone, global policeman. But Trump's US retreat might force it to take up this role, with all the criticisms and exposure that it will present.

Conclusion

The complaint in the 2000s was that PRC leaders were too shy in speaking out more clearly about what their international intentions were. The various evolutions of the BRI until its final formulation seem to at least step towards a more communicative stance on foreign policy. That at least is a very positive thing and something that is hugely significant in particular for its regional partners.

Despite this, the scope and ambition of the idea, while laudable, means that it has proved hard so far to conceptualise adequately. It also partially covers an area in which the PRC's actions have recently seemed at odds with the harmonious intent contained in the formal language around the BRI emanating from within China. So far, therefore, while the maritime BRI has spoken to strengthening the PRC's economic narrative within the region, it has done little to spell out a similarly compelling security one—and it is in this area where there is most lack of consensus amongst the different countries involved in the idea. Even in the economic realm, too, the record of China as a partner and investor in the region is a highly mixed one. If it wishes to develop and improve this, it will need to operate in ways that are more collaborative and communicative than ever before.

Whether the BRI does succeed across the Asia Pacific region will depend on activities that show how it operates in action. Investments by the AIIB for instance, or projects that are clearly badged with the BRI on them, will at least give it some tangible form and visibility. The BRI does show willingness on the part of the PRC to at least seem to be operating on different, new terms with others. The fundamental question in the end is whose interests will ultimately be best served by this—the PRC's, or those seeking to work with it. The Trump presidency might mean that for many in the region, they will have no option but to go along with a Chinese agenda, and the BRI will assume a prominence that it is as yet not ready for, or designed for, but which it will have no choice but to fill.

Notes

1. Robert S Ross, 'Chinese Security Policy: Structure, Power and Politics', London and New York: Routledge, 2009, p 60.
2. Bill Hayton, 'The South China Sea: The Struggle for Power in Asia', Yale: Yale University Press, 2014.
3. A list of these can be found at List of Active People's Liberation Army Navy Ships. https://en.wikipedia.org/wiki/List_of_active_People%27s_Liberation_Army_Navy_ships.
4. See Mark Edward Lewis, 'The Early Chinese Empires: Qin and the Han', Cambridge, Mass and London: Belknap Press of Harvard University, 2007, p 143: 'As for the idea of a "silk road", the term was coined by a German geographer in the late nineteenth century. Neither the Chinese not the Romans, who constituted its two termini, were aware of the existence of such a route or even of the existence of one another'.

5. Full text available on the website of the National Development and Reform Commission: http://en.ndrc.gov.cn/newsrelease/201503/t20150330_669367.html, accessed 27 August 2016.
6. John W. Garver, 'China's Quest: The History of Foreign Relations of the People's Republic of China', Oxford: Oxford University Press, 2016, p. 74.
7. 'China's Xi Says Political Solution for Taiwan Can't Wait Forever', Reuters, October 6 2013, www.reuters.com/article/us-asia-apec-china-taiwan-idUSBRE99503Q20131006.
8. Prashanth Parameswaren, 'Indonesia and China's AIIB', The Diplomat, http://thediplomat.com/2016/07/indonesia-and-chinas-aiib/, accessed 13 November 2016.
9. Gideon Rachman, 'Davos Leaders: Shinzo Abe on WW1 Parallels, Economics and Women at Work', Financial Times, 22nd January 2014, https://www.ft.com/content/7378a719-bd7e-3c99-b63f-330a17ce7a78.
10. Christoker Coker, 'The Improbable War: China, the United States and the Logic of Great Power Conflict', Oxford: Oxford University Press, 2015.
11. Jonathan Holslag, 'China's Coming War with Asia', Cambridge: Polity Press, 2015.
12. Hugh White, 'Excerpt from 'The China Choice: Why America Should Share Power', published by the Lowy Institute, http://www.lowyinstitute.org/files/lowy_institute_extract_-_the_china_choice.pdf.
13. Kurt Campbell, 'The "Pivot": A Reply to Hugh White', Lowy Interpreter, July 2016, at http://www.lowyinterpreter.org/post/2016/07/05/The-Pivot-A-reply-to-Hugh-White.aspx.

PART IV

Corporate Social Responsibilities and Insurance Performance of Chinese Investments

CHAPTER 7

China Power Investment Corporation in Myanmar

Xue Gong

Introduction

Under the previous military government in Myanmar, China became Myanmar's largest foreign investor and wielded the most international influence in the country. China supported Myanmar's military junta largely through economic aid, such as interest-free loans, economic assistance programmes, and technological cooperation. As anticipated, economic statecraft provided China with a new regional ally and helped the development of China's least-developed Yunnan Province. Therefore, China's economic statecraft contributed to the close leaning of Myanmar. Accordingly, China made its presence felt when it supported the military junta through various means, among which economic means has been the most prominent but also the most controversial. Despite its economic success in Myanmar, China's plans were occasionally waylaid by its government counterpart. Since March 2011, the new government has brought significant challenges to China's political and economic relations with Myanmar. The suspension

China Power Investment Corporation (CPI), was merged with State Nuclear Power Technology Corporation (SNPTC) to form the current State Power Investment Corporation (SPIC). This chapter will use CPI as the subject.

X. Gong (✉)
S. Rajaratnam School of International Studies (RSIS), Nanyang Technological University, Singapore, Singapore

A. Arduino, X. Gong (eds.), *Securing the Belt and Road Initiative*,
https://doi.org/10.1007/978-981-10-7116-4_7

of the Myitsone Dam project announced by the quasi-civilian government in 2011 and opposition over other China-invested projects taught the Chinese government a lesson: the 'licence to operate' is becoming more important in protecting its interests overseas. China now has to engage with different actors in the society that influence Myanmar's socio-political landscape and other foreign actors.

In 2013, Chinese President Xi Jinping's Belt and Road Initiative (BRI) was embraced by Myanmar. In December 2013, the two countries signed memorandums of understanding (MOUs) and Economic and Technological Cooperation Agreements (ETCAs) under the framework of Bangladesh–China–India–Myanmar Forum for Regional Cooperation-Economic Corridor (BCIM-EC). Myanmar also responded by becoming the founding member of the Asian Infrastructure and Investment Bank (AIIB). In September 2016, the Chinese-backed AIIB provided a USD 20 million loan to develop a gas power plant in central Myanmar. The Kyaukpyu project, which involves the construction of a deep-water port at the Special Economic Zone (SEZ), is intended to become a key element of China's BRI.

With enormous capital and supportive policies, Chinese companies enjoyed an overwhelming investment advantage in Myanmar, particularly when the military junta faced sanctions and needed foreign investment. However, the implications of China's investments have upset the target country in various issues, such as national security, governance, and environment, with the Myitsone Dam project serving as a warning sign of China's overseas business practice. A case study of Myanmar offers great insights into understanding the backlash on bilateral relations caused by business activities of the Chinese enterprises and the reasons for the behaviour of these Chinese companies. Myanmar possesses a unique set of characteristics. Despite the scarcity of reliable data from both China and Myanmar, this chapter aims to provide a systematic investigation of China's CSR behaviour.

Economic Relations of China and Myanmar

Sino-Burmese Trade Relations

China's trade with Myanmar has been on the rise since 1988 when the focus of its foreign policy was switched from ideology-driven to economic pragmatism. Between 2003 and 2015, the bilateral trade relations appeared asymmetrical and China enjoyed trade surplus with Myanmar (see Fig. 7.1).

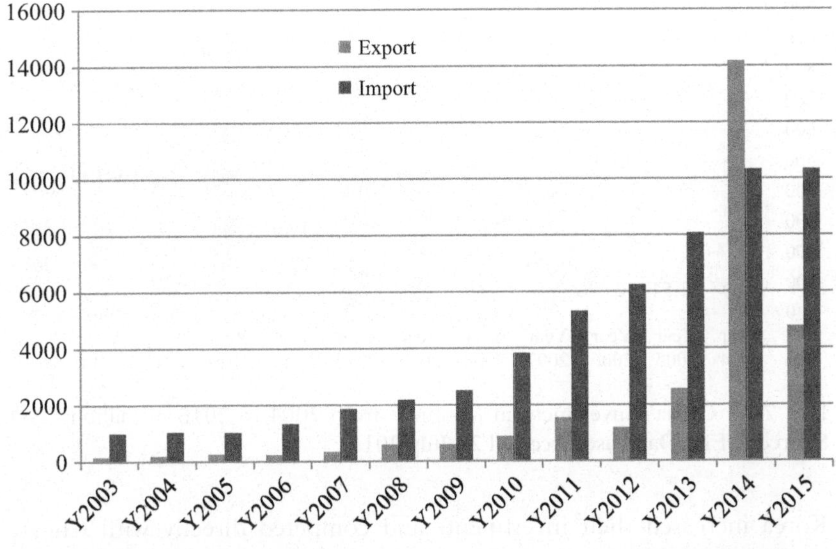

Fig. 7.1 Myanmar's export and import figures with China from 2003 to 2015 in USD million. Source: CEIC Database https://www.ceicdata.com/en?loc=SG&rand=fTaUp, accessed 12 November 2016

China's Investment in Myanmar

In tandem with the growing trade, Chinese investment flows to Myanmar also increased. From 2004 to 2015, the volume of China's investment increased nearly 200 times (see Fig. 7.2). Figure 7.2 shows that 2011 was a turning point of Chinese investment in Myanmar when the Myitsone Dam project suspension was declared under Thein Sein's presidency. After the dam suspension crisis, Chinese investment rose though the pace was slow. This was a result of a series of incidents targeting Chinese investments such as the public resistance in Letpadaung Copper Mine and heavy blows to the Chinese investors' confidence caused by the construction of gas and oil pipelines. Besides, the political transition period of Myanmar's government hindered Chinese investment. Based on project numbers in Myanmar since 2012, Singapore overtook China (excluding Hong Kong) to become the leading investor (see Fig. 7.3). Meanwhile, Myanmar had more diverse foreign investment (FDI) inflows as the sanctions were gradually lifted. Countries such as the United Kingdom, Japan and South

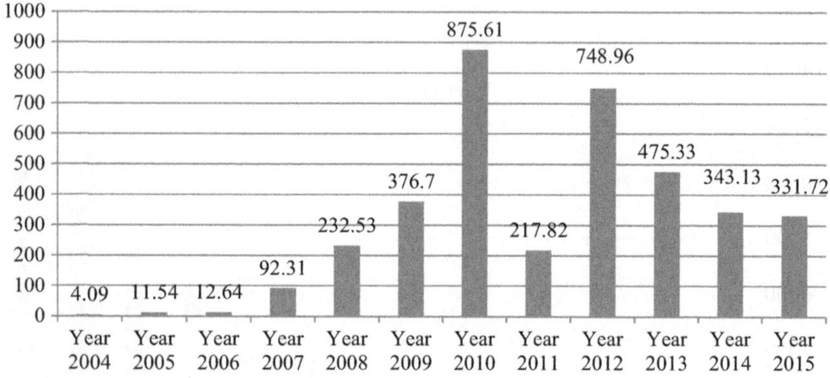

Fig. 7.2 China's investment in Myanmar from 2004 to 2015 in million USD. Source: CEIC Database, accessed 20 July 2016

Korea increased their investments and competed directly with China's investment in Myanmar.

However, the total volume of China's investment in Myanmar reached USD 18,529.301 million, surpassing other countries. Second and third places were taken by Singapore and Thailand (see Fig. 7.4). It is prudent to note that the Chinese ventured into places where investments from other developed countries have shunned. The development of Myanmar currently lags far behind other Association of Southeast Asian Nations (ASEAN) members on most standards, such as poor road connectivity, insufficient power generation capacity, and inefficient port management. The lack of infrastructure also restricted Myanmar's development of trade and manufacturing industries.

Chinese investments would fit in situations where other investors are reluctant to invest in a poor investment environment (Corkin et al. 2008; Urban et al. 2012). More importantly, Chinese investment could offer the local people access to basic infrastructure and the host country a much-needed boost in infrastructure for economic development. For example, developing mining requires stable electricity supply and thus building the Shweli 1 and Tarpein 2 Dams enabled the neighbourhood to access electricity and water (International Rivers 2012; Urban et al. 2012).

China's investments in Myanmar have extended from traditional sectors such as agriculture, industry, and trade, to tertiary sectors such as

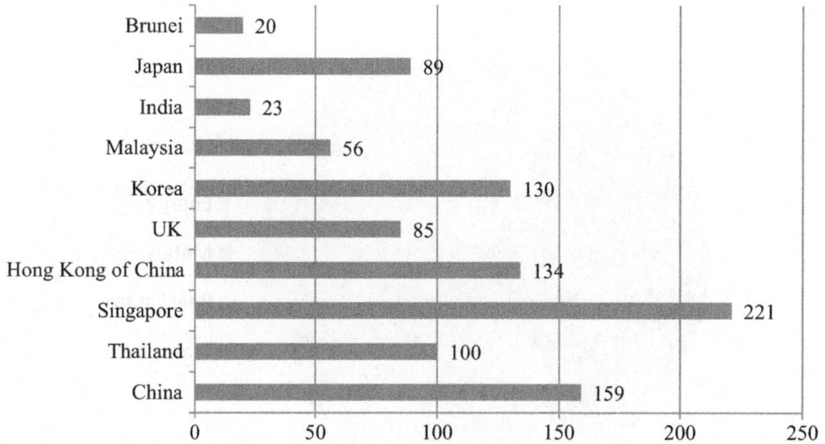

Fig. 7.3 Approved leading projects in Myanmar by October 2016. Source: CEIC Database, accessed 20 July 2016

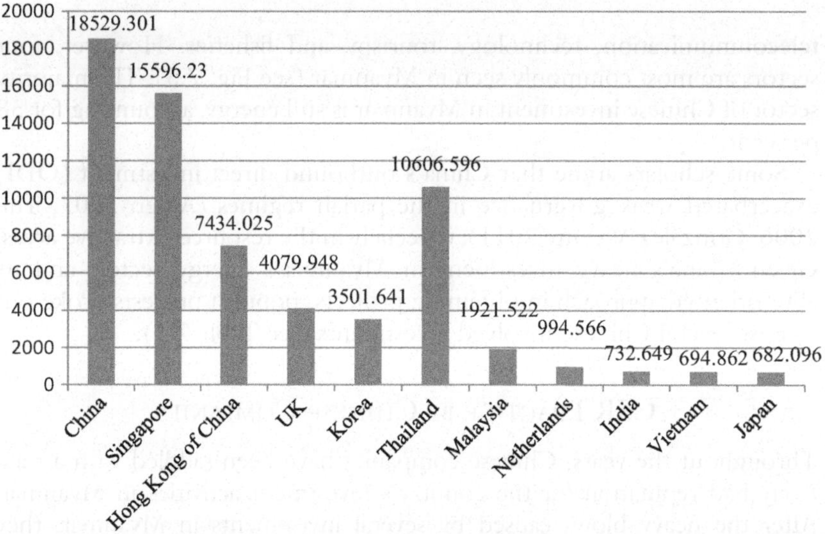

Fig. 7.4 Approved FDI country source in Myanmar by October 2016 in million USD. Source: CEIC Database

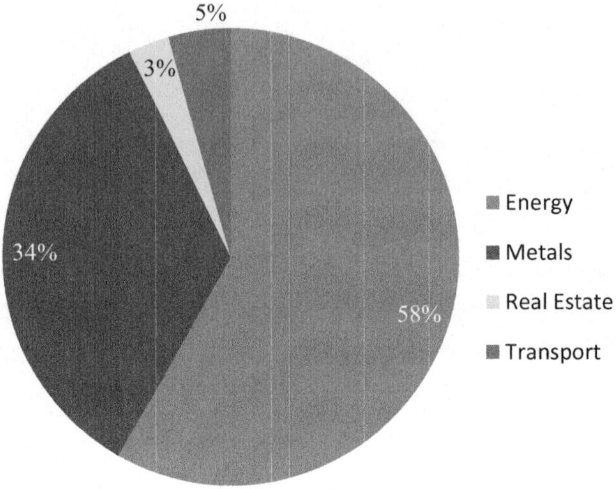

Fig. 7.5 China's investment share in Myanmar by sectors from 2005 to 2016. Source: China Global Investment Tracker by American Enterprises Initiative accessed 4 December 2016

telecommunication, technology, tourism, and fisheries. However, four sectors are most commonly seen in Myanmar (see Fig. 7.5). The majority sector of Chinese investment in Myanmar is still energy, accounting for 58 per cent.

Some scholars argue that China's outbound direct investment (ODI) exacerbated weak governance in the pariah regimes (Alden 2007; Tull 2006; González-Vicente 2011), especially in the resource-extractive areas. Given China's heavy investment in Myanmar's energy sector, and its elite-oriented approach in obtaining projects, populist protests broke out against several Chinese-involved investments (see Table 7.1).

CSR Practice by Chinese Companies

Throughout the years, Chinese companies have been saddled with a relatively bad reputation for the country's investment activities in Myanmar. After the heavy blows caused by several investments in Myanmar, they resolved to improve but with little success. Based on data collected from interviews and media sources, there were major complaints over China's investments.[1] First, Chinese investments were accused of being irresponsible

Table 7.1 Chinese major controversial investment projects in Myanmar

	Projects	*Enterprises*
1.	Sino-Myanmar pipelines project	China National Petroleum Corporation[a]
2.	Myitsone Dam project	China Power Investment[b]
3.	Letpadaung Copper Mine project	Myanmar Wanbao Mining Copper Ltd.
4.	Thanlwin River 6 hydropower projects	Hanergy Holding Company, Hydrochina Corporation, China China Three Gorges Corporation, China Datang Overseas Investment Company, Sinohydro, EGAT International Co., Ltd.[c]
5.	China state, Mt. Mwe and Mt. Pa Nickel mining project	North Mining Investment Corp.
6.	Rakhine state, Rethedaung and Maungdaw titanium mining project	Gold Finder
7.	Kachin state, illegal logging	Unknown
8.	Kyaukpyu-Kunming railway	CREC
9.	Kyaukpyu Special Economic Zone	CITIC Group
10.	Dawei Oil Refinery	Guangdong Zhenrong Energy Co.
11.	Khaunglanphu Dam	CPI
12.	Chibwe Dam	CPI
13.	Lakin Dam	CPI

Source: Adapted from Myanmar media reports

[a]Companies include Daewoo International, Myanmar Oil and Gas Enterprise (MOGE), Oil and Natural Gas Corporation (ONGC) Videsh, Gas Authority of India (GAIL), Korean Gas Corporation (KOGAS), and China National Petroleum Corporation (CNPC). But when people criticise this project, they often mention only CNPC

[b]The company has changed its name to the State Power Investment Corporation in 2015

[c]EGAT International Co., Ltd is a Thai enterprise

and environmentally damaging. China invested heavily in Myanmar's energy sector, yet neglected environmental assessment before and during the projects. For example, the industrial waste from the Letpadaung Copper Mine was released to the nearby village, damaging the soil for farming and harvesting. Similarly for the refinery factory for the oil and gas pipelines, chemical sewage was directly released into Andaman Sea, harming water quality and fish stocks.

Second, Chinese companies were blamed for alienating the local people and depriving them of employment opportunities. In many contracting projects, Chinese companies only hired Chinese workers because the latter have better labour skills and faced fewer language and cultural barriers. The CNPC was said to employ far fewer local workers in the upper section of the Shwe pipeline than the Indian company in charge of the lower section (Walker 2014). The influx of about 2000 Chinese workers hired by CPI in Myitkyina for the hydropower project angered the local people because of the stiff competition for employment and the temporary supply shortage and price spikes (Yang 2012). The Chinese workers and even the Chinese managers behaved badly towards the local people. They were ignorant of the cultural and religious importance to the Burmese society, and this resulted in more resentment against the Chinese investors and workers.

Third, Chinese companies were accused of non-compliance with Myanmar logging law and regulations. Myanmar's laws stipulated that wood and wooden products were allowed to be exported only through the river ports at Yangon. Foreign sales of logs were banned completely in April 2014. However, the lucrative logging trade for both Chinese traders and border officers and the conflict-prone area controlled by the ethnic groups provided the opportunity for illegal logging and log smuggling. In 2015, more than 153 illegal Chinese workers were arrested for the illegal logging.[2] Unauthorised Chinese investments in jade and minerals exploitation were also common in northern Myanmar where it is too remote for the central government to regulate.

Finally, Chinese investment lacked transparency and was carried out under close contact with the military government, resulting in ignorance of the grassroots demands. Most of the investments in the energy sector required land expropriation, and thus Chinese companies relied heavily on the brutal military government to launch the resettlement plan, resulting in inadequate compensation and the lack of sustainable planning for the community. For example, the Letpadaung Copper Mine project, which resulted in the expropriation of 7800 acres of land in 26 villages, provoked a series of protests. Neither Myanmar's government nor the Chinese companies produced a long-term plan for the villagers who had lived on the land for generations. Another outstanding example, the protests and national objection against the construction of the Myitsone Dam project for similar reasons: lack of transparency in the investment, unfair land expropriation, potential environmental degradation, and disrespect for the Burmese culture, and so on. The China-based non-governmental organisation Green Watershed found that, even when the Chinese companies provided public goods to the local population, they usually did so through the unpopular military government, which resulted in limited benefits to the local population (Walker 2014).

Realising the negative impact of its overseas activities, the Chinese government began to show interest in international experiences in implementing CSR for its dam investment (International Rivers 2012). In fact, the CSR implementation of Chinese hydropower companies became a prerequisite, according to government policies. In 2003, China passed a new Environmental Impact Assessment Law, requiring companies proposing projects with significant environmental impact to conduct an environmental impact assessment (EIA) prior to the project construction, and to obtain approval at the environment bureau.

The Chinese government also institutionalised public participation and displacement into its EIA law system. In 2006, the Ministry of Environmental Protection (MEP) (then SEPA) issued *Provisional Measures for Public Participation in EIA and Rules of Land Compensation and People Resettlement in Medium and Large Hydraulic and Hydroelectricity Projects.* In 2007, the MEP and the Ministry of Commerce, People's Republic of China (MOFCOM) announced that Chinese exporters who caused environmental harm would have their export operations suspended.

In addition, financial organisations issued their own policies to improve the CSR of the companies (see Table 7.2). China EXIM Bank funded most of China's overseas dams by providing export credits, guarantees, and concessional loans. It issued the *Guidelines for Environmental and Social Impact Assessment of the China Export Import Bank's Loan Projects* in 2007, requiring the project owner to submit governmental approval documents, particularly the environmental and social impact assessments (SIA), in order to obtain approval for the loan (Hensengerth 2014, p. 237).

However, the activity on the ground failed to abide by the rules laid down on paper (Mang 2015). Although Chinese institutions issued many advanced regulations, their capacity for implementation and supervision remained very weak. It is not specified who should regulate hydropower companies overseas and which domestic regulatory tools should be used for non-compliance. For example, MOFCOM issued the *Guidelines of 2013* requiring Chinese companies to respect the local community and

Table 7.2 Timeline for Myitsone Dam planning from 2006 to 2011

2006	December: CPI signed a memorandum of understanding with the Ministry of Electric Power No.1 of Myanmar
2007	May: Agreement to build the seven dams was signed June and July: Kachin Independence Organisation (KIO) chairman approached Yunnan Province State Council, head of state senior general Than Shwe and head of Myanmar Military Northern Command in Kachin State to express objection December: Changjiang Institute of Survey, Planning, Design and Research (CISPDR) completed planning report for the feasibility of the hydropower projects
2008	March: Terms of reference for the EIA were completed, and subsequently approved December: Yunnan Power Investment Co., Ltd. was created for hydropower projects on the Irrawaddy December 24: The *Biodiversity and Nature Conservation Association* (BANCA) and CPI signed an agreement to conduct an EIA special investigation
2009	January to July: Both Chinese and Myanmar experts conducted a special investigation on the upper Irrawaddy October: The baseline environmental impact assessment by BANCA was finalised December: Stage 1 (out of a total of five construction stages) began on the Myitsone Dam site. The resettlement of people had begun
2010	March: CISPDR finalised the EIA Report April: Four explosions occurred at the Myitsone Dam site September: 1994 Ceasefire Agreement between Myanmar government and the KIO was signed, while communications and cooperation were halted. KIO invited CPI to a discussion but received no response
2011	January: Developers finalised the overall EIA for hydropower projects on the upper Irrawaddy March: The chairman of KIO sent a letter to the Chinese leader June: Fighting erupted, affecting the construction site July: Full-scale construction resumed September 17: The Burmese government hosted a workshop to discuss the impact of hydropower projects on the Irrawaddy River September 30: Thein Sein suspended the construction of Myitsone Dam

Source: Adapted from International Rivers and other media sources

protect the ecology. Nevertheless, the punishment mechanism was absent for non-compliance. Furthermore, the regulatory overlapping jurisdiction embedded in the domestic bureaucracy structure hindered consistent supervision over various aspects of overseas business activities. Several ministries were directly in charge of dam investment issues: Ministry of

Water Resources, Ministry of Environmental Protection, and MOFCOM. However, there was no coordination mechanism among them to instruct the companies. For China EXIM Bank that funded most of the overseas dams, the overseas supervision proved to be 'a really disappointing situation' though the bank made progress in China, according to Peter Bosshard, a senior advisor at International Rivers.[3]

Subsequently, the Chinese companies usually lacked experience in engaging civil society, including labour unions, which was an important reason for the low CSR performance. The governmental legislation on the disclosure of government information came into effect in 2008, and this created a mechanism for the Chinese public to demand governmental information.[4] The regulation required government offices to release information on a timely and regular basis. Such regulations made it easier for the civil society to access information related to the procedures employed in dam projects. The Chinese environment-oriented NGOs grew in power and sought to influence China's policy-making procedures. For example, the *Guidelines of 2013* by MOFCOM and MEP were based on the recommendations by the Global Environmental Institute (GEI).[5] The *Guidelines* also created an opportunity for the Chinese civil society to obtain information on overseas investors that hold the latter responsible. The Chinese NGOs provided communication channels for the government and the local NGOs in the host country. The success of suspending dam construction on the Nu (Salween) River shows that the government consented to the participation of the public after seeking consultation from the Chinese NGOs and those residing along the Salween River from Thailand and Myanmar (International Rivers 2008). China's NGOs also operated overseas as its companies did. In 2008, Chinese NGO Green Watershed and other Chinese organisations launched the Green Banking Innovation Awards in order to encourage banks to cover environmental protection when issuing loans for overseas investment.[6]

However, Chinese NGOs still face challenges in influencing the policy making at home. They have limited financial support and experiences in cooperating with the SOEs and national banks that dominate the overseas investment. Although they have worked to push the government for more information on the activities of the overseas Chinese companies, their success is undermined by institutional barriers of partnering with overseas NGOs, given the deep suspicion of the Chinese government.

Case Study: CPI in Myitsone Dam

China invested in the construction of more than 25 massive dams on the Irrawaddy, Salween, and Sittang Rivers, with its SOEs taking the initiative in Myanmar. China's active involvement in Myanmar could be attributed to several factors. Myanmar's power sector was facing serious shortage, particularly when Western sanctions impeded technological and economic cooperation with potential investors, hindering its economic development. The military junta intended to improve the power shortage to strengthen its political legitimacy. Myanmar's demand for power development would complement China's Going Out Policy whereby Chinese companies can expand the international market to overcome barriers of a saturated domestic market. China viewed the dam investment as a 'win-win' for the two countries because China considered hydropower development as part of its goodwill in providing favourable concessional loans, development of the local economy, and transfer of technology to the host country. To China, the development of hydropower industry in Myanmar served as a boost to its economic and political influence in Myanmar.

As latecomers to hydropower investment, Chinese companies did not have many options in the easily accessible and mature market. Instead, the investments were generally located in controversial and conflict-prone regions. Even China's SINOSURE, a governmental body in issuing insurance for the overseas investment companies, placed Myanmar in the high-risk category[7] for investment (China Export and Credit Insurance Corporation 2007, p. 149). China's investments were vulnerable to political conflicts, ethnic issues, and even terrorism in these destinations. However, the Chinese companies relied on the state-to-state approach to safeguard their projects. Because of the elite-oriented approach, the local communities and NGOs were excluded from the deals, which resulted in the civil society's opposition.

The Myitsone Dam project was signed during then Vice President Xi Jinping's visit to Myanmar in 2009 (see Table 7.2). China Power Investment was backed by China EXIM Bank. This project was contracted to CPI and the Asia World Company with close connections with the military junta.[8] In addition, SINOSURE, the Construction Bank of China, and the Industrial Bank of China all entered into negotiations for supporting construction in the Irrawaddy. When negotiations were finalised, other companies such as Sinohydro and Gezhouba Group were also involved as contractors.[9]

However, the vast scale of Chinese hydropower investment resulted in large-scale protests. Civil society in Myanmar was actively vocal in opposing the Myitsone Dam project. The Kachin Development Networking Group (KDNG) and Burma Environmental Working Group (BEWG), among other organisations, strongly opposed the dam project. As part of the Burma Partnership Network, they demanded community rights within the context of protecting the country's rivers from hydropower development. As early as 2009, the KDNG even sent an open letter to CPI to urge the company to stop the Myitsone Dam project and other dam projects in Kachin State. The anti-dam sentiments began to appear in several influential social media, such as *The Irrawaddy* (a local magazine), after Thein Sein relaxed media control. On 24 September 2011, famous environmentalists, meteorological experts, representatives of local residents from Myitsone, and the media gathered for a CSR seminar in Yangon.

Myanmar Affairs, a Myanmar public opinion survey and environmental protection agency, led a poll of 1059 people in Yangon from 27 to 30 September 2011. Of those polled, 90 per cent objected to the Myitsone Dam project, while 4 per cent agreed, and 6 per cent said they had no idea. In addition, 79 per cent of the people believed that the project would damage national unity if it continued. For the solution of the Myitsone Dam problem, 46 per cent of the people said that it should be re-surveyed by experts, and results were published and made known to the local population, before coming to a decision whether or not to continue.[10]

The Myitsone Dam project remained highly controversial for social, economic, and security reasons. First, the consequences of the construction of the dam proved unfair to the local residents. The cost of the Myitsone Dam project was estimated at USD 3.6 billion and Myanmar's government would receive USD 54 billion for the project over the first 50 years of the project before the operation rights would be transferred to Myanmar. Of the electricity generated by the Myitsone Dam, 90 per cent would benefit China while the remaining 10 per cent would be reserved for Myanmar's own consumption. Many Kachins were primarily engaged in agricultural production for their livelihood, and the reservoir affected the loss of 60 villages and approximately 15,000 people.[11] When Myanmar's military government and the CPI announced that the hydropower project would benefit the local people, the positive news were undermined by a report stating that CPI hired approximately 10,000 workers from China to build the dam (Myint-U 2011, p. 111). Moreover, Chinese companies imported all necessary equipment and construction materials from China, depriving the Burmese of opportunities for investment-related industry development. The Myitsone Dam construction would have an uncertain ecological and cultural impact on the local villagers. A massive reservoir, almost the same size as Singapore, would be created as part of the project, posing potential ecological threats to biodiversity and the livelihood of the local people. Important historical and cultural relics that represent the national heritage of Myanmar would be vulnerable, too.[12]

Second, the project was strongly resented due to the lack of transparency and clarity. The CPI was found to hide the dangers and risks of the project from the public. China actually conducted an EIA on the Myitsone Dam in 2008 at the request of the Power Ministry, but it was not disclosed until the protests broke out in 2011. It was widely criticised for lacking an 'alternative analysis', proper consideration of downstream impact, the cumulative impact of the seven dams, and the absence of social impact assessment. It was found out later by the civil society groups that the Chinese company had concealed the findings and suggestions by the Burmese experts. Contrary to the CPI's official report, the Burmese experts suggested replacing the Myitsone Dam with two smaller hydropower dams to preserve the ecology.[13] The transparency also extended to the land expropriation. While the CPI was not directly involved in the forced relocation of villagers, it had links with the military government because the negotiating process was exclusively government-to-government and the public was kept in the dark.[14] The opposition against Myitsone Dam soon intensified. According to Aung, the leaked report is the flash point of public concern for the project.[15]

The CPI president and party secretary, Lu Qizhou, said in an interview that the suspension of the Myitsone Dam was not informed by the Burmese government.[16] Even before the suspension, they were asked to accelerate the construction. Lu also explained how CPI had followed the legal process in China and Myanmar, how it had given full consideration to project safety, environmental impact, and resettlement of displaced communities, and how the economies of both countries would have benefited from the dam.[17] The Burma Rivers Network (BRN) refuted Qizhou's point and stressed that CPI was late in releasing the environmental assessment report and the process of resettlement was opaque. The Chinese company was also reluctant to interact with NGOs. For example, Li Guanghua, the president of China Power Investment (Yunnan), expressed that it was unnecessary to get in touch with NGOs. He said, 'The environmentalists are all well-fed and clothed, they are not the ones who need to improve their circumstances. There is no need to talk to them'.[18]

Lastly, the construction of the dam heightened ethnic tension while China's business interests were hijacked by the internal conflicts of Myanmar. The interests of the Kachin people in stopping the dam were not only due to the environmental and social impact, but also due to territorial control against the Tatmadaw. Myanmar's military government was seen as using the Myitsone Dam and other hydropower projects in the Irrawaddy River to justify sending troops into the region. While concerns over the dam building began as early as 2007 when it was just announced,[19] the first sign of armed conflict came in 2010, when Chinese workers died in the bomb blast at the site of the Myitsone Dam.[20] In 2011, the chairman of the KIO wrote a letter to the then president Hu Jintao, warning that the Myitsone Dam project could even lead to civil war in Myanmar.[21] While the issue between KIO and the military junta was clearly a domestic affair, the Myitsone Dam became a rallying point against invasive Chinese investments as their opinions were not included in the state-to-state deals.

The building of the Myitsone Dam was not without its domestic reasons. First, CPI was born from the reform of the China Power Corporation in 2002. It operated as a central SOE directly under the leadership of the State-owned Assets Supervision and Administration Commission of the State Council (SASAC). This connection implied that the Chinese government had a major influence over the investment decisions of the CPI. The president of CPI Lu Qizhou would also be a member of the National Committee of the Chinese People's Political Consultative Conference, which advised the National People's Congress. Given Qizhou's position on the Committee, he enjoyed connections with the government. Given such connections and the importance of energy security, it would be no surprise that CPI invested in the Myitsone Dam project. Yu Xiaogang, the founder of Watershed, referred to the domestic state-business relations in a comment on the China model. China's large SOEs had significant resources and huge capital and this marginalised private companies. SOEs enjoyed domestic monopoly and had no worries about the costs of conducting CSR. They also did not have to worry as much as the private companies about the environmental and social impact of their operations in Myanmar.[22]

Second, domestic competition led to the extensive hydropower venturing in Myanmar. In the past two decades, Chinese companies were involved in the construction and investment in many dam projects as well as power plants in Myanmar. For example, the China National Machinery Corporation signed three contracts with Myanmar to provide equipment for generating electricity for the Kun and Kabaung Hydropower Plants and also for the Yeya Hydropower Project. China's Gezhouba Group participated in the construction of hydropower projects in Yeya and Tasang as well, while providing equipment for hydro-electricity generation to the Papun, Shwe Gin, and the Tasang Hydropower projects. Li Guanghua, the CPI's president, explained the investments in Myanmar, 'There are over a dozen Chinese firms, including CPI, working on hydropower in Myanmar .... we may be based in China, but we compete in Myanmar-almost always with other Chinese firms, and fiercely'.[23]

Behind each leading SOE, there were various subsidiary Chinese companies involved in the Myitsone Dam project. For example, in the Dapein Power Plant project, the Sinohydro Corporation was in charge of the construction, while the Datang Corporation and Central China Power Group were investors. The Jiangxi Provincial Water Conservancy Planning and Designing Institute were in charge of the design and impact survey of the project.

Third, the building of Myitsone Dam was a reflection of China's belief and experience of reliance on hydropower for its own domestic economic development. By the same token, the development of the Myitsone Dam would greatly benefit Myanmar's economy and accelerate industrialisation. According to Li Guanghua,

> The 10 percent of electricity given to Myanmar is equivalent to two gigawatts, and the entire country only has three gigawatts of generating capacity. And if that is not enough, CPI will give priority to meeting Myanmar's needs...we are just doing business and it is nothing but good news for Myanmar. Over a century, there will be one trillion Chinese yuan of profit to Myanmar.[24]

Given the importance and the amount of Chinese investment in the Myitsone Dam project, the Chinese government intervened by calling for action from both CPI and Myanmar's government. On the one hand, while the Chinese government was aware of the negative impact of its companies' overseas activities and the need to improve corporate behaviour (McDonald et al. 2009), the Chinese companies in charge of the dam construction and design failed to fulfil the international standard of environmental and social impact. The official guidelines on Chinese business activities overseas gave the following warning:

> China's companies …should actively work with the local society participate in social welfare and build some small projects benefiting the Myanmar people, in order to get support from the places where the construction project is located and to ensure China's investments' and projects' steady and sustained development.[25]

On the other hand, the Chinese government urged Myanmar's government to address the suspension issue. Hong Lei, China's spokesman for the Foreign Ministry, noted that the dam had undergone thorough examination by specialists in both countries, and urged Myanmar's government to 'protect the legal and legitimate rights of Chinese firms abroad'. According to Li Guanghua, Myanmar's government did not accuse CPI of not complying with the EIA and SIA procedures, and CSR implementation. He implied Myanmar's government assured them that the responsibility of suspension was not on the Chinese side, but rather it was Myanmar's own difficulty.[26]

There were also voices demanding for the reassessment of the relationship between China and Myanmar. They believed that the suspension of the Myitsone Dam project was not due to the poor CSR standards implemented by the Chinese companies. Instead, they held the internal political conflict and ethnic conflict in Myanmar accountable for the Chinese loss. They also believed that the suspension was indirectly caused by the Western conspiracy to contain China by provoking tensions between China and its neighbouring countries through supporting NGOs and media (Zhang 2012; Chu and Huang 2016).

The CPI thought that it was taking responsibility by following the agreement with Myanmar's government. Therefore, Chinese companies tended to think that as long as they followed the domestic laws and rules of Myanmar's government, they would be acting as responsible investors (Soe 2016). However, what most Chinese investors tended to overlook is that the decades of dictatorship instilled in the Burmese people a deep mistrust for their government. Any foreign company that would only deal with the government but ignored the local society would be at risk of condemnation from the Burmese people.

In fact, the sponsor of the Myitsone Dam project for CPI, China EXIM Bank, failed to supervise the activities of CPI in terms of assessing the EIA and SIA for providing loans. The CPI Yunnan conducted the EIA according to the requirement (*Guidelines for the EIA and SIA of China EXIM Bank's Loan Project of 2008*) mandated by China EXIM Bank even though EIA is not mandatory in Myanmar.[27] The Biodiversity and Nature Conservation Association (BANCA) said, 'Regarding hydropower development of Irrawaddy (Ayeyarwady) River, we should appreciate China's concern on EIA and should refer to their EIA procedure'.[28] However, it proved that the Chinese company did not strictly follow the guidelines as it was found out that the CPI also did not wait for the EIA to be finalised before commencing construction and resettlement. Construction began in December 2009, three months before the final EIA was reportedly available to CPI from Changjiang Institute of Survey, Planning, Design and Research (CISPDR) in March 2010.[29] Local people were asked to relocate by the authorities at the start of the EIA while the SIA was omitted during the resettlement. During the process of relocation, there was no specific long-term arrangement for the local people's living arrangements (Soe 2016, pp. 144–176) despite the fact that the company had paid compensation to the villagers.

Although the Chinese institutional setting improved after the application of environmental and social impact assessment, China EXIM Bank's failure to act as a supervisor for the CPI implied that there was still a gap for actual implementation. It was found that staff of financial institutions still viewed environmental protection under the jurisdiction of the MEP in China and the local government's responsibility if the investment was overseas.[30] To the Chinese banks, loan repayments outweighed issues such as environmental protection. Moreover, China EXIM Bank lacked accountability and transparency in issuing loans. The CPI received the financial support from the bank even before submitting the EIA and SIA reports. When protests broke out, China EXIM Bank did not respond to questions.

To be fair, the CPI did carry out certain forms of CSR, though mainly in philanthropy and infrastructure building. From 2009 to July 2011, in addition to the construction of new resettlement houses, the CPI donated a large amount of study supplies and school uniforms to students, malaria-preventive medical kits, television sets, allowances, as well as rice and cooking oil to all the villagers affected.[31] Moreover, the Chinese company also built roads, bridges, telecommunication stations, hospitals, temples, and churches for the resettlement of the local people. However, the CPI failed to publicise its activities timely online until the suspension of the Myitsone Dam project. Some people believed that Chinese companies lacked public relations skills in reaching out to the local people, taking blame away from China's inept CSR practice. Even Li Guanghua's claim of 'just do but not say it' led to more misunderstanding towards Chinese investments.[32]

After the suspension of the Myitsone Dam project, the company's official website showed that its CSR activities became more diversified even though philanthropic activities still dominated CSR implementation. Their activities included the following:

- Flood relief:[33] In August 2015, the company contributed MMK 2 million to the disaster area and visited the Magway Region to distribute relief supplies together with the Chinese Embassy in Myanmar. The CPI handed more than MMK 50 million of relief to the Ministry of Electricity of Myanmar despite the suspension of the dam project. At the end of August, the company provided rice valued at MMK 4.2 million to two newly relocated villagers.
- Malaria disease investigation and medical services:[34] The CPI launched a 100 per cent malaria-eradication campaign in Myanmar. By fumigation and providing malaria prophylactic drugs and mosquito nets at the project site, hotels, and other public areas, the medical team achieved its goal. This is the fourth time in two years that the company provided malaria-disease investigation and medical services to the local population.
- ACHC Scholarship award ceremony:[35] The scholarship award ceremony was launched in 2013 in order to support education opportunities for the local people. A total of MMK 5.61 million was awarded to 163 students by the end of 2015.

With the suspension of the Myitsone Dam project, the Chinese government and companies realised the importance of the 'license to operate' to China's overseas investment and thus the concept of CSR emerged in Chinese investments in Myanmar. On 5 July 2013, more than 100 Chinese companies that invested in Myanmar hosted a press conference and also launched a proposal emphasising China's CSR implementation in Myanmar. In the proposal, the Chinese companies agreed to abide by the bilateral laws and regulations, strictly implement investments based on contracts, protect the environment, as well as enhance the employability and safety of the labour force.

The Chinese companies started their own CSR efforts. The CNPC formed the Friends of the Sino-Burmese Pipeline Association, liaised with local community groups, and invited the civil society stakeholders to a meeting in Beijing. The China Nonferrous Metal Mining (Group) Co., Ltd agreed to become a member of the multi-stakeholder group of the Myanmar Extractive Industries Transparency Initiative (EITI) that is working to implement the EITI in the country. Wanbao Mining began its environmental and social assessment by inviting an Australian consultancy company. The CPI directly engaged different stakeholders, Myanmar military government, the NLD, Kachin government, civil society groups such as 88 Generation Students Group, the media such as *7Day Daily*, and the general public such as the representative of the villagers. Starting in early 2012, the CPI distributed pamphlets disclosing the design of the dam and the impact of the dam. In April 2012, Lu Qizhou visited villagers in Kachin State to negotiate with the environmentalists, and offered an extra year's worth of free electricity and rice in exchange for support for the project to continue.

As a Chinese company in Myanmar, the CPI was the first to release a detailed CSR report. Despite the absence of the United Nations Global Compact company (UNGC),[36] the CPI issued the 2010–2012 CSR Report, borrowing the advanced standards of the UNGC and Global Reporting Initiative (GRI).[37] In this report, the CPI acknowledged its shortcomings in communicating and cooperating with the local society, given the restrictions set by the military government. It also acknowledged the negative impact of the dam project and provided scientific solutions for crisis management. Moreover, the report provided detailed information on a large number of areas such as project planning, environmental protection, safety management, quality control, social security, long-term vocational training for the relocated villagers, and employability development. The Report even adopted the assessment from the third party to increase transparency.

In October 2015, a company official from CPI commented that the company already invested USD 800 million on the Myitsone Dam project for the following:[38]

- The soil and water flow assessment at construction sites for Myitsone, Chipwe, Lasa, or Maliyan hydropower plants
- EIA for the total construction of dam sites
- A dam construction on the Chipwe stream that flows into the Maykha River
- Relocation and compensation expenses for households living at watershed areas after dam construction
- Miscellaneous expenses

The Chinese representatives from NGOs such as Green Watershed based in Yunnan also conducted investigations regarding the Myitsone Dam project. The Chinese NGO GEI helped to arrange an informal visit by a vice-minister from the Chinese Ministry of Environment Protection to attend a one-day workshop organised by EcoDev in Myanmar. As an alternative to the state-to-state relationship, the citizen-to-citizen exchange created a more transparent and acceptable mechanism for the information exchange. Go Mingbo, the former head of the political section at the Chinese Embassy in Myanmar, boosted the image of Chinese companies by creating a Facebook account in Myanmar, even though Facebook is blocked in China.

'Meet-the-press' gatherings and the CSR Report gained some positive feedback. However, such attempts were made under the false assumption that the problems faced by Chinese companies originated not with the projects per se but with the lack of public understanding about these projects and the good deeds done by the Chinese companies. In other words, Chinese companies assumed that the local resistance against Chinese operations in Myanmar can be traced to weak Chinese public relations skills, civil society's resentment against the Myanmar military junta, as well as the provocation by Western NGOs. Such ideas were unlikely to win over the local population.

In March 2016, 61 civil society organisations, political parties, and religious groups released a statement calling for a halt to all resource extraction in Kachin State until conflicts were resolved.[39] At the same time, ethnic civil society organisations and environmental activists with local communities joined the International Day of Action for Rivers and Against Dams in the eastern border where Chinese investments were involved in many projects along the Salween River across Shan, Kayah, and Karen States.[40]

To be fair, one should acknowledge that Chinese investments were treated with bias by the civil society. Under-developed civil society in Myanmar did not have the financial or technical resources in communicating and establishing a professional relationship with the government and CPI. They also lacked knowledge on verifying news and sources regarding CPI's activities. Some organisations slandered CPI as participating in illegal activities such as panning for gold or stealing livestock of the villagers that are forbidden in Myanmar. When the CPI invited the local media and conducted interviews to investigate the truth, CPI became a scapegoat.[41] Some Chinese interviewees said given China's vast scale of investment in Myanmar, companies with Asian faces are easily mistaken as Chinese companies. The non-compliance of the local laws and regulations were the result of Myanmar's corrupted and backward investment environment. But the local people remained unaware of the truth and thus only trusted the Western media and NGOs, which aimed at containing China's investment.[42] However, approaching communities with the idea that the Burmese people are uninformed, ignorant, or pro-West will only further damage the business reputation of Chinese companies.

Nonetheless, questions concerning the capability of Myanmar's government in monitoring Chinese business activities arose, despite ongoing political reforms. After Myanmar's government established the Myitsone Dam project investigation commission in 2016 and visited Myitgyinar for inspection in September, 53 NGOs in Kachin State submitted a proposal that had five statements requesting the committee to stop the Myitsone project completely. According to the interviewee, one of the reasons for perpetual termination was that the local people had doubts about the Burmese government's financial, intellectual, and political capacity to monitor the business activities. The roles of the governmental agency were not yet defined as the government was still in the transitional phase. Moreover, Myanmar's government lacked the enforcement mechanism for non-compliance. The local people believed that Myanmar still has a long way to go in eradicating corruption in businesses.

Conclusion

The suspension of the Myitsone Dam project highlights the need for Chinese companies to deal with key weaknesses in their business model. Chinese weak CSR performance was a result of heavy reliance on the corrupted military regime, lack of transparency, and isolation from the civil society. China's weak supervision from domestic institutions also hindered efficient CSR implementation.

The suspension of the Myitsone Dam project had become a watershed for China to start to work with different sectors in Myanmar, especially the local communities and NGOs. Amid the transition of Myanmar's government after the election, ethnic conflict, and border stability, many challenges remain. Chinese investments would continue to be subject to the instability of Myanmar's politics and its limited capability in creating a fair and transparent environment for foreign investors. Only concerted efforts in improving the CSR supervision and enforcement from both Chinese and Burmese sides can enforce strict CSR compliance among Chinese companies.

NOTES

1. For example, http://burma.irrawaddy.com/article/2014/03/06/55850.html.
2. http://www.economist.com/news/asia/21665030-chinese-firms-are-still-stealing-myanmars-forests-stumped, accessed 29 November 2016.
3. China's dams: both welcome and worrying, http://www.thenational.ae/news/world/asia-pacific/chinas-dams-both-welcome-and-worrying, accessed 16 December 2015.
4. Regulation of the People's Republic of China on the Disclosure of Government Information, No. 492. 5 April 2007. http://www.gov.cn/zhengce/node_327.htm, accessed 13 June 2015.
5. https://www.internationalrivers.org/resources/chinese-government-guidelines-for-overseas-investment-7934, accessed 11 January 2016.
6. https://www.chinadialogue.net/article/show/single/en/3825-Following-the-money, accessed 28 December 2015.
7. SINOSURE has nine rankings for referring the risk level of the investment destination. The first ranking indicates the safest while the ninth implies the most risky country. Myanmar is ranked eighth in the report.
8. The Myitsone Dam on the Irrawaddy River: A Briefing, International Rivers, 28 September 2011, https://www.internationalrivers.org/resources/the-myitsone-dam-on-the-irrawaddy-river-a-briefing-3931, accessed 17 December 2015.
9. http://www.atimes.com/atimes/Southeast_Asia/NB07Ae01.html, accessed 18 December 2015.
10. Myanmar Affairs, "The poll of Ayeyarwady Myitsone hydropower project", *Myanmar Affairs Newsletter*, http://www.myanmaraffairs.com/mmaffairs2015/sites/default/files/poll_pdf/2011_Survey/Opinion%20Poll%20on%20Ayeyawaddy%20Myitsone%20Dam%20Hydropower%20Project_Sept_2011.pdf, translated by the Myanmar student in Yunnan, accessed 19 December 2015.
11. Dam Forces Relocation of 60 Villages, Burma Rivers Network, 28 October 2009, http://www.burmariversnetwork.org/index.php?option=com_content&view=article&id=262:concern-over-forced-relocation-of-60-kachin-villages&catid=11&Itemid=46, accessed 17 December 2015.
12. https://www.internationalrivers.org/campaigns/irrawaddy-myitsone-dam-0, accessed 27 November 2015.
13. https://www.internationalrivers.org/resources/the-myitsone-dam-on-the-irrawaddy-river-a-briefing-3931.
14. BRN responds to interview on Myitsone dam by CPI president, *Mizzima News*, 5 October 2011, http://www.burmalibrary.org/docs12/Mizzima-BRN-Dams.pdf, accessed 27 November 2015.

15. http://burmese.dvb.no/archives/15756, translated by a student in Yunnan, accessed 19 December 2015.
16. President Lu Qizhou's Answers to Media about the Suspension of Construction of Myitsone Hydropower Station, 4 October 2011, *CPI News*, http://eng.cpicorp.com.cn/NewsCenter/CorporateNews/201110/t20111004_163111.htm, accessed 27 November 2015.
17. https://www.chinadialogue.net/article/show/single/en/4574-Lessons-from-the-Irrawaddy, accessed 17 December 2015.
18. https://www.chinadialogue.net/article/show/single/en/4852-Chinese-power-Burmese-politics, accessed 26 December 2015. Yang Meng, 2 April 2012.
19. Five anti-Irrawaddy dam detainees freed in Myitkyina, Kachin News Group, 16 November 2007, http://www.kachinnews.com/news/326-five-anti-irrawaddy-dam-detainees-freed-in-myitkyina.html, accessed 13 December 2015.
20. Four killed, 12 injured in bomb blasts in Irrawaddy-Myitsone dam site, 17 April, 2010, Kachin News Group, http://www.kachinnews.com/news/1512-four-killed-12-injured-in-bomb-blasts-in-irrawaddy-myitsone-dam-site.html, accessed 13 December 2015.
21. KIO warns China: Myitsone Dam could spark 'civil war', May 20, 2011, *Mizzima*, http://archive-1.mizzima.com/special-29517/myitsone-dam-controversy/5295-kio-warns-china-myitsone-dam-could-spark-civil-war, accessed 13 December 2015.
22. Yu Xiaogang in Liao, Ruo, Lessons from the Irrawaddy, China Dialogue, 10 October 2010, https://www.chinadialogue.net/article/show/single/en/4574-Lessons-from-the-Irrawaddy, accessed 26 November 2015.
23. Li Guanghua, in Meng, Y., Chinese Power, Burmese Politics. China Dialogue, 2 April 2012, https://www.chinadialogue.net/article/show/single/en/4852-Chinese-power-Burmese-politics, accessed 26 November 2015.
24. Ibid.
25. Chinese Academy of International Trade and Economic Cooperation of Ministry of Commerce, Investment Promotion Agency of MOFCOM, Economic and Commercial Counsellor's Office of the Embassy of China, Duiwai Touzi Hezuo Guobie Zhinan (Miandian), Guidelines for Overseas Investment and Cooperation in Other Countries and Regions (Myanmar), 2014, pp. 66 and 69, http://aaa.ccpit.org/Category7/Asset/2015/Mar/13/onlineeditimages/file71426207826381.pdf, accessed 28 November 2015.
26. http://www.cec.org.cn/xinwenpingxi/2013-08-16/107538.html, accessed 28 December 2016. China Electricity Council.
27. The Myitsone Dam on the Irrawaddy River: A Briefing, https://www.internationalrivers.org/resources/the-myitsone-dam-on-the-irrawaddy-river-a-briefing-3931, accessed 25 December 2015.

28. http://burmese.dvb.no/archives/15756, translated by a student in Yunnan, accessed 19 December 2015. Aung 2011.
29. https://www.internationalrivers.org/resources/the-myitsone-dam-on-the-irrawaddy-river-a-briefing-3931, accessed 17 December 2015.
30. Personal communication, Beijing, 7–8 December 2015.
31. Canyu Gongyi Shiye, Lvxing Shehui Zeren, (Participate in Philanthropy, Fulfil Social Responsibility), http://www.cpiyn.com.cn/Liems/site/zeren/zerenNews.jsp?nid=6827, accessed 15 April 2016.
32. Xinhua Wang: Chongqi Zhongmian Hezi Misong Dianzhan Husheng Jianqi, (Xinhua Agency: Emerging Claims to Restart co-funded Myitsone Dam), http://www.spic.com.cn/mtbd/201309/t20130906_222956.htm, accessed 29 December 2015.
33. Luo YongChan and Zhang Ruogu, Guojia Diantou Xiang Miandian Shuizai Diqu Tigong Zhenzai Jiuzhu, "CPI participated in the flood relief of Myanmar", http://www.cec.org.cn/hangyewenhua/qiyeyushehuizerenbaogao/zhongdiantoujituangongsi/2016-08-26/157547.html, accessed 2 December 2016.
34. Jituan Gongsi Jianxing 'Yidaiyilu', Zuo Fuzeren Quanqiu Gongmin, 16 August 2012 http://www.spic.com.cn/ttxw/201608/t20160811_266402.htm, accessed 26 September 2016.
35. Ibid.
36. CPI was a member of UNGC in 2009. However, it was removed from the membership in 2014 due to communication problems, https://www.unglobalcompact.org/what-is-gc/participants/2076-China-Power-Investment-Corporation, accessed 3 January 2016.
37. Yijiang Shangyou Shui Dian Youxian Zeren Gongsi 2010–2012 Nian Shehui Zeren Bagao (Upstream Ayeyawady Confluence Basin Hydropower CSR Report from Year 2010–2012) 25 December 2013. http://www.cpiyn.com.cn/Liems/site/zeren/zerenNews.jsp?nid=8813, accessed 28 December 2015.
38. http://www.mmtimes.com/index.php/business/16882-cpi-calculates-cost-of-myitsone-dam.html, accessed 28 November 2015.
39. Kachin Groups Urge Halt to Resource Extraction in Northern Burma, *The Irrawaddy*, 8 March 2016, http://www.irrawaddy.com/news/burma/kachin-groups-urge-halt-to-resource-extraction-in-northern-burma.html, accessed 17 March 2016.
40. Salween in Focus for Burmese Civil Society on Rivers Day, Irrawaddy, 15 March 2016, http://www.irrawaddy.com/news/burma/salween-in-focus-for-burmese-civil-society-on-rivers-day.html, accessed 17 March 2016.
41. Yijiang Shangyou Shuidian Youxian Zeren Gongsi Shengming (Declaration of Upstream Ayeyarwady Confluence Basin Hydrowpower Co. Ltd). http://www.mhwmm.com/ch/NewsView.asp?ID=16616, accessed 11 November 2016.
42. Anonymous, personal communication, Yunnan, 17 December 2015.

References

Alden, C. (2007). *China in Africa: Partner, Competitor or Hegemon?* London: Zed Books.

China Export and Credit Insurance Corporation. (2007). *Handbook of Country Risk* (Vol. I). Beijing: China Finance Press.

Chu, Y., & Huang, R. (2016, January 15). Suspension of a Chinese Project in Myanmar Due to Two Lies Believed by Local People. *International Herald Leader*. Retrieved from http://www.uachc.com/Liems/esiten/detail/detail.jsp?newsNo=11203

Corkin, K., Burke, C., & Davies, M. (2008). *China's Role in the Development of Africa's Infrastructure*. SAIS : The Johns Hopkins University.

González-Vicente, R. (2011). China's Engagement in South America and Africa's Extractive Sectors: New Perspectives for Resource Curse Theories. *The Pacific Review*, 24(1), 65–87.

Hensengerth, O. (2014). Between Local and Global Norms: Hydropower Policy Reform in China. In W. Scheumann, & O. Hensengerth, *Evolution of Dam Policies*. Berlin: Springer.

International Rivers. (2008, July). The Great Walls: A Guide to China's Overseas Dam Industry in China.

International Rivers. (2012). The New Great Walls: A Guide to China's Overseas Dam Industry.

Mang, G. (2015, June 23). China's Global Dam Builders: Talking the Talk, Walking the Walk? Retrieved June 25, 2015, from International Rivers: https://www.internationalrivers.org/node/9063Walk

McDonald, K., Bosshard, P., & Brewer, N. (2009). Exporting Dams: China's Hydropower Industry Goes Global. *Journal of Environmental Management*, 90(Supplementary 3), S294–S302.

Myint-U, T. (2011). *Where China Meets India: Burma and the New Crossroads of Asia*. New York: Farrar, Straus and Giroux.

Soe, M. (2016). *Myitsone Problem and Myanmar-China Relations*. Yangon: Moemaka.

Tull, D. (2006). China's Engagement in Africa: Scope, Significance and Consequences. *Modern African Studies*, 44(3), 459–479.

Urban, F., Nordensvard, J., Khatri, D., & Wang. (2012). An Analysis of China's Investment in the Hydropower Sector in the Greater Mekong Sub-Region. *Environment, Development and Sustainability*, 15(2), 301–324.

Walker, B. (2014, May 13). Anti-Chinese Sentiment on Rise in Myanmar. Chinadialogue.

Yang, M. (2012, April 2). Chinese Power, Burmese Politics. Chinadialogue.

Zhang, B. (2012, April 5). Why Was the Myitsone Dam Suspended? China Energy News.

CHAPTER 8

CSR as a Tool to Mitigate Risk for the B&R Initiative: The Case of Thailand

Zhimin Tang

The Silk Road Economic Belt and the 21st Century Maritime Silk Road policy initiatives (B&R Initiative) is a strong driver for Chinese firms venturing into more than 60 foreign countries.[1] Chinese Outward Direct Investment (ODI) in B&R countries amounted to US$50 billion from 2014 to 2016, and is expected to reach US$150 billion in the next five years, one fifth of the total Chinese ODI in the world.[2] The risk and risk management of these B&R investments attract increasing attention inside and outside China. For example, at the World Economic Forum on ASEAN 2017, it was commented that "risks accentuated in B&R projects, particularly from a geopolitical, funding and operational perspective" (Wijeratne, D. 2017).

This chapter focuses on why and how Corporate Social Responsibility (CSR) can be a tool to mitigate risks for Chinese firms involved in the B&R Initiative. Following a widely accepted definition in the literature, CSR here refers to the integration of an enterprise's social and environmental responsibilities into its operations and core business strategy in cooperation with relevant stakeholders. In other words, its triple bottom-

Prof. Dr. Tang Zhimin is the Dean of International College, and Director of China ASEAN Studies, Panyahpiwat Institute of Management, Thailand.

Z. Tang (✉)
Panyahpiwat Institute of Management, Bangkok Metropolitan, Thailand

A. Arduino, X. Gong (eds.), *Securing the Belt and Road Initiative*,
https://doi.org/10.1007/978-981-10-7116-4_8

line of economic, social and environmental performance (Rasche et al. 2017; Aguinis et al. 2012; Crane et al. 2008; Lee, 2007; Windsor, 2006; McWilliams et al. 2001). In the part of theoretical background, the rational for CSR as a tool to mitigate the B&R risk will be established, followed by the guidance of its implementation. The CSR performance of Chinese firms overseas is then discussed with a case study of Thailand.

Theoretical Background

Why CSR Could Mitigate the B&R Risks

In the literature of risk and risk management, risk of a firm could be understood as the threat to the firm and the firm's vulnerability to the threat (Kytle et al. 2005). The mitigation of the risk involves the management system to create controls and countermeasures that minimize or eliminate the threat and shorten the recovery time from disruption, thereby reducing its impact on the business.

The risk of B&R investment abroad can be analyzed with the STEP framework of international business, in other words, the threats from the Social, Technological, Economic and Political systems of the host country (Table 8.1). Beside direct impacts from the laws, regulation and administrative decisions of the government, these threats may enter the firm in concern through its interaction with its stakeholders of investors, customers, employees, suppliers and NGO/civil society (Fig. 8.1).

CSR is relevant to B&R risk because the mismanagement of a Chinese firm's responsibility towards the environment and society of the B&R countries may directly or indirectly evoke threats to the firm in local political, economic, social and technological systems through its interactions with its stakeholders and local governments. For example, Corporate

Table 8.1 STEP framework of risk in international business

System	*Threats from*
Political	Change in laws, regulation and administrative decisions of government
Economic	Change in the market parameters: demand and supply, price of goods, service and factors of production
Social	Change in structure, sentiment and behavior of social groups
Technological	Change in technology or adoption of technology

Source: Author's compilation

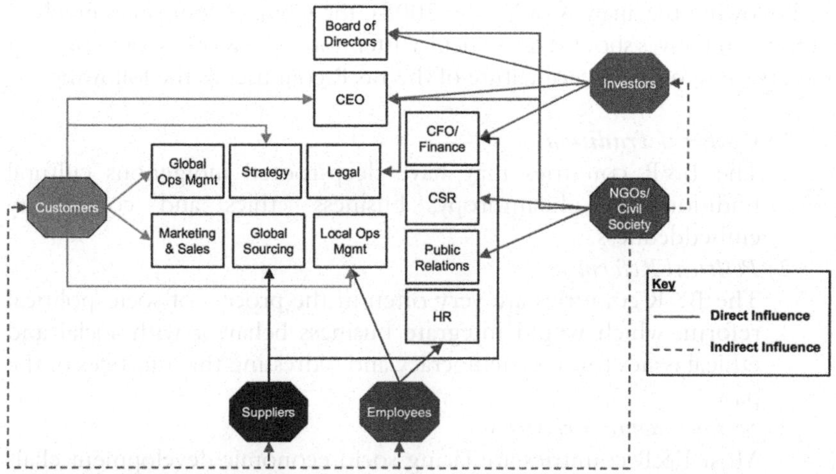

Source: Adapted from Kytle et al. 2005

Fig. 8.1 Entry points of threats to a firm

Social Irresponsible (CSI) behavior that damages local environments may cause operations prohibited by government, boycott or low acceptance of its products by consumers or disruption of its supply chain.

On the other hand, CSR programs may give a Chinese firm the "social license" to operate, that is, local community's acceptance or approval of a company's project or ongoing presence in an area. Moreover, the active engagement with the local stakeholders for the firm's social and environmental responsibility may help to mitigate the STEP risks listed above by receiving intelligence about what those threats are, and by generating an effective means to respond to them.

According to Kytle et al. (2005), what a firm may learn from engagement with local stakeholders through CSR may include: the issue or problem of a threat, its complexity and scope, the parties involved, the workable approach to the problem and what would be accomplished by engaging others in the dialogue.

The relevance of CSR to B&R risk could also be examined through the looking glass of special drivers of CSR in developing countries (Visser 2008). Most B&R countries are indeed developing countries where social and environmental crises are usually most acutely felt, and globalization and economic growth are likely to have the most dramatic social and environmental impacts.

Following the analysis of Visser (2008), the Chinese companies involved in B&R Initiatives should pay particular attention to CSR issues for mitigating risks because of the special nature of the B&R countries as the following:

1) *Cultural Tradition*
The B&R countries may have deep-rooted indigenous cultural traditions of philanthropy, business ethics and community embeddedness.
2) *Political Reform*
The B&R countries are very often in the process of socio-political reform, which would integrate business behavior with social and ethical issues towards democracy and redressing the injustices of the past.
3) *Socio-economic Priorities*
Most B&R countries are facing socio-economic development challenges, including poverty alleviation, health-care provision, infrastructure development and education.
4) *Governance Gaps*
Many B&R countries are plagued with the "governance gaps" left by weak, corrupt or under-resourced governments that fail to provide adequate social services (housing, roads, electricity, health care, education, etc.).
5) *Crisis Response*
Various kinds of crises in B&R countries may catalyze CSR responses. These crises can be economic, social, environmental, health or industrial related.
6) *Market Access*
Some least developed B&R countries may have a large untapped market at the "bottom of the pyramid." The CSR activities may enable Chinese firms to access these segments.

How CSR Could Mitigate the B&R Risks

To mitigate the risks, a Chinese firm involved in the B&R Initiative may follow the guidance of the theory of neo-institutionalism to gain its legitimacy in a new environment with CSR activities through three mechanisms (Matten et al. 2008):

1) *Coercive Isomorphism*
Coercive isomorphism occurs when an organization is forced to change by external forces such as governmental mandates or contract law. A Chinese firm may follow the codified rules, norms or laws in B&R countries.
2) *Mimetic Process*
The mimetic process refers to the tendency of an organization to imitate another organization's structure, where the environment is uncertain. A Chinese firm may follow the "best practice" in their organizational field, where the codified rules are not well established.
3) *Normative Pressure*
The normative pressure comes from the profession. A Chinese firm may also follow the guidance set up by a third-party professional authority.

ISO 26000 and GRI Sustainability Reporting Standards are two well-established international standards for CSR practice and disclosure. The ISO 26000 has seven core subjects covering "organizational governance," "human rights," "labor practices," "environment," "fair operating practices," "consumer issues" and "community involvement & development" (ISO 2010). Table 8.2 lists the seven core subjects with examples of the

Table 8.2 Core subjects of ISO 26000

Core subjects	*Examples*
Organizational governance (12)	Commitment to social responsibility System of incentives
Human rights (8)	Discrimination and vulnerable groups Civil and political rights
Labor practices (5)	Health and safety at work Human development and training
Environment (4)	Prevention of pollution Sustainable resource use
Fair operating practices (5)	Anti-corruption Fair competition
Consumer issues (7)	Consumer data protection and privacy Education and awareness
Community involvement & development (7)	Community involvement Health

Source: ISO (2010)

Table 8.3 GRI sustainability reporting standards

Set	*Standards*
Universal standards	GRI 101: Foundation GRI 102: General Disclosures GRI 103: Management Approach
GRI 200: Economic	201: Economic Performance 202: Market Presence 203: Indirect Economic Impacts 204: Procurement Practices 205: Anti-corruption 206: Anti-competitive Behavior
GRI 300: Environmental	301: Material 302: Energy 303: Water 304: Biodiversity 305: Emissions 306: Effluents & Waste 307: Environmental Compliance 308: Supplier Environmental Assessment
GRI 400: Social	401: Employment 402: Labor/Management Relations 403: Occupational Health and Safety 404: Training & Education 405: Diversity & Equal Opportunity 406: Non-discrimination 407: Freedom of Association and Collective Bargaining 408: Child Labor 409: Forced or Compulsory Labor 410: Security Practices 411: Rights of Indigenous Peoples 412: Human Rights Assessment 413: Local Communities 414: Supplier Social Assessment 415: Public Policy 416: Customer Health Safety 417: Marketing and Labeling 418: Customer Privacy 419: Socioeconomic Compliance

Source: GRI (2016)

standards. The numbers in parentheses in the first column indicate the number of standards in each core subject.

The newly revised "GRI Sustainability Reporting Standards" is another popular set of standards for CSR (GRI 2016). After a set of universal standards for the disclosure practice and management approach, it has three topic-specific sets covering the triple bottom-lines of a firm: its economic, environmental and social performance (Table 8.3).

Another approach for implementing CSR is to check each stage of the value chain of a firm (Porter and Kramer 2006). The CSR issues should be addressed in primary activities such as inbound logistic, operations, outbound logistics, marketing and sales, and after-sale services (Table 8.4), as well as the supporting activity such as procurement, technology, HR and firm infrastructure (Table 8.5).

Table 8.4 CSR issues in the value chain of a firm (1)

Supporting activity	*CSR issues*
Procurement	Procurement practices (bribery, child labor, pricing to farmers) Use of particular inputs (e.g., fur), & natural resources
Technology	Relationships with universities Ethical research practices (e.g., animal testing, GMOs) Product safety, conservation & recycling
HR	Education & job training, safe working conditions Diversity & discrimination, health care & other benefits Compensation, layoffs
Firm infrastructure	Financial reporting practices, governance & transparency Lobbying for policy change, stakeholder engagement

Source: Adapted from Porter and Kramer (2006)

Table 8.5 CSR issues in the value chain of a firm (2)

Primary activity	*CSR issues*
Inbound logistics	Transportation impacts (e.g., greenhouse gases)
Operations	Emissions & waste, ecological impacts Energy & water usage, worker safety & labor relations Hazardous materials
Outbound logistics	Transportation impacts (e.g., greenhouse gases) Packaging disposal
Marketing & sales	Truthful & suitable marketing & advertising Pricing practices (anti-trust, pricing for the poor) Consumer information & Privacy
After-sales service	Disposal of obsolete products & consumables Customer privacy

Source: Adapted from Porter and Kramer (2006)

CSR of Chinese Firms

CSR of Chinese Firms in the Literature

There are increasing interests in CSR of Chinese firms in the literature (Xu et al. 2010). The earlier studies focused on the perception of CSR and its drivers by Chinese firms in China (Wang et al. 2009; He et al. 2012), the disclosure of CSR practice (Yao et al. 2011) and linkage between CSR practice and financial performance (Chen et al. 2011).

The difference in CSR perception and practice between Chinese firms and Western firms operating in China was also scrutinized. Xu et al. (2010) found the unique dimensions of CSR perception of Chinese firms such as "Increase job opportunities" and "Ensure social stability and harmony."

Tang et al. (2009) studied the difference between Chinese firms and their Western counterparts in terms of "what" they do and "how" they do it in CSR practice. The CSR activities are targeted towards community (with programs for youth and senior citizens, education, sports, art and culture, development, disaster relief, environment conservation), customers (with programs for product quality and safety) and employees (with programs for employee health and safety, welfare, development and equal opportunity). The Western firms seemed to be more active on programs for environment conservation and product safety. The CSR practices include company policy, CSR report, foundation, volunteering, sponsorship, donation, award, partnership with governments, partnership with NGOs and partnership with universities. The Western firms seemed to emphasize more on CSR policy and report.

However, there are few empirical studies on CSR practice of Chinese firms overseas besides some general description (Shen et al. 2016; Zhang 2015; Wu 2013).

CSR of Chinese Firms in Thailand

Thailand as a Case

Thailand boasts a strategically important position in the B&R Initiative. It not only links the Silk Road Economic Belt to Southeast Asia, but also bridges the 21st Century Maritime Silk Road from Pacific Ocean to Indian Ocean. Following the B&R Initiative, many Chinese firms entered Thailand and made it a regional center for markets in the continental ASEAN. According to data from the Board of Investment (BOI), China has become the second largest investor in Thailand in 2016, with approved FDI of 54 billion Baht (around US$1.5 billion).[3]

There are more than 3000 registered Chinese firms in Thailand.[4] Their sectoral distribution covers: manufacturing (e.g., machinery, cars and motorbikes, electric and electronic (E&E) appliances, food and chemicals); agriculture (e.g., rice, rubber, fruit farms); resource (e.g., lead recycling);

infrastructure (e.g., roads and bridges, telecommunication); service (e.g., banking, logistics and tourism); and real estate (e.g., industrial parks and residences). As illustrated in the six case studies that follow, some of those firms have started their CSR programs at different levels.

Framework and Methodology

This study on the CSR practice and performance of Chinese firms in Thailand follows the grounded theory approach; no prior framework or hypothesis is set up before the case study of the six firms. Through several rounds of interviews and field observation, several key concepts were distilled. In the end, a framework emerges based on which the research findings are presented.

Six Chinese firms were selected for the case study based on their representation for sectors, ownership structure and size. They are:

A. a multinational manufacturer for electric appliances
B. a marketing branch for electronic products
C. a small and medium-sized enterprise (SME) for processed food
D. a joint venture for infrastructure development
E. a real estate operator
F. a subsidiary of a state-owned enterprise (SOE) in the financial sector

The six cases cover E&E, food, infrastructure, real estate and financial service. It reflects the sectorial distribution of Chinese investment in Thailand. There are joint ventures and subsidiaries of SOEs, large and medium-sized publicly listed companies as well as a small private company.

After the qualitative analysis of the interview and observation notes, a 4I model is constructed as a framework to describe the CSR of Chinese firms in Thailand (Fig. 8.2). Their practice and performance are described though four dimensions: "Intention" (how CSR is positioned in the firm);

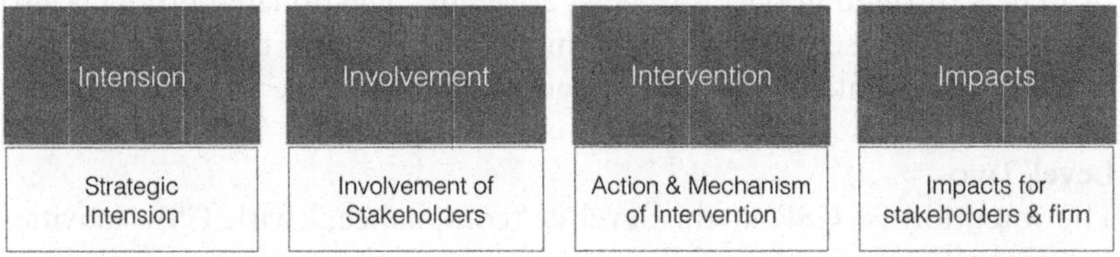

Fig. 8.2 A 4I model for CSR practice and performance. Source: Author

Table 8.6 Three levels in the four i model

Level	*Intention*	*Intervention*	*Involvement*	*Impacts*
1	Philanthropy	Ad hoc donation	Community initiated	Brand awareness Tax deduction
2	Compliance	Systematic good practice	Firm initiated	Operational efficiency Brand association
3	Strategy	Built-in mechanism Competency enhancement	Two-way communication	Competitive advantage Brand loyalty

Source: Author

"Involvement" (how stakeholders are involved in CSR activities); "Intervention" (what CSR activities are conducted); and "Impacts" (how CSR activities impact the firm).

Findings and Implications

It is found that in terms of their CSR activities, Chinese firms in Thailand could be grouped in three levels with different features in the 4I model (Table 8.6), supported by the evidence in the case examples (Table 8.7).

The letters A through F in parentheses in Table 8.7 correspond to the six cases listed above.

Level One

The intention of CSR at this level is "philanthropy," with CSR activities as "ad hoc donations" normally initiated by the communities who will send a request for such donations. For example, firms may donate money, books, sports equipment or their products (like old TV sets) to schools or areas devastated by flood. They may even sponsor sports competitions or initiate "Clean Beach" programs to collect garbage. The firms achieve brand awareness through good PR in news coverage. The donated products also served as advertisement for the firm. In some cases, the donation also brings a tax advantage when the expenses can be double or triple counted.

Level Two

The intention of CSR at this level is "compliance," with CSR activities as "systematic actions" to follow the good practice to comply with laws, regulations or industrial standards normally initiated by the firms.

Table 8.7 Case examples of the three levels

Level	*Intervention case examples*	*Impacts case examples*
1	Flood donations, book donations (A) Donation of TV sets, sports equipment to schools (B) Sponsor of GO competition (C) & (F) "Clean beach" initiative (F)	PR through news media (C) Donated products as advertisement (B)
2	Compliance to use foreign labor (C) & (E) Zero discharge of polluted water (C) & (E) Issue of radiation to environment (D) Localization: training & developing local staff (A)	Skilled & happy labor force (A) Energy saving with solar power (C)
3	Organization & communication department (A) New products for Thai consumers (low-voltage washing machine) (A) Product knowledge lecturing & activity nurturing new customers (A) Consumer education on healthy food (C)	Local-oriented innovation (A) Nurture new customer base to enhance competency (A) (C)

Source: Author

For example, firms may voluntarily comply with the rules of government in hiring foreign labors from neighboring countries, achieving zero discharge of polluted water or responding to the government's call for "localization" to train and develop local staff. The positive impacts may be operation efficiency as a result of energy saving or well-trained and happy employees. Customers may also have a good brand association with these firms who are environmentally friendly or society friendly.

Level Three

The intention of CSR at this level is "strategy." In other words, CSR is a built-in mechanism and is positioned as a strategic tool for the firm to enhance its competitive advantage. For example, a formal department under the name of Organization Development is set up to integrate CSR with the strategy of the firm. New products are specially designed for local customers. Product knowledge lectures (e.g., healthy food and knowledge about electric appliances) are conducted to actively nurture the new customers. The involvement with the stakeholders is normally a two-way communication, with a project initiated with the inputs from both parties. The firms achieve local-oriented innovation and extend and consolidate their customer base.

As an overall assessment, most large Chinese firms in our case study have achieved the first level of CSR. The achievements at this level for SMEs are uneven, possibly due to their unequal financial resources. Some SMEs may not have adequate financial resources in their early stage of development. The second level of CSR is partially achieved by large as well as small and medium-sized Chinese firms. Some Chinese firms have started to position CSR as a strategic tool to enhance their competitive advantage.

It is also a consensus of the Chinese firms interviewed that mismanagement of CSR is indeed a risk for Chinese firms involved in B&R Initiatives. In extreme cases, mismanagement may be a threat to the survival of a firm. It would certainly be a threat to a firm's market share and profit, as well as future development opportunity.

In terms of impacts on business, the case studies show the benefit of CSR could vary from "brand awareness" and "tax deduction" (at philanthropy level), to "operational efficiency" and "good brand association" (at compliance level), and towards "competitive advantage" and "brand loyalty" (at the strategy level).

The adoption of CSR by Chinese companies in Thailand may be also traced back to the political, economic and social backgrounds of the country (Visser 2008). The cultural traditions of philanthropy, the governance gaps to provide adequate infrastructure, the transition towards poverty relief and inclusive development create necessity and opportunities for CSR activities for Chinese companies.

Conclusion

The risk and risk management of B&R investment attracts increasing attention inside and outside China. CSR is relevant to B&R risk because the mismanagement of a Chinese firm's responsibility towards environment and society of the B&R countries may directly or indirectly evoke threats to the firm in local political, economic, social and technological systems through its interactions with its stakeholders and local governments.

The active engagement with the local stakeholders through CSR activities may help to mitigate the risks by receiving intelligence to identify the threats, and by generating an effective means to respond to them. In this regard, international CSR standards like ISO 26000 or GRI Sustainability Reporting Standards may help Chinese firms to plan and disclose their CSR activities to cover every stage of their value chain. Efforts have been made for setting up CSR standards for certain industries in China (Zhang et al. 2017). It is suggested that such standards or similar standards based on the CSR practice of overseas Chinese firms should be adopted, and platforms for exchanging the information on demand and supply of CSR activities and CSR best practices should be enacted.

The case studies of Chinese firms in Thailand show that some Chinese firms, especially SOEs, have understood and indeed engaged in CSR activities overseas. They are advised to move from the "philanthropy" level towards the "compliance" and "strategy" levels of CSR. CSR is a critical factor for the B&R Initiative as it is a license for Chinese firms to operate and thrive, a component of China's soft power in the world.

Notes

1. In the "Vision and Actions on Jointly Building Silk Road Economic Belt and 21st Century Maritime Silk Road" issued by the Ministry of Foreign Affairs and the Ministry of Commerce of China in 2015, the geographic coverage of B&R countries is defined as: "The Silk Road Economic Belt focuses on bringing together China, Central Asia, Russia and Europe (the Baltic); linking China with the Persian Gulf and the Mediterranean Sea through Central Asia and West Asia; and connecting China with Southeast Asia, South Asia and the Indian Ocean. The 21st Century Maritime Silk Road is designed to go from China's coast to Europe through the South China Sea and the Indian Ocean in one route, and from China's coast through the South China Sea to the South Pacific in the other."
2. Data of Ministry of Commerce, China quoted in "一带一路"投资大数据 (Big Data of B&R Investment) in 北京商报 (Beijing Business Today) May 17, 2017.
3. BOI Thailand 2017: <u>FOREIGN INVESTMENT FROM MAJOR COUNTRIES</u> The figure is the FDI from China (excluding Hong Kong and Taiwan), approved by BOI.
4. Data from "Chinese Thai Enterprises Association".

Bibliography

Aguinis, H. et al. 2012: "What We Know and Don't Know About Corporate Social Responsibility: A Review and Research Agenda" in <u>Journal of Management</u>. Vol. 38, No. 4.

Chen, H. et al. 2011: "Corporate Social Responsibility and Corporate Financial Performance in China: An Empirical Research from Chinese Firms" in <u>Corporate Governance: The International Journal of Business in Society</u>. Vol. 11, No. 4.

Crane, A. et al. ed. 2008: The Oxford Handbook of CSR. Oxford: Oxford University Press.

GRI 2016: GRI Sustainability Reporting Standards.

He, H.Y. et al. 2012: "Corporate Social Responsibility Perspectives and Practices in Chinese Companies: A Brief Overview on Environment, Consumers and External Communication" in Journal of Management and Sustainability. Vol. 2, No. 1.

ISO 2010: Guidance on Social Responsibility.

Kytle, B. et al. 2005: "Corporate Social Responsibility as Risk Management: A Model for Multinationals." Corporate Social Responsibility Initiative Working Paper No. 10. Cambridge, MA: John F. Kennedy School of Government, Harvard University.

Lee, M.D. 2007: "A Review of the Theories of Corporate Social Responsibility: Its Evolutionary Path and the Road Ahead" in International Journal of Management Reviews. Vol. 10, No. 1.

Matten, D. et al. 2008: ""Implicit" and "Explicit" CSR: A Conceptual Framework for a Comparative Understanding of Corporate Social Responsibility" in Academy of Management Review. Vol. 33, No. 2.

McWilliams, A. et al. 2001: "Corporate Social Responsibility: A Theory of the Firm Perspective" in Academy of Management Review. Vol. 28, No. 1.

Porter & Kramer 2006: "Strategy & Society: The Link Between Competitive Advantage and Corporate Social Responsibility" in Harvard Business Review. 2006 No. 12.

Rasche, A. et al. ed. 2017: Corporate Social Responsibility: Strategy, Communication, Governance. Cambridge: Cambridge University Press.

Shen M.H. et al. 2016: "中国企业海外投资的企业社会责任：基于案例分析的研究 (CSR of Chinese Oversea Investment: A Study Based on Case Analysis)" in 中国社会科学院研究生院学报 (Journal of Graduate School Chinese Academy of Social Science). 2016 No. 2.

Tang, L. et al. 2009: "Corporate Social Responsibility Communication of Chinese and Global Corporations in China" in Public Relations Review. Vol. 35, No. 3.

Visser, W. 2008: "Corporate Social Responsibility in Developing Countries" in Crane, A. et al. ed. 2008: The Oxford Handbook of CSR. Oxford: Oxford University Press.

Wang, J. et al. 2009: "Corporate Social Responsibility Engagement and Communication by Chinese Companies" in Public Relations Review. Vol. 35, No. 3.

Wijeratne, D. 2017: "How Can We Realize the Opportunities of China's Belt and Road Strategy?" World Economic Forum on ASEAN 2017. Phnom Penh, World Economic Forum.

Windsor, D. 2006: "Corporate Social Responsibility: Three Key Approaches" in Journal of Management Studies. Vol. 43, No. 1.

Wu, F.F. 2013: "中国对外投资合作中的企业社会责任问题研究 (Study on the CSR Issue in Chinese Outward Investment and Cooperation)" in 产业与科技论坛 (Industry & Science &Technology Forum). Vol. 12, No. 4.

Xu, S.K et al. 2010: "Indigenous Characteristics of Chinese Corporate Social Responsibility Conceptual Paradigm" in Journal of Business Ethics. Vol. 93, No. 2.

Yao, S.J. et al. 2011: Determinants of Social Responsibility Disclosure by Chinese Firms. Discussion Paper No. 72. China Policy Institute, University of Nottingham.

Zhang, L.X. et al. 2017: "政府推动企业社会责任认证的策略研究 (Government Promotion for CSR Certification)" in 科技和产业 (Science Technology & Industry). Vol. 17, No. 5.

Zhang, Z.Y. 2015: "中国海外投资企业社会责任" 现状规范与展望 (CSR of Chinese Oversea Investment: Situation, Standard and Prospect)" in 国际经济合作 (International Economic Cooperation). 2015 No. 12.

CHAPTER 9

China, Securing "Belt and Road Initiative": Risk Management

HaoMing Zhou

China's International Expansions: Construction Project Contracting and Direct Investment

China's international expansion in the form of construction project contracting and foreign direct investment has progressed significantly in the last 10 years.

Estimated by a leading global reinsurer Swiss Re,[1] the requirement for infrastructure development in Belt and Road countries between 2015 and 2030 is about USD 20 trillion, equivalent to about 3 percent of the GDP collectively. China will be the leading provider of the funding and construction capability.

Construction Project Contracting

According to the Ministry of Commerce, Chinese contractors have completed projects abroad with the revenue of USD 159 billion in 2016, of which 48 percent is from the Belt and Road countries. According to the *Engineering News-Record* (ENR), seven of the top 10 global contractors are from China, and China has the largest numbers of contractors listed in

H. Zhou (✉)
Brit, Shanghai, China

A. Arduino, X. Gong (eds.), *Securing the Belt and Road Initiative*,
https://doi.org/10.1007/978-981-10-7116-4_9

the Global Contractor 250, and has achieved revenue of USD 95 billion collectively. In 2007, the highest revenue ranking of a Chinese contractor was 14th and there were 49 contractors among the Global Contractor 225, with total revenue of USD 7.6 billion.

There are various kinds of risks associated with project contracting. Many Chinese contractors often try to bid using a low-price strategy. Some bidding prices were based on their experience from their practice back in China (such as labor and material cost), which is not necessarily applicable in other countries. Some countries require employing all or a certain percentage of labor forces in the countries where the labor cost could be much higher than the cost of using Chinese labor. Some contracts have appointed the designers for some sub-contracts; as such, the costs of the sub-contracts are often influenced by the designer appointed. When a Chinese enterprise bids for the Engineering, Procurement, Construction (EPC) Contractor, without knowing the hidden cost of some sub-contracts, it would possibly bid at an inadequate price. The only way to avoid bidding at inadequate price is knowing, before bidding, the exact cost (material and labor) and the law and regulations around the material and labor supply in the project country. This can be achieved by engaging the relevant professional services in the project country.

China Railway Construction Corp., the builder of more than half of China's railways, was booking a loss of RMB 4.1 billion on its Mecca Light Rail Project, which is 18 kilometers of track linking religious sites around Mecca and Medina in Saudi Arabia, pending compensation talks with the project owner.[2] After the construction contract was signed, the project owner raised planned capacity, changed other instructions and delayed land purchases. China Railway Construction, as the contractor, had to add resources to ensure on-time completion. China Railway was in negotiations with the owner for the compensation for the aforementioned variations. It is unknown if the loss fully resulted from the owner's variations and ultimately recovered from the owner, or only partially recovered due to the underprice bidding by the contractor. The truth is probably somewhere in between. This is the largest loss Chinese enterprises have ever suffered from an overseas project.

Underprice bidding for international projects is often an outcome of the competitions between Chinese companies. China South Locomotive & Rolling Stock Corporation (CSR) and China North Locomotive and

Rolling Stock Corporation (CNR) had similar market shares in China and had competed often for the same tendering, mainly on price, for the railway projects in the international markets. They were merged in 2015, and it was considered a good move for China as it enhances their market influence and eliminates "internal" price competition.

Foreign Direct Investment (FDI)

In 2004, China State Council issued "Decision on Investment System Reform,"[3] which formalized the market-oriented investment system (instead of the government-driven approach). This policy, together with other government policies thereafter, clearly defined the different roles between the government and the enterprises (one supervising and the other investing) and helped to establish a formal platform of Chinese overseas expansions.

According to the Ministry of Commence, China's FDI during 2015 of USD 146 billion was historically high and ranked the second highest FDI after the United States (USD 300 billion). The accumulative FDI (i.e., "stock") is almost USD 1100 billion, ranking 8th. In 2005, the FDI outflow was only USD 12 billion and the stock was USD 57 billion. The Belt and Road Initiative will further fuel the expansion in the targeted geographic areas (more than 60 countries) and the targeted segments—infrastructure including natural resources, energy, road, railways and so on.

There are different reasons for China to make FDI. It could be considered to secure natural resources for China, to avoid trade barriers by establishing a manufacturing facility for domestic consumers and to secure international market shares. Ultimately, the objective is to achieve financial profits.

Some of the FDI, such as a greenfield manufacturing facility or energy facility, is constructed by Chinese contractors; as such, the construction part of the FDI has the same risk exposure as construction project contracting.

More and more project tendering favors construction contract bidders who provide or help source full or partial project financing. There are increasing numbers of projects awarded to Chinese contractors with projects financed partially from China. Chinese enterprises will face risks associated with both categories of project contracting and FDI.

The risk landscape of construction project contracting and direct investment can be better understood through the following risk categories and the risks can be best dealt with under a risk management framework.

The Risk Landscape

The Belt and Road countries represent more than 60 percent of the world's population and only about 30 percent of the world's Gross Domestic Product (GDP). They are mostly developing countries at the political, social and economic transition phase. The uncertainty in security, inadequate political governance and development direction commonly prevails in most of these countries, particularly in some countries in the Middle East, North Africa, Central Asia and South Asia.

Political Risks

Terrorism, political violence, armed conflicts and anti-establishment political movements are in the category of political risks, and we have witnessed their continuous growth in both emerging and developed countries. For example, the Islamic State (IS) is not only in Iraq and Syria, but also expands its presence in North America, Europe and Asia.

Many multinational risk professionals are reasonably well equipped with knowledge and skills for some of these threats. Chinese enterprises and workers are increasing their awareness and developing such skills. According to "Sustainable Overseas Development of Chinese Enterprise 2015,"[4] the higher the investment level and the longer experience of investment practice, the better the risk management capability of Chinese investors. The companies with individual investment exceeding USD 100 million are doing noticeably well in all aspects of risk management. It is not difficult to understand this survey outcome as risk management requires resources and professionals that smaller companies may not consider necessary.

Chinese contractors had about 50 large construction projects in Libya with a contracting value of USD 18 billion before the war in 2011 (according to the Ministry of Commerce of China). Political risk insurance claims of only USD 130 million were recovered, according to the China Export and Credit Insurance Corporation (SINOSURE). The total losses of the Chinese contractors are unpublished, but it can be estimated that a large number of projects were uninsured for the specific political risks because this type of insurance is not mandatory.

Financial, Legal and Operational Risks

The global financial segment is heavily impacted by the quantitative easing in Europe and Japan, the interest rate hike in the United States and other possible geo-political events (such as the potential conflict in the Korea peninsular, Middle East, or the South China Sea).

Financial Risk is a term for types of risks associated with financing, typically including risks of interest rate, credit and commodity price. These risks are quite obvious in any international trading and investment.

Legal Risk is the risk of financial or reputational loss that can result from lack of awareness, misunderstanding of, ambiguity in, or uncertainty of the way law and regulation apply to the business, its relationships, processes, products and services. Typical examples are heavy expenses of litigation and change in law that makes a project or investment void or not executable.

Operational Risk is the risk of financial or reputational loss caused by inadequate or failed internal processes, people and systems. Some will put external events, including legal risk, under this category. Operational risk in projects starts from project design, construction and operation. These risks are not specific to Belt and Road countries, but Chinese operations in the Belt and Road countries would have higher risks in comparison to the operations by local people. The Chinese would probably not be able to understand "local elements" as well as the local people because of, for example, the difference in language or in culture.

Geo-Risks (also Often Called Act of God)

Geo-risk includes earthquake, cyclone, typhoon and flooding, which are not specific to the Belt and Road countries, but is part of the considerations for the investment location.

The Chinese know the natural hazards in China well, but some companies do not know these risks in other countries.

Risk Management

Risk management is the identification, assessment and prioritization of the effect of uncertainty on objectives followed by coordinated and economical application of resources to monitor, minimize and control the probability and/or impact of unfortunate events or to maximize the realization of opportunities.

The risk management process consists of the following elements (in the following order): Identify, characterize threats; Assess the vulnerability of critical assets to specific threats; Identify ways to reduce those risks; and Transfer and retain residual risks.

Risk Identification

Risk identification is the starting point for the risk management process to determine what risks or hazards exist or are anticipated, their characteristics, and remoteness in time, duration period and possible outcomes.

The significance of individual types of risks differs from country to country, for example, environmental risks in North America are more costly than say in a developing country. Political instability in some African countries is a bigger concern than in some other countries.

Different risks require different risk identification methods. Here are some examples.

Geo-Risks

Geo-hazards are assessed in feasibility study reports, but the risk of earthquake, storm, flooding and so on is also available from public information.

The leading reinsurer, Munich Reinsurance Company, has online interactive tools to assess natural hazard risks by inputting a location. Most project companies engage consultants, and the project geo-risks are analyzed in a project feasibility study report.

Political Risks

Maps are available from the global leading firms for risk management, Marsh and Aon. Marsh publishes Political Map, which provides the overall risk scores based on three categories of risk—political, economic and operational—and reflect both short- and long-term threats to stability. The Aon Political Risk Map examines political risk in 162 emerging economies, considering risks through nine types of risk, namely: exchange transfer, sovereign non-payment, political interference, supply chain disruption, legal and regulatory risk, political violence, risk of doing business, banking sector vulnerability and inability of government to provide stimulus.

Kidnaping, Ransom and Extortion

These risks are increasingly and particularly high in less political-stable countries such as in some countries in the Middle East and Africa. It is often more important to reduce and manage the risks to our people than to our assets. Specialist risk management firms such as Terra Firma Risk Management produces the Kidnapping Map, and NYA International publishes the Kidnap and Piracy Map.

Risk Assessment

Risk assessment is the determination of quantitative and/or qualitative estimate of risk related to a defined situation and a recognized hazard. Quantitative risk assessment requires calculations of two components of risk: the magnitude of the potential loss and the probability that the loss will occur.

Methods for risk assessment may differ between industries and whether it pertains to general financial decisions or environmental, public security or health risk assessment.

Here are some examples of well-known risk assessment methods.

HAZOP and Fault Tree Analysis

Hazard and Operability Study (HAZOP) was initially developed in the 1960s to analyze major chemical process systems, but has since been extended to other areas, including mining operations and other types of process systems and other complex systems such as nuclear power plant operation. It is a structured and systematic (qualitative) examination of a complex process or operation in order to identify and evaluate problems that may represent risks to personnel or equipment.

Fault Tree Analysis (FTA) is a top-down, deductive failure analysis in which an undesired state of a system is analyzed using "false or true" logic to combine a series of lower-level events. This analysis method is mainly used in the fields of safety engineering and reliability engineering to understand how systems can fail, to identify the best ways to reduce risk or to determine event rates of a safety accident or a particular system level (functional) failure. FTA is used in the aerospace, nuclear power, chemical and process, pharmaceutical, petrochemical and other high-hazard industries.

When the critical hazard is identified through HAZOP, the undesirable state can be further analyzed through FTA.

Total Risk Profiling

This is no standard terminology, but often it represents a systematic approach to addressing an organization's major exposures. It delivers a comprehensive assessment of business objectives, the associated challenges and the mitigation strategy to help you identify, prioritize and manage business risks across your enterprise. It is often conducted by a consultant.

In the insurance community, a similar process is engaged, but focusing on insurable risks, to determine the key risks, understand their financial impact and determine the optimal insurance requirement for the organization.

Different risk assessment methods normally apply to different types of risk. The risks around the Belt and Road Initiative can be quite different from the risks in other countries. Political risks, social unrest and kidnapping risks are in practice easy to identify, but not easy to assess and reduce.

Risk Reduction

Risk reduction is either to reduce the probability or the undesirable consequence of the event.

Safety and risk management has been a key focus in the Chinese policy for outbound investment. Out of the 33 government polices from 2000, eight of them are related to Safety of Personnel and Production.[5] For example, China's Ministry of Commerce published "Safety Risk Early Warning and Information Reporting System"[5] in 2010 to establish the system of early warning and information communication for the security risks in outbound investment.

For example, good intelligence and security will reduce the probability of terrorism and sabotage. Stronger construction will reduce the causality or property damage from earthquakes, and sprinkler systems could contain and extinguish the fire spread, but both are unable to eliminate the probability of the events.

An important step in the risk assessment and reduction for the Belt and Road projects is the approval of project financing. Most of the insurance is driven by the lenders' requirement, and is very comprehensive. Some Chinese banks have less restrictive requirements for project financing than most multinational banks and some banks have less restrictive requirements for public projects than for private projects. There are various reasons for this including inadequate awareness and less comprehensive internal procedures. When the projects are important for a bilateral relationship with the Belt and Road country, Chinese state-owned banks may exercise some flexibility in risk management.

Different types of risks can be dealt with by different types of risk reduction methods; some examples are provided as follows.

Due Diligence

Due diligence is a term used for involving either the performance of an investigation of a business or person, or the performance of an act with a certain standard of care. It is more commonly applied to voluntary investigations. In particular, due diligence is a process through which a potential acquirer evaluates a target company for acquisition. Due diligence is often performed by the specialists from within the potential acquirer or from external sources.

Specialist risk management firms such as Terra Firma and NYA International help the clients to review the risks of the operational environment, provide risk management solutions and deal with the incident/crisis when it occurs.

Natural Hazards

These are also called "Acts of God" and include disasters such as earthquakes, tsunamis, hurricanes and typhoons, floods and inundations. Risk reduction aims to reduce socio-economic vulnerabilities to disaster as well as deal with the environmental and other hazards that trigger them. The United Nations Office for Disaster Risk Reduction (UNISDR) was created in December 1999 to ensure the implementation of the International Strategy for Disaster Reduction. In addition, there are similar national strategies. For enterprises, the risk reductions are about to select the location of investment at less hazardous area, to apply minimum construction codes.

Fire Risk Management Programs

Fire, next to natural hazards, is another major cause of losses. As such, many risk management programs in the insurance community are fire-prevention focused, such as fire protection equipment inspection and pre-emergency planning.

Emergency Response Plan and Crisis Management

An emergency response plan or crisis management system is also part of risk reduction. It effectively prevents, controls or mitigates the occurrence of accidents and reduces bodily injuries and financial losses. Terra Firma and NYA International provide crisis management services to clients and design a strategy to deal and negotiate with the parties on behalf of the client until a conclusion is reached. They have in many instances reduced the risk of bodily injury and financial losses.

In contrast to risk management, which involves assessing potential threats and finding the best ways to avoid those threats, crisis management involves dealing with threats before, during and after they have occurred.

Contractual Obligations

Contractual obligations are negotiable before the contract is agreed upon. Each party wishes to maximize the responsibility and obligation of the other parties in the contract, and the parties who understand the relevant rules and practices well will have an advantage in the negotiations.

A public-private partnership (PPP) practice is a good example. Different governments play different roles in PPP projects depending on the types of projects. The obligation, willingness and effectiveness of the government to reinforce a PPP contract differ.

Often, different terms are used in PPP contracts such as "exert due care to, on a best effort basis, be obliged to, be responsible, warrant." If they are the requirement to the government, it is better to use the term requiring the highest levels of engagement possible. The best practice is to have the government be on the panel of investors (it is the case for many PPPs in China); as such, the government will be more proactive in executing the project and there is a better chance for the project to be successful.

Commercially we see Chinese enterprises shift their international engagement from EPC to BOT (Build–Operate–Transfer) or PPP. Inadequate funding for infrastructure projects, which is often the case in the Belt and Road countries, leads some owners to invite some Chinese enterprises to invest (BOT) or to jointly invest (PPP). The risk exposure landscape to BOT or PPP participants is much broader than to EPC, as BOT or PPP involves operations to produce revenue and profit over a long period of time, which are subject to the law, regulation and market risks. The risks around PPPs are the highest as it involves with dealing with other PPP partners.

Risk Transfer and Retention

Risk can be reduced, but not always possible to be eliminated. The residual risks are dealt with by risk transfer and retention.

An acceptable risk is a risk that is understood and tolerated, usually because the cost or difficulty of implementing an effective countermeasure for the associated vulnerability exceeds the expectation of loss. If the residual risk is acceptable, it would be the best to retain it.

Insurance is the most common and effective vehicle for risk transfer. There are deductibles in monetary amount and/or as percentage of the loss and exclusions for insurance coverage, which are risks to be retained by the insured. Insurance policy deductibles and exclusions are required for careful review to ensure the insured is able to retain these risks.

Basically all types of risks can be insured to a certain extent. The following insurance types are most relevant to China's international expansions. Insurance was not on the priority list for SOEs; still only basic insurance coverage is bought today. But it is getting better as the bank's requirement and tight scrutiny in case of incidents not insured. PPP is a good example, where the lenders require much boarder coverage than BOT or EPC projects to deal with bigger risks.

Political Risks

The following insurance is only offered by SINOSURE China according to the current insurance regulation:

Overseas Investment Insurance covers loss of capital and realized earnings directly caused by expropriation, restriction on transfer and conversion, war damage, liability to operate due to war and breach of understanding (political risks in host country). It consists of Equity Insurance and Credit Insurance.

Overseas Investment Equity Insurance is for the shareholders and Credit Insurance is for the financial institutes (such as the bank) for its loan overseas. A variation is Overseas Leasing Insurance, which is to protect a company leasing its equipment overseas.

Export Credit Risks

Export Credit Insurance is used to protect against the default of payment due to certain political and commercial risks. The lending bank is insured and the policy holder can be an exporter or a lending bank.

Political Risks and Mid- to Long-Term Credit Insurance is more or less monopolized by SINOSURE in the Chinese market.

Political insurance is also provided by other foreign (re)insurers such as Lloyd's, but they often have little risk appetite for certain unstable countries and for investment in some industries.

Terrorism and Sabotage Risks

Terrorism is, in its broadest sense, the use of intentionally indiscriminate violence as a means to create terror or fear, in order to achieve a political, religious or ideological aim. Various legal systems and government agencies use different definitions of terrorism in their national legislation.

In practice, one organization or individual may be identified and announced as a terrorist by one government, but not by another government, often for political reasons.

The international insurance community has formulated a standard definition: "an Act of Terrorism means an act or series of acts, including the use of force or violence, of any person or group(s) of persons, whether acting alone or on behalf of or in connection with any organisation(s), committed for political, religious or ideological purposes including the intention to influence any government and/or to put the public in fear for such purposes."[6,7] "An Act of Sabotage means a subversive act or series of such acts committed for political, religious or ideological purposes including the intention to influence any government and/or to put the public in fear for such purposes."[8]

Kidnap and Ransom

The typical perils are kidnap, extortion, wrongful detention and hijacking, and the insurance provides financial reimbursement for the loss incurred for ransom demand, negotiator costs and medical care. Access to specialist response consultants who offer support to the crisis management team and the victim's family through an incident can be provided.

Warranty and Indemnity Risks

Warranty and Indemnity Insurance can help bridge the gap between a buyer and seller (of a mergers and acquisitions deal) and benefit both with the policy helping protect against financial loss as result of a breach of warranty in the mergers and acquisitions contract.

Construction and Delay in Start-Up Risks

Construction Insurance covers any direct and sudden physical loss of or damage to the *Property Insured*, which the *Insured* could not reasonably have foreseen and which occurs at the construction site during the *Period of Insurance* due to any cause not specifically excluded. The policy period runs from the commencement date to the completion of the project construction.

The Delay in Start-Up policy indemnifies a loss of gross profit and/or other associated charges when the project completion is delayed as it suffers indemnifiable loss or damage under Construction Insurance.

There are key exclusions under these insurances; terrorism is one of them.

Cargo and Delay in Start-Up

Project Cargo Insurance covers any damage to the project cargo from the time of departure from the manufacturer to the project warehouse due to any cause not specifically excluded.

The Delay in Start-Up policy indemnifies a loss of gross profit and/or other associated charges when the project completion is delayed as it suffers indemnifiable loss or damage under Project Cargo Insurance.

Property and Business Interruption Risks

Property Insurance covers any direct and sudden physical loss of or damage to the *Property Insured*, which the *Insured* could not reasonably have foreseen and which occurs. This is normally an annual insurance policy.

Business Interruption Insurance indemnifies a loss of gross profit and/or other associated charges when the business is interrupted and suffers indemnifiable loss or damage under Property Insurance.

More and more Chinese insurance companies have placed great importance on the Belt and Road Initiative and have provided insurance products and other services to the risk under the Belt and Road Initiative. However, many of them had little experience in doing so overseas, and some are competing with low-price strategy. In order to avoid a loss-making outcome, some companies have started working with the international (re)insurance community in terms of insurance terms, risk management and client services.

It is a natural progression for the Chinese insurance companies to follow their clients' international expansion. It has been the approach for many global companies and some of the Japanese and Korean companies as well.

Insurance and Reinsurance Community
The insurance communities are interlinked globally. When an insurance company considers a risk bigger than its underwriting capacity (which is a function of its paid-up capital), it normally turns to reinsurance companies for reinsurance.

The Chinese insurance market enjoys support from the global reinsurance community despite the difficulty of making some profit for the reinsurers. The global reinsurance companies are struggling with their business growth other than in the emerging markets. China's non-life insurance market has grown its premium income significantly to RMB 1,351 billion in 2016[8] and become the second largest market after the United States, according to Swiss Re Sigma (while the premium was only RMB 109 billion in 2004). China has been the growth engine for many reinsurance companies in terms of premium income, but not necessarily in terms of profit.

Reinsurance is in business to make profit. When the underlying insurance terms are too competitive, and could lose money, the reinsurer suffers loss too. The reinsurers will request better insurance terms, which will then push up the price for insurance and ultimately the insured will have to pay bigger premiums.

The global capital market has been flooded with cheap capital in the last many years; as such, the capital return expectation has not been high. The capital market will require better return as the interest rate increases, and it will transpire in the insurance community to push up the premium rates.

Concluding Comments

Globalization of free trade is likely to suffer a setback, the Belt and Road Initiative to promote trade and investment has become the main force to continue globalization. That is why the Initiative is also welcome by countries beyond the Belt and Road.

China is playing an increasingly important role to lead the world economically, and a sound risk management framework and practice will ensure a sustainable development for China and for the world.

Insurance is not only a mean to transfer risks, but often requires sound risk management by the insured. Chinese domestic insurers, despite the huge market premium (the majority from simple motor insurance), offer standard insurance products, while the multinational insurers and reinsurers offer many specialty insurance products and relevant risk management. Specialty insurance products such as political risk, kidnapping, and Delay in Start-Up for BOT or PPP are much more required for the Belt and Road projects than the projects domestically.

The cooperation between Chinese domestic insurers and multinationals under the Belt and Road Initiative helps the Chinese enterprises (the insured) and Chinese insurers in terms of risk management and specialty insurance products. This, in turn, will further promote good risk management and sophisticated insurance products in China.

Notes

1. Interview of Jayne Plunkett Asia Head of Swiss Reinsurance Company by China Economy Weekly, June, 2017.
2. China Railway Construction Corp filing 25 Oct 2010 to Hong Kong Exchanges and Clearing Co.
3. 2004 China State Council issued "Decision on Investment System Reform" 《国务院关于投资体制改革的决定》国发[2004]20号.
4. Sustainable Overseas Development of Chinese Enterprise 2015《2015 中国企业海外可持续发展报告》.
5. Safety Risk Early Warning and Information Reporting System 2010《对外投资合作境外安全风险预警和信息通报制度》.
6. NMA2918 Lloyd's Underwriters' Non-Marine Association (a business and employers membership organizations).
7. LMA3030, Lloyd's Market Association.
8. *sigma*3/2017: World insurance in 2016: the China growth engine steams ahead, Swiss Reinsurance Company.

PART V

Risk Forecasting and Crisis Mitigation along the Eurasian Landmass and Middle East

CHAPTER 10

One Belt, One Road in Central Asia: Progress, Challenges, and Implications

Farkhod Tolipov

"Silk Road" as a New Brand of Central Asia

In September 2013, Chinese President Xi Jinping proposed the new strategic initiative called the "Silk Road Economic Belt" (SREB). In October of the same year, he proposed the "21st Century Maritime Silk Road" (MSR). These two strategic initiatives are combined in the concept "One Belt, One Road" (OBOR).

The OBOR mega-project in Central Asia is mostly understood in terms of the broadly propagated and discussed concept of the SREB. The very notion of "Silk Road" is currently used by Central Asian states—Kazakhstan, Kyrgyzstan, Tajikistan, Turkmenistan, and Uzbekistan—for, so to speak, self-branding, which manifests itself, particularly, in various semiotic exercises by which these states advertise their territories, resources, economic potential, reliability, perspectives, and even history. They more often than not refer to such semiotic designations as "bridge," "crossroad," "corridor," "hub," "center," "segment," and even "strategic location."

However, such seemingly normal aspiration to gain a more attractive image has implicit geopolitical implications. From this perspective, such a motion can have both its benefits and detrimental effects. The notion of Silk Road is not simply about revitalization of the erstwhile vast network

F. Tolipov (✉)
Non-governmental Research Institution "Knowledge Caravan",
Tashkent, Uzbekistan

A. Arduino, X. Gong (eds.), *Securing the Belt and Road Initiative*,
https://doi.org/10.1007/978-981-10-7116-4_10

of land transport and trade routes that used to connect eastern shores of China to western edges of Europe in the ancient time and Middle Ages. It is also about modern geopolitical interactions of great and mid-ranking powers as well as small countries of Central Asia—very specific types of interactions of the globalized era. The specificity of type of interactions that I am talking about reveals itself in what I call the third "*transportization*" of Central Asia.

The first *transportization* of Central Asia was, in fact, the mission of the ancient Silk Road, which, on the one hand, ascribed the region the transit function, and on the other hand, raised Central Asia to the world arena. With the advent of oceanic trade and sea routes, the significance of the Silk Road declined. The second *transportization* of the region played the opposite role and is related to the creation, beginning from the mid-nineteenth century, of the network of northward-oriented railroads that served the strategic task of supplying the "dominating power," that is, Russia, with natural resources and other products, and at the same time creating a buffer zone between Russia and southern powers by cutting off Central Asia from the external world. That's why, during the Soviet rule, the entirety of transport arteries in the region were disrupted in all directions but north. The modern third *transportization* has a mission of bringing the region back to the world system. The first tokens of what is discussed and advanced as Modern Silk Road projects at the dawn of the twenty-first century—the mega idea of creating the system of railroads, highways, and pipelines stretching from this region to the north, south, east, and west—arose with the gaining of independence by countries of the region.

Therefore, the mega idea implies mega projects and the latter means mega-scale interactions. Moreover, the New Silk Road, should it come to pass, will have long-term substantive implications in terms of a triple diversification—economic, geopolitical, and security. "A new Silk Road of modern railroads and highways that would effectively give China a land route far to the west, ultimately to Europe and to an Iranian opening on the Persian Gulf, would have enormous strategic consequences, possibly comparable to the impact that the advent of Suez and Panama Canals once had."[1]

Actually, the OBOR is an integral part of the mega connectivity projects. These are the China-Mongolia-Russia economic corridor; New Eurasia land bridge economic corridor; China-Central Asia-West Asia economic corridor; China-Pakistan economic corridor; Bangladesh-China-India-Myanmar economic corridor; and China-Indochina economic corridor.

The OBOR-related projects would also provide an outlet for China to use its overcapacity in steel, cement, and construction materials, as also its surplus financial reserves. Through this Chinese expression of expansion, China aims at promoting a whole range of Chinese interests. The protection of resources such as oil, gas, uranium, copper, and gold is another key motive, along with the setting up and expansion of new trade routes and sales markets. According to a report by the news agency Reuters, Xi told a delegation of Chinese entrepreneurs that he hopes to achieve a trade volume of more than 2.5 trillion dollars with the OBOR countries in around ten years' time. The main focus of the initiative is on the countries within Central Asia, which is where these interests are precisely highly complex.[2]

Besides, China is being driven both by domestic and foreign considerations. The urge to achieve development in all of China's 31 provinces is a major factor and all provinces have already affirmed their active participation in different aspects of the enterprise.[3]

It has to be noted that "Silk Road" is a new brand of not only Central Asia but also even more of China. Moreover, China is actually building three Silk Roads, one through Central Asia to Europe; a second, maritime one through Southeast Asia to India and South Asia; and third, China is building a robust commercial network through the Arctic to connect it with Europe. In pursuit of these geoeconomic and geopolitical goals that would bind Asia to China ever more closely through commercial means, Beijing has recently allocated US$40 billion for the first Silk Road alone, on top of all of its previous large-scale investments in Central Asia, information systems, telecommunications, transportation, energy pipelines, and infrastructure.[4]

Therefore, the overall transportization of Central Asia should be considered not simply per se or as a "*thing-in-itself*," but rather in a broader context of the special variant of New Silk Road, which in turn pushes China to the forefront of the implicit or explicit geopolitical reformatting of the space around this rising global power. In China, the intercontinental railroad connecting it with Europe through Central Asia and Iran was labeled "second Eurasian terrestrial bridge" (the first being the road through Russian territory).

Progress

The following selected list of ongoing projects illustrates that, although they all can be combined under one mega brand, "Silk Road," in fact some of them were started before the OBOR was initiated. Some of them at the very onset didn't even include China. That's why these projects were and are stipulated with multiple interests of multiple actors.

In 1996, the construction of the Tedjen-Serakhs-Mashhad railroad was completed. This connected the network of Iranian railroads to those of Turkmenistan and other Central Asian countries and opened the shortest way from the Central Asian region towards the Middle East and Europe. It was done more than a decade before the OBOR, but today it can become one of the links in the chains of OBOR.

In April 1997, three states—China, Kyrgyzstan and Uzbekistan—signed a memorandum on the construction of the new railroad, Andijan (Uzbekistan)-Osh (Kyrgyzstan)-Irkeshtam (Kyrgyz-Chinese border)-Kashgar (China), which would connect the region and ultimately connect the eastern shores of China all the way through to Amsterdam. With the construction of that strategically important segment, the railroad systems of China, Central Asia, Iran, and Trans-Caucasus can be connected. Thereby the eastern Chinese export-import port of Lyanyungan and Amsterdam will become two ends of one vast transport system. The distance between them is 8000 km shorter than the sea route through the Suez Canal. It is likely that no less than 30 countries will benefit from the construction of this road. However, this project still faces geopolitical problems related to diverging positions of two neighbors—Uzbekistan and Kyrgyzstan—regarding the ways of adjusting their local territorial interests.

Kyrgyzstan President Almazbek Atambaev is skeptical of this project. He stated that despite its attractiveness, it is more beneficial for China and Uzbekistan, not Kyrgyzstan, since this projected railroad doesn't help connect northern and southern regions of this country, which is vital for Kyrgyzstan.[5]

In 2011, at the initiative of Uzbekistan President Islam Karimov, an agreement was signed on the construction of the new international transport-communication corridor Uzbekistan-Turkmenistan-Iran-Oman (Central Asia-Persian Gulf). This is another example that the overall future outlines of the OBOR space are shaped not only from east (China) to west, but also independently as some clusters of roads and infrastructure that are to be combined gradually within OBOR.

Of special significance is the international multi-modal transport hub and logistical center created in the Uzbek city Navoi. This project was realized jointly with the airline Korean Air and offers a combination of air transport, highways, and railroads services of export, import, and transit of goods and passengers. Currently, 12 flights a week are made by Korean Air on such itineraries as Incheon (Korea)-Navoi (Uzbekistan)-Milan (Italy), Incheon-Navoi-Brussels, and Shanghai-Navoi-Milan. Uzbeck Airways itself makes 11 flights a week on the itineraries Navoi-Delhi, Navoi-Mumbai, Navoi-Bangkok, and Navoi-Frankfurt, as well as chartered flights Navoi-Dakka и Navoi-Frankfurt. The cargo terminal center in Navoi has a processing capacity of 300 tons of cargo a day.[6]

On 22 June 2016, in Tashkent, an official ceremony took place devoted to the completion of the most strategically important grand project symbolizing Uzbekistan-China cooperation—the construction of the railroad segment Angren-Pap (in the southeast of Uzbekistan) and the Kamchik tunnel. The general contractor of the project was China Railway Tunnel Group. During the opening ceremony, Uzbekistan President Islam Karimov and the chairman of the PRC, Xi Jinping, made solemn speeches and emphasized that the project was accomplished within 32 months, resulting in a tunnel 19.2 km long.

It has to be said that the Kamchik tunnel represents in itself the biggest construction of this type in the post-Soviet space and in the world ranking by its complexity; it is the eighth longest tunnel in the world. The tunnel began its operation in August 2016.

Currently, intra-regional highways and railroads are being constructed between Central Asian countries; thereby, the regional clusters of the New Silk Road are being shaped. Especially, this is peculiar to two key countries of Central Asia—Kazakhstan and Uzbekistan. The reconstruction of the old 99 km-long highway connecting Uzbek city Tashkent with Kazakh city Shymkent is underway. Soon it will be the first category international road and an important segment of the "West China–West Europe" transit corridor. Its length in the territory of Kazakhstan is 2787 km.[7] Besides, the railroad is about to be constructed soon, connecting the Uzbek town Uckuduk with the Kazakh town Kyzylorda, which further has connection to the Russian Ural and Siberia regions.

The OBOR in Central Asia cannot be considered separately from the Shanghai Cooperation Organization (SCO). By and large, since the very inception until now, the SCO has served, so to speak, as a litmus test for checking suppleness of Central Asian countries and as a ground for gradual seeding of the Chinese idea of the modern Silk Road. It is noticeable, in this regard, that both Ufa (2015) and Tashkent (2016) declarations of the SCO display member-states' support of the Chinese SREB initiative. Former Uzbekistan President Islam Karimov stated at a June 2016 summit that one of the key conditions for achieving programmatic goals and tasks of the organization is the further expansion and deepening of economic cooperation. "Our common task in this direction," he said, "should be the realization of priority economic and infrastructural projects matching interests of all states of the region, above all in the sphere of transport communications."

One can firmly assume that from its inception, the organization has laid the groundwork for OBOR. Dialectically speaking, the old SCO has shaped the modality of OBOR and vice versa; OBOR is shaping the modality of the new SCO.

Analyzing the OBOR perspectives one cannot overlook one specific phenomenon—the so-called shuttle trade of ordinary people, traders, and businessmen. The scale of shop tours from Central Asian countries to Chinese cities such as Beijing, Shanghai, Urumqi, and others is increasing from year to year. In fact, the shuttle trade can also be regarded as a symbol of renaissance of the Great Silk Road. Alongside the shuttle trade, sizable trucking with various types of transport was established between Central Asian and Chinese cities.

Alongside inter-state (macro-) and people's (micro-) trade, "culture follows trade!" Since millennia, the emergence of the Silk Route gave a boost not only to political contacts of states, but also led to development of cities and regions. These cities were not only centers of trade but centers of learning as well.[8] Hundreds of students from Central Asian countries currently are engaged with famous Confucius Institutes, which the Chinese state sponsors.

Uzbekistan President Shavkat Mirziyoev, who participated in the OBOR Forum in Beijing on 15 May 2017, made a speech in which he expressed Uzbekistan's full support of the initiative and stated that Tashkent expects the realization of major projects in the sphere of transport, logistics, trade, investments, energy, and high technologies. The OBOR will help not only China in its westward movement, but also help Central Asian countries to connect through China with markets of South and Southeast Asia as well as Europe.

He also spoke for the creation along the SREB of industrial techno parks, scientific-innovative clusters, and free economic zones. Mirziyoev advanced the proposal of encouragement of direct dialogue between business communities within the frameworks of the OBOR as well as of strengthening cultural-humanitarian ties, including tourism.[9] Meanwhile, during his visit to China in May 2017, an unprecedented investment package of agreements was signed between the two states totaling about US$23 billion.

Chinese investments and trade with Central Asian countries have been growing significantly since these five countries gained their independence in 1991. Energy and trade cooperation between China and the Central Asian republics was further boosted during the visit of Chinese President Xi Jinping to Central Asia in September 2013 when Xi promoted the idea of the "Silk Road Economic Belt" and signed an estimated US$48 billion worth of investment and loan agreements (US$15 billion with Uzbekistan, US$30 billion with Kazakhstan, US$3 billion with Kyrgyzstan, and an undisclosed sum with Turkmenistan) with a focus on energy, trade, and infrastructure.[10]

Illustrative in this regard is the construction of four gas pipelines (A, B, C, and D lines) from Turkmenistan through Uzbekistan and Kazakhstan to China (lines A, B, and C), and from Turkmenistan through Uzbekistan, Tajikistan, and Kyrgyzstan to China (line D). It is envisaged that by 2020 the annual gas supply from Turkmenistan to China will reach 65 billion cubic meters.

Challenges

When it comes to the overall challenges that the OBOR project can be faced with, one can group them into three categories: those caused by national interests, those related to security issues, and technical ones.

National Interests Conundrum

This challenge stems from what some experts call the "geographical trap"—fluctuation of the states' regional relationships between self-isolation from each other dictated by the attributes of sovereignty and regional integration dictated by historical commonality and indivisibility of the single region.

On one hand, two countries of Central Asia—Kazakhstan and Kyrgyzstan—are members of the Russia-led Eurasian Economic Union (EEU), three others—Tajikistan, Turkmenistan, and Uzbekistan—are not. But even for those two countries, membership in the EEU was not so much economically beneficial but rather a politically motivated decision. That's why the expert community and political elites in these countries are divided in their attitudes towards the EEU based on their perception of the national interests.

On the other hand, until recently there has been no unity among Central Asians themselves regarding the future shape of the region-wide transport networks to be covered by the OBOR; moreover, there are competitions for transit corridors. The countries of the region have yet to solve the number of issues stemming from one or another vision of their national attitude towards the regionalism as to custom tariffs, common market, regulation of border control and management, mutual trade, intra-regional migration, and many others. One example in this regard is quite illustrative. Until recently, Tajikistan and Uzbekistan have had chronic disputes over management of water flow of the Amu Darya River. In order to resolve this dispute to its advantage, Uzbekistan often had used transport blockage tactics towards Tajikistan (whose transport arteries traverse Uzbekistani territory) to exert pressure upon the latter.

Therefore, the national interests' conundrum reflects a threefold controversial situation: the intermingling of national interests of individual Central Asian countries, their common regional interests, and interests of neighboring great powers—Russia and China. This issue was well described in the following analysis: "For both Russia and China, an important issue is whether the 'one belt, one road' (OBOR) project will be based primarily on bilateral agreements with individual countries, or multilateral agreements with regional organizations. Russia would much prefer multilateral agreements. This is because Russia has been seeking to expand the significance of regional groupings such as the Eurasian Economic Union (which, besides Russia, includes Kazakhstan, Belarus, Armenia, and Kyrgyzstan) and the Shanghai Cooperation Organization (Russia, China, Kazakhstan, Kyrgyzstan, Tajikistan, and Uzbekistan, and, soon, India and Pakistan). Through these organizations, Russia can exert an influence more proportional to its political and military weight, whereas a series of bilateral agreements would lessen Russia's potential influence over China's relations with countries in Central Asia. So far, however, it appears that China leans toward using bilateral agreements with individual countries along the route, ultimately leading toward the formation of a huge trade and investment zone for China. China also envisions expanding cultural and academic exchanges through the project."[11]

Security Conundrum

Since the beginning of their independence, Central Asian countries have been exposed to threats and risks of different types and different degrees, such as terrorism and religious extremism, interethnic conflicts, territorial claims in the border areas, disputes over water sharing of major regional trans-boundary rivers Syr Darya and Amu Darya, as well as a dangerous situation in neighboring Afghanistan. However, so far, states of the region have been able to cope with such challenges and keep them in check, with a few exceptions, like a civil war in Tajikistan that lasted five years from 1991 to 1997, and a few days-long massacre in June 2010 between local Uzbeks and Kyrgyz communities in Osh, the southern city of Kyrgyzstan.

The term "security conundrum" means not only a set of threats and risks to security but also providers of security. Many point out the division of labor between great powers—Russia and China. Russia is a provider of a "security umbrella," China provides economic assistance. However, with growing domestic economic stagnation in Russia, in the long term China could still challenge Moscow's monopoly as a main security guarantor and may gradually increase direct engagement with Central Asian states in military and security spheres. Consequently, this could lead towards a more assertive Chinese policy, where Beijing will frame its own security agenda in the region, rather than following Moscow's steps. This is particularly important as Chinese investment and capital in the region increases, indicating that China will need to protect its interests.[12]

At the same time, there is another school of thinking according to which China's growing presence in Central Asia is regarded as a challenge because it causes the perception of its geopolitical expansion (see later in the chapter).

Security conundrum can be well illustrated with the consideration of the challenges that the China-Pakistan Economic Corridor (CPEC) is facing nowadays. "In December 2016, China's Ambassador to Pakistan, Zhao Lijian, stated that 'CPEC is working well' with the support of the Pakistani people, notwithstanding certain opposition. The statement is characteristic of China's and Pakistan's praise for the China-Pakistan Economic Corridor (CPEC) as a game changer for their respective economies and regional connectivity. Yet in reality, the project faces a variety of intricate economic challenges as well as security threats. Its success will therefore depend upon an inclusive, balanced and sustained China-Pakistan approach towards the forces hostile to the project. Even then, the project will have various geopolitical, geo-economic and geo-strategic implications for the region and the world."[13]

Technical Conundrum

The vast space covered by OBOR and its very ambitious character cannot help but cause questions about its technicalities. Some experts, for instance, point out to complexities of the combination of physical components of infrastructure and transportation projects and such spheres as services, financing, management, involvement of economically weak countries, and even such costs as corruption.[14] This is, as one can see, a multifaceted issue. Only the railway transportation, for instance, has a number of serious infrastructural limits ranging from the issue of track width divergence (Central Asians use 1520 mm, while European and Asian countries, China and Iran included, use 1435 mm) to the wagons standards, to the average speed of goods movement (it is necessary to have 80–100 km/h speed to compete with sea transportation, while currently the speed is about 65–70 km/h), to underdeveloped processing facilities, and so on.[15] The reduction of transport costs depends on the increase of tonnage. Consequently, land transportation is not able to compete either in price for the freight or in terms of transit volumes. The speed of delivery is the only competitive advantage in these circumstances.[16]

However, even the speed is not too critical an issue for a number of reasons. First, 90 percent of Chinese foreign trade freight traffic are shipped by sea. Second, most export-oriented clusters of China are located in its eastern seashore. Third, the difference in speed is not a decisive feature of the land transport, since relatively slower shipment of goods from China to Europe doesn't yield a deficit of Chinese goods there. Finally, there is a serious problem of insufficient reverse loading of trains by goods on the way back from Europe to China.

Finally, conjugation of OBOR with other similar projects advanced by other states (such as transport corridor Europe-Caucasus-Asia [TRACECA]; gas pipeline from Iran, Iraq, Central Asia, and Azerbaijan to Europe [NABUCCO]; north-south, and others) is another important question that has, besides technical aspects, also geopolitical implications (see next section).

Implications

The implications of the OBOR are considered here from two perspectives—strategic and geopolitical. On the strategic level, two questions have to be explored related to the notion of "connection" because

OBOR's connotation is connectivity. If connection implies only transport-logistical, that is, a transit-related question, we will have one approach to the problem; but, if connection implies a broader question of the comprehensive regional development, we will have another approach. Today, many are primarily focused on the former approach thereby simplifying the task of the exploration. However, even consideration of the problem through transport-logistical lenses encounters various challenges, as was indicated earlier. In general, strategic implication can be understood as a dilemma: Transit and/or development?

From this viewpoint, "if tangible benefits are not identified and communicated to local populations, then the SREB will not only fail to reach its full potential; it could also raise suspicions that this is more of a geopolitical project than China says, with China benefiting far more than the Central Asian populations and gaining further leverage over the region's political elites through economic influence."[17]

Meanwhile, there are reports that "both Chinese firms and the Chinese government realize the necessity of localization to make projects palatable to local populations. Wages in China are also much higher than in Central Asia (except for perhaps Kazakhstan) which provides an economic incentive to hire locals. Questions remain around the patchiness of local employment, but it is clear that broad statements about Chinese only hiring their own no longer hold true."[18] Anyhow, much, in this respect, will depend on Chinese self-identification and self-positioning not only internally but also internationally. As former President Hu Juntao said, China should try to establish a new type of foreign relations that can "satisfy the Chinese public and at the same time reassure people of all nations."[19]

On the geopolitical level, the implications are even less clear. It must be noticed that right after the collapse of the Soviet Union, Central Asia found itself and has remained until today a geopolitically galvanized area. Central Asian countries invoked the spirit of the ancient Silk Road and felt temptation to return to their erstwhile glory and niche in the international system. They desperately need to break the landlocked status, but interestingly, such a position is not merely geographical destiny, it is rather a geopolitical condition due to such circumstance that the unlocking of the region depends largely on neighboring great powers—China and Russia.

The ancient Great Silk Road was in essence a mere trans-continental trade route. But the modern one, which OBOR is supposed to create in the turbulent era of globalization and the shaping of the new world order, will likely be more than a trade route. It will be facing, symbolically speaking, explicit and implicit "geopolitical stations" on the way, that is, numerous encounters in unprecedented scale of various subjects who will interact in uneasy conditions. In particular, the vast space is expected to be shaped by means and in the form of rising China's westward impulses. Yet in 2005, former Uzbekistan President Islam Karimov stated that "a situation of geopolitical uncertainty emerged in Central Asia, and the real interests of great powers in the region remain ambiguous."

That's why many today correlate the OBOR with the current geopolitical trends, which should stipulate Beijing's one or another form of geopolitical activation. These trends explicitly and implicitly manifest themselves, in particular, in the two following situations.

1. The scenario of possible direct Chinese involvement in Central Asian regional security affairs. American analyst Stephen Blank points out the creeping Chinese military involvement in Central Asia in order to defend Chinese interests and investments in these states rather than rely on unreliable local governments or Russia. This trend can increase dependence of the Central Asian states on the Chinese security umbrella. Blank puts forth a question as to whether a Chinese move to upgrade its powers and obligations in the region would be "met with equal and opposing countermoves from other powers who also have important equities and interests there? Given the nature of contemporary international relations, the answer to that question is almost certainly yes. In other words, a new chapter of the contemporary great game in Central Asia is underway."[20] This argument sounds quite strong. However, the region currently is not facing security threats to the degree that would require a great power "umbrella." Even the decades-long conflict in Afghanistan hasn't raised the level of security threats in Central Asian countries to the highest point. The region is relatively peaceful and stable in sharp contrast to the area where, for instance, the CPEC is supposed to be built.
2. There is also a strong perception that the OBOR can in part be seen as China's response to the "pivot" or "rebalance" to Asia under US President Barack Obama and to Russia's relative decline in Central Asia.[21] However, the geopolitical dimension is more ambiguous than it can seem in a linear approach. This can be illustrated in the possible long-term implications of the Northern Distribution Network (NDN). One report made by the Washington-based Center for

> Strategic and International Studies noticed: "While the creation of the NDN was motivated by the U.S. military's immediate logistical needs, its establishment nonetheless offers a unique opportunity for Washington to further broader strategic objectives. This opening will not last forever. With prompt attention, adequate coordination, and the correct set of policies, the U.S. government could leverage the NDN to lay a foundation for the so-called Modern Silk Road. This development would help stabilize Afghanistan in the long term and have a transformative effect on Eurasia."[22]

Add to this picture other geographical areas where respective geopolitical equations can also come into being, since the countries, companies, and development banks involved in New Silk Road-related projects are also international, and span across the entire Eurasian theater:[23]

- The Trans-Siberian Railway, a vital link in both of the main China-Europe rail routes, is still Russian.
- Poland, Belarus, and Germany are building key Silk Road Economic Belt-related dry ports and corresponding industrial zones without much in the way of Chinese funding or direction.
- Georgia chose an American-led consortium to build their Silk Road-connected deep-sea port rather than a Chinese-led one.
- Azerbaijan is building a new port, highways, rail lines, and other trans-Eurasian transportation infrastructure with their own oil money and loans from the World Bank.

Conclusions

So the OBOR will be created in the geopolitically galvanized area where trade, movement, transit, services, communications, exchanges, and so on will be affected by geopolitics and, in turn, affect geopolitics. OBOR is a Chinese initiation, but its embodiment will be the derivative of various international and regional conditions. That's why a dialectical and systems approach is required for strong and correct comprehension of nuances and modalities of the real development of the OBOR process, multiple challenges the stakeholders can face, and all implications of this process for regional countries and great powers.

Many analysts and officials point to, and emphasize, the fact that this mega-project embraces more that 60 percent of the world's population. However, taken as it is, this figure can mislead stronger analysis of the project's perspectives. Out of this 60 percent, about 37 percent live in China. Dozens of other nations are much smaller and very diverse with diverse interests and political and economic systems. As one analyst argues: "Where the Silk Road network begins and ends is unclear, when it actually got started is debatable, and inquires into what countries it even includes are often inconclusive. It is perhaps easier to simplify the issue and just label the project as a" Chinese "initiative and look at it through the lens of the Belt and Road but it just isn't correct: the New Silk Road is international."[24] When it comes to the Central Asian segment of the OBOR, the main strategic task for the countries of this region would be consolidation of a common five-lateral vision of the project emanating from much higher value and goal—unification, not fragmentation, of the region—a goal that was proclaimed yet in 1991 as their own mega-project in itself.

Notes

1. Munro, R.H. "China, India, and Central Asia," in J.Snyder, ed., *After Empire. The Emerging Geopolitics of Central Asia* (Washington: National Defense University Press, 1995), p. 130.
2. Bessler, Patrick, "China's 'new Silk road': Focus on Central Asia," EU-Asia Economic governance Forum, www.kas.de/wf/doc/kas_43841-1522-2-30.pdf?160401030733.
3. Nirmala Joshi and Kamala Kumari. "China's Silk Road Economic Belt and the Central Asian Response," in *World Focus, Annual number*, on Indian Foreign Policy, December 2016.
4. Blank, S. "China's Silk Roads and Their Challenges," 01/07/2015 issue of the CACI Analyst, http://cacianalyst.org/publications/analytical-articles/item/13119-chinas-silk-roads-and-their-challenges.html.
5. http://rus.azattyk.org/content/article/25205660.html.
6. www.mfa.uz.
7. Капитал, 05.11.2013, http://kapital.kz/gosudarstvo/22958/opredelen-podryadchik-po-stroitelstvu-trassy-tashkent-shymkent.html.
8. Nirmala Joshi and Kamala Kumari. "China's Silk Road Economic Belt and the Central Asian Response," in *World Focus, Annual number*, on Indian Foreign Policy, December 2016.
9. https://www.gazeta.uz/ru/2017/05/15/belt-road/.
10. Fabio Indeo. "China as security provider in Central Asia post 2014: a realistic perspective," in *Central Asia Security Policy Briefs* (Bishkek), No.17, January 2015.
11. Thomas F. Remington. One belt, one road, one Eurasia. http://blogs.nottingham.ac.uk/chinapolicyinstitute/2016/04/06/one-belt-one-road-one-eurasia/#.VwTDUGK0pg0.twitter April 6, 2016.

12. Kosnazarov, D. and Akylbaev, I. "The great bargain between Russia and China for Central Asia" in *China and Central Asia*, November 6, 2016, http://chinaincentralasia.com/2016/11/06/the-great-bargain-between-russia-and-china-for-central-asia/.
13. Mushtaq A. Kaw "The China-Pakistan Economic Corridor Between Hope and Fear," the CACI Analyst, April 26, 2017, http://cacianalyst.org/publications/analytical-articles/item/13440-the-china-pakistan-economic-corridor-between-hope-and-fear.html.
14. https://reconnectingasia.csis.org.
15. See for details: Aset Ordabayev. "The Geopolitics of Transport Corridors in Central Asia," in Working paper of the Institute of World Economics and Politics. – Almaty, June, 2015.
16. Ibid.
17. Sarah Lain. "Trade Connectivity: the missing link in the belt and road," in China and Central Asia, December 11, 2016, http://chinaincentralasia.com/2016/12/11/trade-connectivity-the-missing-link-in-the-belt-and-road/.
18. Dirk van der Kley. "Chinese companies increasingly employ Central Asians," in *China in Central Asia*, December 27, 2016 http://chinaincentralasia.com/2016/12/27/chinese-companies-increasingly-employ-central-asians/.
19. Quoted in Wang Yizhou. *Creative Involvement: A New Direction in Chinese diplomacy.* – Mark Leonard edited, "China 3.0" (European Council on Foreign Relations, 2012), p. 123.
20. Blank, S. "New signs of Chinese military interest in Central Asia," in *CACI Analyst*, 16 January 2017 http://cacianalyst.org/publications/analytical-articles/item/13421-new-signs-of-chinese-military-interest-in-central-asia.html.
21. Clarke, M. "Beijing's 'March West': One Belt, One Road and China's Quest for Great Power Status," http://centralasiaprogram.org/blog/event/michael-clarke-beijings-march-west-one-belt-one-road-and-chinas-quest-for-great-power-status/?instance_id=822.
22. The Northern Distribution Network and the Modern Silk Road. Planning for Afghanistan's future. (Washington, DC: A Report of the CSIS), December 2009.
23. http://www.forbes.com/sites/wadeshepard/2016/10/14/regardless-of-what-beijing-says-the-new-silk-road-is-not-chinese/#7f746f907289.
24. Shepard, W. "The New Silk Road Is Not Chinese, It's International," Forbes, Oct. 14, 2016 http://www.forbes.com/sites/wadeshepard/2016/10/14/regardless-of-what-beijing-says-the-new-silk-road-is-not-chinese/#7f746f907289.

CHAPTER 11

Securing CPEC: Challenges, Responses and Outcomes

Khuram Iqbal

Introduction

Chinese economic expansion led to a sense of optimism throughout South Asia, a region that was beset with armed conflicts, impoverishment and massive youth bulges. For Afghanistan, One Belt One Road (OBOR) offered an opening to maximize its economic potential as a transit state connecting South and Central Asia. Bangladesh welcomed the shift in global centre of economic gravity from west to east and saw this as an opportunity to restore its historic connectivity with China.[1] Sri Lankan polity, initially divided over the role of China, came to recognize that initiatives such as OBOR fit into the capital city of Colombo's goals of connectivity, increased trade and rebuilding a war-torn economy.[2] With anti-Indian sentiments running unprecedentedly high in Nepal, Kathmandu stands prepared to develop cross-border road and railway connectivity with China[3] with a view to reduce the landlocked nation's dependence on India. The Maldives perceives China as a counter-weight to the "Western colonial powers" bent upon altering the Islamic identity of the small island nation.[4] Most importantly for Pakistan, the Chinese-financed mega developmental project the China–Pakistan Economic Corridor (CPEC) has come to be seen as Beijing's version of the "Marshall

K. Iqbal (✉)
National Defence University of Pakistan, Islamabad, Pakistan

A. Arduino, X. Gong (eds.), *Securing the Belt and Road Initiative*,
https://doi.org/10.1007/978-981-10-7116-4_11

Plan" for its "all-weather" iron friend. The Marshall Plan witnessed the United States intervene in continental Europe to deliver prosperity from the ruins of the two world wars, while China today attempts to provide Pakistan with a similar opportunity to shed the debilitating scars of war, and establish sustainable peace within the fractured self, and extend it beyond to temper regional perspectives.

CPEC had the immediate effects of raising Pakistan's global profile. From "the world's most dangerous country"[5] in 2007, Pakistan came to be seen in 2015 as the next economic success story.[6] Economic and financial indicators published by *The Economist* in January 2017 highlighted Pakistan to be the world's fastest-growing Muslim economy in 2017 ahead of Indonesia, Malaysia, Turkey and Egypt.[7] This data reinforced a Harvard University study that predicted Pakistan to grow by more than 5% in the next decade. The fear that Pakistan may convert its newly acquired wealth into military muscle to obstruct India's rise as a global power has led New Delhi to vocally oppose the CPEC.[8] In opposition to CPEC, India has invoked the disputed nature of territory in the Gilgit–Baltistan region from where the Pakistani section of the CPEC commences. Besides strengthening Pakistan economically, CPEC is seen as detrimental to Indian security interests for its potential to internationalize the Kashmir dispute by increasing Chinese economic stakes. The Indian strategic community is also apprehensive that the initiative may also challenge New Delhi's role as a net security provider to the island states of the Indian Ocean as the regional environment becomes ever more conducive for China.

Indian opposition to CPEC has further complicated the South Asian geopolitics and the regional threat environment alike. Violent extremist organizations, which hitherto operated purely as ideological entities, are now keen on seeking New Delhi's patronage to fight a common enemy, that is, Pakistan. It seems with the inception of CPEC and subsequent Indian opposition the era of ideological terrorism has ended and is replaced by Cold War–era "proxyism" where different states are increasingly relying on non-state and sub-state actors to pursue their strategic and commercial interests. Besides external threats, internal political dynamics of Pakistan can also hinder the timely and smooth implementation of CPEC. This chapter aims to outline the significance of CPEC for Pakistan and China, internal and external risks to its implementation, Islamabad's counter-measures and their outcomes. The first section highlights the economic and strategic significance of CPEC for both Pakistan and China, followed by an overview of Indian and American response to the project. The subsequent discussion elaborates the implications of powers-competition on the regional terrorism landscape, as to how some terrorist organizations are seeking convergences with some state actors to challenge the CPEC. An overview of security and strategic measures by China and Pakistan is also provided to evaluate their effectiveness for smooth implementation and utilization of the project.

Understanding CPEC

In 2013, Chinese President Xi Jinping unveiled one of the most important infrastructure construction projects of the human history. The project was entitled One Belt One Road (OBOR) or the Belt and Road Initiative (BRI). BRI has two components: one over land and another over/through sea. The New Silk Economic Road consists of a web of six interconnected economic corridors. On land, the initiative will connect Asia, Europe and Africa through six Economic corridors: (1) New Eurasian Land Bridge (NELB); (2) China-Mongolia-Russia Economic Corridor (CMREC); (3) China-Central and West Asia Economic Corridor (CCWAEC); (4) China-Indo-China Peninsula Economic Corridor (CICPEC); (5) China-Pakistan Economic Corridor (CPEC); and (6) Bangladesh-China-India-Myanmar Economic Corridor (BCIMEC). The 21st Century Maritime Silk Road (MSR) will start from eastern ports of China and travel via the South China Sea, East China Sea, Strait of Malacca, Bay of Bengal, Arabian Sea, Persian Gulf and Gulf of Aden, diverging towards the Red Sea in the north and African ports in the south. In the north, through the Mediterranean Sea, it will end at Rotterdam, and in the south, it will encircle Africa. It will connect three gigantic oceans—Pacific, Indian and Atlantic—and geo-strategically important navigational choke points, and different East Asian, South Asian, European and African ports through extended phenomena of "Neo String of Pearls." Silk Railway routes, energy silk routes and trans-state supper highways are other important elements of this hitherto mysterious and magical project.

The project would be financed by the Asia Infrastructure and Investment Bank (AIIB), the BRICS New Development Bank, the Silk Road Fund, the China-ASEAN Interbank Association and the SCO Interbank Association. The Chinese maintain that OBOR will be funded initially by

$40 billion from China's Silk Road infrastructure fund, $100 billion in Asian AIIB pledges, and an initial $50 billion commitment from the New Development Bank of the BRICS countries—Brazil, Russia, India, China and South Africa—with a promise to increase that to $100 billion.[9]

CPEC is one of six pillars of the OBOR. It is both geopolitical and geo-economic paw of both China and Pakistan in reconfiguring geo-economic-cum-political realities. It is an extension of China's 21st Century Silk Road initiative. The peculiar attribute of CEPC is its intersection between the oversea 21st Century Maritime Silk Road (MSR) and the land-based Silk Road Economic Belt (SREB). Its total length is approximately 3000 km spanning from Pakistan's Gwadar Port to Kashgar, northwestern China's Xinjiang Uygur Autonomous Region. It consists of railway lines, roads, fibre optics, energy pipelines and industrial zones.

Table given below summarizes the number of projects identified so far, along with estimated cost under CPEC.

Sr. no.	*Sector*	*No. of projects*	*Estimated cost (Million $)*
01	Energy	21	33,793
02	Transport infrastructure	4	9,784
03	Gwadar	8	792.62

Source: Author

Significance for Pakistan

Pakistan has been worst hit by terrorism since the outset of the twenty-first century. It has faced huge monetary, political, social, and human losses under active engagement in regional conflicts. The US-led intervention in Afghanistan has further compounded historical fault lines, and the subsequent global war against the Taliban has immersed Pakistan as a direct participant in the War on Terror. This has also served to nurture extremism, which, in turn, has certainly retarded the economic development within the state. The CPEC project between these Asian neighbors is an emerging opportunity for Pakistan. It will not only help Pakistan in overcoming economic opportunities missed due to involvement in the War on Terror, but will also transform the country into an economic hub, resurrecting its path to development. The $56 billion bilateral project has multi-dimensional implications for Pakistan promising to renew its strategic significance in a rapidly altering world. This study attempts an in-depth analysis of the benefits and the drawbacks accompanying the proposed economic corridor between Pakistan and China, with a structured approach focusing on three tiers of geopolitical and socio-economic realities:

- Domestic / Internal
- Regional; and
- International

The CPEC is located in the hub of the OBOR and is the cornerstone of the MSR. This belt is intended for the promotion of systematic opening of financially viable investments, complete with the allocation and distribution of vital resources and deep assimilation of the markets.[10] South Asia, as a region, is understood as one that is marred by instability, economic under-development and conflict. When mutual avenues of cooperation, which lead towards development, are forged, it will naturally strengthen the prospects for a stronger and stable region. Chinese President Xi Jinping's visit to Pakistan (April 20–21, 2015) carried forth with it the hopes of this stability in the coming years for Pakistan as 51 memorandums of understanding (MoUs) were signed between the premiers of both states during the visit.[11] The idea of developing the CPEC was visualized by Chinese Premier Li Keqiang during his visit in May 2013, and found a legal framework in the subsequent visits. The proposed economic corridor will ultimately connect southwestern China, via the province of Xinjiang, with Pakistan's emergent port city of Gwadar interlinked via a network of roads and railways measuring roughly 3000 km, providing energy-starved Pakistan with much needed economic infrastructure.

Pakistan and China's all-weather friendship stems from their shared interests and mutual rivalry with India, with varying reasons for each state. Both neighbours have developed strong ties and have been collaborating with each other in terms of economics, military and politics for decades. With China emerging as a major trading partner, and according to the Pakistan Economic Survey 2013–2014, China and Pakistan's trade volume of US$4.1 billion in FY 2006–2007 jumped 124%, increasing to US$9.2 billion during FY 2012–2013.[12] Whereas China's exports to Pakistan increased nominally, Pakistan's exports during this period increased from US$600 million to US$2.6 billion, an increase of 400%.

Consequently, bilateral trade between the two increased from 4% in FY 2008–2009 to more than 10% in 2013–2014.

The CPEC is further anticipated to bolster the developing trade and commerce between the two nations. With the enthusiasm for the project displayed by the leadership of China and Pakistan, the rapid development of the project will make Gwadar not only fully operational, but also a noteworthy deep-sea port in the region. Inaugurated in 2007, the control of Gwadar Port was transferred to China Overseas Ports Holding Company in February 2013, a Chinese state-owned enterprise (SOE). Since then, Gwadar is transforming under a major expansion into a full-fledged, deep-water commercial port. When constructed, the corridor will serve as a primary gateway connecting China, the Middle East and Africa. The corridor is also expected to cut the 12,000-km route Middle East oil suppliers now take to reach Chinese ports. Any and all transit trade stemming from the corridor will naturally work to the benefit of Pakistan.

Aside from boosting the trade of both countries through the economic corridor, Pakistan's energy sector is the primary focus with approximately 61% of the total CPEC investment specifically targeted at energy infrastructure development, enhancing capacity, distribution and transmission networks. Around 36% of the CPEC investment has been earmarked for infrastructure in the transport and communication sector. The energy sector projects are being built by Independent Power Producers (IPP) with the investment from Exim Bank of China at the interest rate of 5–6%, while at a later phase, the government of Pakistan is committed to purchasing electricity from these projects at pre-negotiated prices. Through the projects under CPEC, an estimated 17,045 megawatts of energy will be added to Pakistan's national grid by 2020. Thus, these projects garner hope to make Pakistan self-sufficient in the energy sector, traditionally a major hurdle for the country on the quest for development.

Additionally, development in the infrastructure of the communication sector, centred upon road and rail networks, most essentially along the Gwadar Port, will not only provide an opportunity for Pakistan to generate massive foreign direct investment (FDI), but will also transmute the country into a prized investment destination for global markets. Positioned as an economic powerhouse, a post-CPEC Pakistan aligns all immediate neighbours and regional states to further diversify their economic ventures across Europe and Africa via accessing the Middle Eastern states through the transit route under the corridor.

Significance of CPEC for China

China's peaceful rise to the status of global power goes through diversification of its energy and trade routes. The "Malacca Dilemma," however, has always constrained China's global ambitions. The concept was first articulated by China's former president, Hu Jintao, in 2003 when he used the phrase "the Malacca Strait Dilemma" in the Central Military Commission. Currently, more than 80% of China's crude oil passes through this strait. In 2013, the Chinese economy surpassed Japan's economy to become the world's second largest economy with growth of 7.7% for 2012–2013.The important component of it industrial growth is energy. China is the largest consumer of the world's energy. China is largely dependent on crude oil imports from far-flung regions, including East Africa, West Africa and the Middle East. It is dependent on sea routes for its energy imports. The Strait of Malacca is a narrow 850-km stretched water body between the Malay Peninsula and the Indonesian island of Sumatra; at some points, it is as narrow as 15 km or even 2.5 km at its narrowest.

To mitigate and pull itself out of the Malacca Dilemma, China started to diversify both its energy sources and routes to ensure its energy security. The most important phenomenon of the diversification principle has a paramount position in the policy-making process not only in China but also in the entire international community. The diversification principle emerged as a main element in global power transformation. Different states such as India, Great Britain, France, Saudi Arabia and Russia embarked on the diversification principle. The main purpose is to diversify market, customers, sources and friends. Russia is heavily investing in the Far East in order to connect with Far East states to diversify its energy market. Similarly, through the BRI, China wants to diversify its energy source. Investment in Iraq, Iran, Nigeria, Angola, Russia and many more countries' energy sources are just to diversify its market. It is also diversifying its access routes to far-flung energy sources to ensure a smooth flow of oil even in any crisis situation. Oil pipelines in Myanmar's Gwadar Port, oil and gas pipelines and rail and routes to Central Asia and Middle East all are alternatives to the Straits of Malacca.

For China, CPEC is a game changer in both the strategic and economic senses. First, in any crisis at Andaman and Nicobar Islands, the Straits of Malacca and the South China Sea, Gwadar provides safe and smooth access from China to the Arabian Sea. CPEC gives China's trade cargo direct access to the Indian Ocean Region (IOR), circumventing Malacca and reducing the 12000-km distance to 3000 km. The first pilot cargo was dispatched from Gwadar during Prime Minister Nawaz Sharif's visit on November 13, 2016. The trade consisted of 160 convoys that reached Gwadar and were dispatched to the Middle East, the European Union and African countries.[13]

Strategic aspects are more bright and pivotal for China in reconfiguration of global power structure. Alfred Thayar Mahan was an American naval captain and wrote extensively on sea powers and their influence on economics and trade. He enumerated five conditions that affect the sea power of nations. The five principal conditions are Geographical Position, Physical Conformation, Extent of Territory, Number of the Population, Character of the People and Character of the Government. Regarding Geographical Position, Mahan says that if a country is situated in such a position that it needs neither to defend itself by land nor seek territorial extension, then it diverts maximum energies to strengthen its naval force. In the twenty-first century, being a nuclear power, China could not be invaded by land. Feeling secure by land, China has been concentrating its energies to develop its blue water navy. The naval modernization process, which was actually started by Liu Huaqing, the father of the modern Chinese navy, is moving towards new heights with the induction of the Liaoning aircraft carrier, Jin nuclear power submarine and modern destroyers.

China, owing to a 9000-mile temperate coastline with many good natural harbors, is both a land power and a sea power.[14] Projecting true sea power the geographical position may be such as of itself to promote a concentration, or to necessitate dispersion, of the naval force.[15] Gwadar is bolstering China's geostrategic leverage both in the Pacific and Indian Ocean regions. The most important element of China's outward approach is establishing, investing, building and leasing seaports. Gwadar Port can be a launching pad for China's naval expeditions in the IOR. Gwadar is China's Asian Djibouti. Where Djibouti effectively controls the Red Sea, Gwadar performs a similar function for the Persian Sea. Djibouti and Gwadar are two important Chinese dragon wings in the IOR.

Political Risks to CPEC

Since the announcement of the CPEC and its ratification, the route designated under the corridor triggered much debate and controversy. The major bone of contention here was regarding the distribution of economic, development and infrastructure projects of this mega venture within the provinces. It was alleged and counter alleged that the route of the corridor had been manipulated to better serve the interests of existing and established industrial zones in Punjab. Terms such as the Eastern Route and the Western Route began gaining currency, whereby it was accepted that the Central Route was the original one approved by the federal government, and was listed to pass through as follows:

Gwadar – Turbat – Panjgur – Khuzdar – Ratodero – Kashmore – Rajanpur – Dera Ghazi Khan – Dera Ismail Khan – Bannu – Kohat – Peshawar – Hasanabdal – onwards to the Karakoram Highway.

Under the Eastern Route, cities along the eastern half of Pakistan were more highlighted, and this version of the route specified by the federal government is designed to pass through the following:

Gwadar – Turbat – Panjgur – Khuzdar – Ratodero – Kashmore – Rajanpur – Dera Ghazi Khan – Multan -Faisalabad – PindiBhatian – Rawalpindi – Hasanabdal and onwards along the Karakoram Highway.

Subsequently, after the controversy was highlighted over electronic media, a third route was purported as well, later referenced as the Western Route. This route heavily favoured the oft-neglected northeastern Balochistan, and was designed to pass through the following:

Gwadar – Turbat – Panjgur – Khuzdar – Kalat – Quetta – Zhob- Dera Ismail Khan – Bannu – Kohat – Peshawar – Hasanabdal – and the Karakoram Highway.

The route to be designated as the economic corridor within Pakistan was suddenly the hotbed of controversy, fueled initially by the government's silence and subsequent contradictory statements while providing justification. The initial position taken by the federal government was that there had been "no changes" made to the original route, however, statements failed to specify what was the original route in question. Later, the federal government took the position that the three routes existed, and all three would be built. Dr. Bengali in his paper implored that:

This explanation cannot be accepted as plausible; as the resources to build all three routes are not available and China would certainly not allocate resources to pander to political disagreements in Pakistan.

The latest explanation—an acknowledgement that the federal government is prioritizing the Eastern Route—is that it is cheaper and faster to route the corridor through areas with pre-existing road connections. This implies that the corridor will be routed through areas of the country that are already relatively developed.

Pakistan sits at geographic crossroads of ancient empires and civilizations and thus inherits a myriad labyrinth of inter-provincial conflicts spanning generations of active conflict and ancient rivalries. Under the CPEC route controversy, particularly with the decision of the government to construct the Eastern Route first, these intricate problems are rising once more under political garb. As the Eastern Route largely passes through Punjab, it is heavily criticized by the political leadership from other provinces. Chairman of Pakistan Tehreek-e-Insaaf, Imran Khan, was of the opinion that any preferential treatment shown by the government will give birth to enmity between provinces.[16]

Originally, the western alignment was scheduled for construction first, covering and rapidly developing areas mostly located under Balochistan and Khyber Pakhtunkhwa. However, the federal government's decision stems from the fact that it is both easier and more secure to construct first. Further emphasis is laid on the claim that construction of the Eastern Route does not mean the abandonment of the original plan.[17] Evidence to this fact is granted by the National Logistics Cell (NLC) construction of the 55-km-long road along the the Hakla–Dera Ismail Khan Motorway, which directly feeds into the Western Route.[18]

One of the key reasons for prioritizing the Eastern Route was the marked difference in security, and another motive, ulterior or not, is interpreted to boost existing industrial complexes in the east. The government claimed it decided to change the route to ensure better security for workers and later on for the transit convoys once deployed. On the other hand, the Western Route-first debate, holds that it would have been better for both Balochistan and Khyber Pakhtunkhwa, since these are the two provinces traditionally lesser developed and more prone to violence as they share borders with active conflict zones in Afghanistan. Whereas the law and order situation is much improved under recent military operations, positive peace can be established only through competitive trade and commerce, where the populace of these marginalized provinces is integrated into the national mainstream. Furthermore, economic corridors by design are better operated across the shortest distance, where the Western Route is decidedly shorter, with the Eastern Route being 700 km longer.

According to "CPEC: The Route Controversy," a study conducted by the provincial government of Balochistan in May 2015, heavy analysis is laid upon the term "opportunity costs" involved in the CPEC. Here it is surmised the Eastern Route is costlier than the Central or Western routes. The acquisition of land itself is lower in either case, compared to the Eastern Route, which was designed to pass through highly populated areas. However, the Eastern Route still offers better security. Another report states the following:

> *The Western Route is likely to be the shortest and cost least in terms of opportunity cost and dislocation compensation cost. By comparison, the Eastern Route is likely to be the most expensive in terms of land acquisition and dislocation compensation. Arguments that pre-existing sections therein are likely to save time and costs are not tenable, as most sections will have to be widened and re-laid to cater to the volume and load of the traffic that is likely to be generated. The Eastern Route is also likely to be politically divisive and emerge as a source of political instability and carries the danger of imperiling the entire Corridor plan. If selection of the Eastern Route is made on grounds that the 'Western' and 'Central' routes carry security risks, then security considerations today will be traded for interprovincial discord and political instability in the future. Security considerations are important, of course; however, bombardment of disaffected areas with jobs is a better option than bombardment with drones.*[19]

Security Risks

Andrew Small, in his work, *The China-Pakistan Axis*, maintains that the biggest concern for the Chinese is the growing menace of terrorism within the region, especially within its most trusted ally Pakistan,[20] where Beijing has pledged and commenced an investment of $46 billion for CPEC. This can be interpreted as a rise in violence may be the most effective way to scare Beijing off from implementing the CPEC. Islamabad has repeatedly accused India and other opponents of the CPEC of fomenting attacks with this ulterior goal in mind. During Iranian President Hassan Rouhani's state visit to Pakistan on March 25, 2016, Pakistani law enforcement agencies disclosed the arrest of a RAW spy, Kulbhushan Yadav. Pakistani authorities claimed Yadav had entered Pakistan from Iran and was actually arrested on March 3, 2016. The Indian government admitted that Yadav was a former naval officer, but categorically denied any involvement with the captured man, whereas the Pakistani government maintains he was an "Indian spy" assigned to sabotage CPEC-related activities in Balochistan, especially around Gwadar Port. Pakistan asserts that India is bent on sabotaging the CPEC by funding and training anti-state elements in Balochistan. The claim is supported by India's official concern over CPEC and a potential Chinese naval base in Gwadar to ensure Chinese maritime hegemony in the Indian Ocean. During India's Independence Day celebrations, the comments made by Prime Minister Narendra Modi added fuel to this fire.[21] In his address to the nation, Modi especially mentioned that the Kashmiri and Baloch people alike have thanked him for raising concerns regarding human rights violations by the Pakistani state in these territories.[22] Pakistan has subsequently termed these remarks as a proof of Indian involvement in its internal affairs and territory.

Another creeping danger in Balochistan is the growing footprints of ISIS. In 2014, Jundallah spokesperson Fahad Marwat had claimed that a delegation of ISIS met the head of Jundallah in Balochistan.[23] The purpose of the meeting was how to unite the Islamic militants in Pakistan under one banner. In August 2014, Abdul Rauf Rigi was killed in an intra-Baloch conflict and Iranian press TV claimed that before his murder he had joined ISIS.[24] The most shocking proof emerged when ISIS claimed responsibility for the suicide attack targeting lawyers and journalists in Quetta on August 8, 2016. The responsibility for the blasts was claimed by Tehreek-i-Taliban Pakistan (TTP) splinter group, Jamaat-ul-Ahrar (JuA) and ISIS. The next day, in a high-level official meeting, it was acknowledged that the blast was aim at sabotaging the CPEC.[25]

Hardly one and half months later in October 2016, three terrorists stormed the Balochistan police college in the outskirts of Quetta and 61 recruits were killed. Inspector General of Frontier Corps Major General Sher Afgan claimed that intercepted communication revealed that the attack was carried out by the Al-Alimi faction of the Lashkar-i-Jhangvi (LJ) militant group.[26] A day before the groundbreaking ceremony for Gwadar Port, 52 people were killed when a suicide bomber blew himself up at the shrine of Shah Norani in the Khuzdar district of Balochistan.[27] The Islamic State of Iraq and the Levant (ISIL) claimed responsibility.

Besides violent extremism and terrorism, Baloch and Sindhi ethno nationalist groups are another daunting challenge for the economic corridor. On May 30, 2016, a Chinese engineer was targeted by the Sindhudesh Revolutionary Party. Luckily, the Chinese engineer and his driver sustained only minor injuries. The terrorists left a pamphlet denouncing "foreign control over Sindh's natural resources."[28] Another Chinese engineer escaped when a planted bomb on a bike exploded in the

Rohri area of the Sukkur District.[29] On September 30, 2016, the head of the Balochistan Liberation Front (BLF), Allah Nazar Baloch, pledged that he would orchestrate further attacks on the CPEC.[30] He also welcomed Indian help against Pakistan. In September 2016, the Baloch separatist, Switzerland-based Brahamdagh Bugti, president of the outlawed Baloch Republican Party and the grandson of Baloch nationalist leader Nawab Akbar Khan Bugti, sought asylum in India.[31]

Following terrorist attacks on Chinese workers in the Federally Administered Tribal Areas (FATA) and Balochistan, Chinese ambassador to Pakistan Sun Weidong called for security of its workers in Pakistan. To ensure foolproof security, both China and Pakistan agreed on a four-layer security plan for the more than 3000-km-long trade route from Xinjiang to Gwadar Port. Round about 32,000 security personnel consisting of the Frontier Corps, police and Balochistan Levies would guard more than 14,321 Chinese workers in Pakistan.[32] A separate security division under the title of Special Security Division (SSD) was raised in April 2015 to protect the $46 billion economic corridor. The SSD is comprised of nine composite infantry battalions (9000 personnel) and six civilian armed forces (CAFs) wings (6000 personnel) to be headed by a serving major-general of the Pakistan Army.[33] On February 19, 2016, the then Chief of Army Staff General Raheel Sharif visited the headquarters of the newly established SSD. During his visit, Sharif said "We are totally aware of all campaigns against the corridor and I vow that the security forces are ready to pay any price to turn this long cherished dream into reality."[34] The government spent Rs 23 billion on raising SSD to ensure the security of CPEC being commanded by Major General Abid Rafique.[35]

The next level of security was maritime domain. Gwadar has immense geostrategic importance in the Arabian Sea. In September 2014, an attempt was made to hijack PNS Zulfiqar, Pakistan's naval frigate.[36] Another important reason for maritime security is shifting trends from land to naval warfare and supremacy to keep safe and open sea lines of communication (SLOCs) for trade. On December 13, 2016 the Pakistan Navy raised a task force to protect the CPEC and the Gwadar Port.[37] The main task of "Task Force-88" (TF-88) is to protect the CPEC and Gwadar Port against traditional and non-traditional threats. The newly assembled force would comprise ships, fast attack craft, aircraft, drones (unmanned aerial vehicles) and surveillance assets.[38] The two components of CPEC, the 3000-km-long land route that had already been secured by SSD and now Gwadar Port and sea lanes, would be guarded by TF-88. Commodore Muhammad Waris will serve as first commander.

China also handed over two maritime patrol ships that are equipped with Chinese state-of-the-art guns. The ships—named after the Hingol and Basol rivers near Gwadar—were received by commander of the Pakistan Navy, Vice-Admiral Arifullah Hussaini. China is expected to provide two more ships, "Dasht" and "Zhob," to the Pakistan Navy.[39] According to *IHS Jane's Navy International* "Armament to be fitted onboard includes either a 37 mm or a 30 mm gun as a primary weapon, in addition to mountings for two 12.7 mm machine guns. An artist's illustration of the MPV [Maritime Patrol Vessel], shown at the ceremony, suggests that the PMSA has opted for an automatic stabilized naval gun system as the platform's main weapon."[40]

Conclusion

China's growing trade and defence relationships with South Asia have created fears of encirclement in India and hardened its attitude towards Beijing, Islamabad and their joint economic ventures, which are seen entirely through a strategic lens in New Delhi. Pakistan's policy of "peaceful neighbourhood" intended to woo India to share the dividends of CPEC seems not to be paying off, as India has not responded positively to Pakistan's offer to join CPEC. Against this backdrop, New Delhi can seek alliances and cooperation from state and non-state actors to undermine CPEC.

Success of the CPEC is highly dependent upon Pakistan's internal security situation and how it manages its relations with India. It is of paramount importance that Pakistani political leadership resolved their internal differences over the route controversy and distribution of benefits under the CPEC in order to maximize Pakistan's output from this mega project. The current state of Pakistan's economy is in dire straits, severely relying on loans from international monetary institutions and lending bodies in order to cover large deficits in fiscal budgets. Further stress is exerted under the rampant pilferage of extremist and terrorist ideologies. Resultantly, economic opportunities have rapidly shrunk, causing additional strain on the social fabric of the nation. Within this reality, projects inaugurated under the corridor have sparked a wave of rapid development in Pakistan, bringing with it opportunities anew; those of increased and sustained economic growth, driven by the Chinese juggernaut, which will not only benefit the state of Pakistan, but will directly benefit the people of multiple countries. In our current arrangement of the globalized world, nation-states now focus on progress and development through mutual cooperation. Under this new mantra, the CPEC is a prospect that directly benefits Pakistan, in tandem and under the direct collaboration of China, to amplify its sway among the comity of nation.

Notes

1. Historically, China was connected with the Indian sub-continent through three Silk Roads and the Southern route linked the Middle Kingdom with the East Bengal (now areas comprising modern-day Bangladesh).
2. Debasish Roy Chowdhury, "Exclusive: How China-Sri Lanka relations are getting new wings" This Week in Asia, 03 December 2016, http://www.scmp.com/week-asia/geopolitics/article/2051323/exclusive-how-china-sri-lanka-relations-are-getting-new-wings, last visited 05 March 2017.
3. Staff Reporter, "China hopes Nepal could become member of B&R Initiative soon" Xinhua English, 28 February 2017, http://english.sina.com/news/2017-02-28/detail-ifyavwcv9259202.shtml, last visited 05 March 2017.
4. "China-Maldives Friendship Bridge "project launched" Maldives Independent, 31 December 2015, http://maldivesindependent.com/business/china-maldives-friendship-bridge-project-launched-121081, last visited 04 March 2017.
5. David Blair, "Pakistan: the world's most dangerous country" The Telegraph, 06 Nov 2007, http://www.telegraph.co.uk/news/worldnews/1568535/Pakistan-the-worlds-most-dangerous-country.html, last visited 05 March 2017. Also see Ron Moreau, "Pakistan: The Most Dangerous?" Newsweek, 20 October 2007, http://europe.newsweek.com/pakistan-most-dangerous-102955?rm=eu, last visited 05 March 2017.
6. Daniel Runde, "Pakistan: The Next Colombia Success Story?" Forbes, 03 August 2015, https://www.forbes.com/sites/danielrunde/2015/08/03/pakistan-the-next-colombia-success-story/#13d498b330da, last visited 05 March 2017.
7. Wali Zahid, "Pakistan predicted to be world's fastest-growing Muslim economy in 2017" The Express Tribune, 10 January 2017, https://tribune.com.pk/story/1290084/pakistan-predicted-worlds-fastest-growing-muslim-economy-2017/, last visited 06 March 2017.
8. Staff Reporter, "CPEC 'unacceptable' to India, Modi tells China" Geo News, 02 June 2015, https://www.geo.tv/latest/3473-cpec-unacceptable-to-india-modi-tells-china, last visited 05 March 2017.

9. Marc Grossman, "Two Visions, One Collaboration? Part of a Future for US-China Relations?" The Asia-Pacific Journal: Japan Focus, accessed January 17, 2017, http://apjjf.org/2017/02/Grossman.html.
10. The Silk Road Economic Belt and the 21st Century Maritime Silk Road, May 2015, Flung Business Intelligence Centre. Source cited on November 2, 2016 https://www.fbicgroup.com/sites/default/files/The%20Silk%20Road%20Economic%20Belt%20and%2021st%20Century%20Maritime%20Silk%20Road%20MAY%2015.pdf.
11. Mateen Haider and Irfan Haider," Economic Corridor in focus as Pakistan-China sign 51 MoUs", April 20, 2015, Dawn.com. Source cited on November 2, 2016 http://www.dawn.com/news/1177109.
12. Mubarak Zeb Khan, "FTA's hurting Pakistan's Trade Balance", November 7, 2014, Dawn.com. Source cited on November 2, 2016 http://www.dawn.com/news/1142776.
13. Zafar, Muhammad. "First Chinese trade convoy arrives in Gwadar through CPEC." *The Express Tribune* (Karachi), November 12, 2016.
14. Kaplan, Robert D. "The Geography of Chinese Power." Foreign Affairs. Last modified June 2010. https://www.foreignaffairs.com/articles/china/2010-05-01/geography-chinese-power.
15. Mahan, Alfred T. "Discussing of The Elements of Sea Power." In *The Influence of Sea Power upon History*, 29. London: Methuen & Co Ltd, 1890.
16. Web Desk, "Eastern Route for CPEC May Foster Enmity Between Provinces, Warns Imran – the Express Tribune," Tribune (The Express Tribune), September 30, 2015, http://tribune.com.pk/story/965041/eastern-route-for-cpec-may-foster-enmity-between-provinces-warns-imran/.
17. Safdar Sial, The China-Pakistan Economic Corridor: Assessment of Potential Threats and Constraints, (2014): 3.
18. "CPEC – Pkg1 Inauguration – National Logistics Cell," National Logistics Cell, May 17, 2016, accessed August 24, 2016, http://www.nlc.com.pk/news/352-pm-inaugurates-package-1-of-cpec-western-route.
19. Aarish U. Khan, "Pak-China Economic Corridor: The Hopes and Reality," Regional Studies XXXIII, no. 1 (2014).
20. Andrew Small, "The China Pakistan Axis: Asia's New Geopolitics", Oxford University Press, 2015.
21. Modi, Chaarvi. "Highlights: Narendra Modi's Speech on India's 70th Independence Day." (2016).
22. Usman Shahid," Balochistan: The troubled heart of the CPEC", August 23, 2016, The Diplomat. Source cited on December 8, 2016 http://thediplomat.com/2016/08/balochistan-the-troubled-heart-of-the-cpec/.

23. DAWN. "IS Visits Militants in Balochistan." DAWN.COM. Last modified November 12, 2016. https://www.dawn.com/news/1143997.
24. Notezai, Muhammad A. "Can ISIS Gain a Foothold in Balochistan?" The Diplomate, January 7, 2016.
25. DAWN. "Consensus That Quetta Attack Targeted CPEC." DAWN.COM. Accessed February 27, 2017. https://www.dawn.com/news/1276337.
26. Sherani, Hafeezullah. "61 killed in twin suicide attacks as terrorists storm police training college in Quetta." *DAWN* (Karachi), October 25, 2016.
27. "Attack on Shah Noorani Shrine in Pakistan Kills Dozens." Al Jazeera. Last modified November 13, 2016. http://www.aljazeera.com/news/2016/11/dozens-casualties-attack-pakistan-shrine-161112141000715.html.
28. Boone, Jon. "Chinese Engineer and Driver Injured in Karachi Separatist Bombing." The Guardian. Last modified May 30, 2016. https://www.theguardian.com/world/2016/may/30/chinese-worker-driver-injured-karachi-bombing-claimed-separatists.
29. PTI. "Pakistan: Chinese Engineer Survives Roadside Bombing in Sindh." The Indian Express. Last modified December 14, 2016. http://indianexpress.com/article/world/pakistan-chinese-engineer-survives-roadside-bombing-in-sindh-4427239/.
30. Hashim, Asad. "Pakistan: BLF Chief Baloch Says Indian Help 'welcome'." Al Jazeera. Last modified September 30, 2016. http://www.aljazeera.com/news/2016/09/pakistan-blf-chief-baloch-indian-160929153641899.html.
31. The Newspaper's Correspondent. "Brahamdagh Bugti to Seek Asylum in India – Pakistan." DAWN.COM. Last modified September 20, 2016. https://www.dawn.com/news/1284917.
32. Gishkori, Zahid. "Economic corridor: Pakistan, China agree on four-layer security." *The Express Tribune* (Karachi), November 1, 2015.
33. Haider, Mehtab. "17,177 soldiers deployed for security of Chinese workers of CPEC." *The NEWS* (Karachi), December 15, 2015.
34. Bajwa, Lieutenant General Asim S. "Press Release:No PR-60/2016-ISPR." ISPR. Last modified February 19, 2016. https://www.ispr.gov.pk/front/main.asp?o=t-press_release&id=3207.
35. Gishkori, Zahid. "Pakistan raises Special Security Division successfully." *The News* (Karachi), February 3, 2016.
36. Ali, Naziha S. "Dockyard attackers planned to hijack Navy frigate." *DAWN* (Karachi), September 13, 2014.
37. Maj Gen Asif Ghafoor, Maj Gen Asif. "Press Release Navy:No PR-PN479/2016-ISPR." ISPR. Last modified December 13, 2016. https://www.ispr.gov.pk/front/main.asp?o=t-press_release&id=3629&cat=navy.

38. The Newspaper's Staff Reporter. "Special force set up to guard Gwadar port's sea lanes." *DAWN* (Karachi), December 12, 2016.
39. "China Gives Pakistan Two Ships for Security of CPEC." The Times of India. Last modified January 15, 2017. http://timesofindia.indiatimes.com/world/pakistan/china-gives-pakistan-two-ships-for-security-of-cpec-sea-route/articleshow/56558924.cms.
40. Rahmat, Ridzwan. "KSEW cuts steel on Pakistan's first MPV" IHS Jane's 360, May 4, 2016.

CHAPTER 12

Uyghur Militant Activity in Southeast Asia and Its Security Implications

Pinjie Sun

Introduction

Southeast Asia constitutes an important transshipment hub for illegal Uyghur migration, some of which has cross-fertilized with local and transnational jihadist extremism. The large-scale movement of Uyghurs to the region commenced in 2013 and has continued to grow annually since then with more than 10,000 using the route by the end of 2015.[1] While the vast bulk of these individuals are seeking an alternative passage to Turkey either as economic migrants or political refugees fleeing persecution in the Xinjiang Uyghur Autonomous Region (XUAR), there are indications that a small number have joined with active militant entities in Indonesia and may be looking to establish additional bases in the southern Philippines. In addition, there is a growing concern that experienced battle-hardened Uyghurs who departed for Turkey not as a sanctuary but to fight in the Middle East will increasingly seek to return to Southeast Asia as a result of the recent territorial losses that have beset so-called Islamic State (IS) and other rebel organizations in Syria and Iraq.

This chapter looks at the scope and dimensions of illicit Uyghur movement through Southeast Asia and the implications it holds for local terrorism in this part of the world. It first discusses the main triggers for the

P. Sun (✉)
Shanghai University, Shanghai, China

A. Arduino, X. Gong (eds.), *Securing the Belt and Road Initiative*,
https://doi.org/10.1007/978-981-10-7116-4_12

recent exodus from Xinjiang, how China's on-going national security policies might impact on these flows and the principal logistics that are utilized to gain entry to the region as a subsequent "jump-off" point for Turkey. The chapter goes on to analyze the interaction between Uyghur and Indonesian jihadists and why this could have practical impact in the event that Chinese Muslim foreign fighters start returning to Asia from the Middle East. Finally, the implications of these dynamics for the southern Philippines is discussed and assessed in terms of how it could extend the Uyghur logistical and operational footprint in Southeast Asia. The conclusion looks at how China is working with regional governments to enhance joint action against common terrorist threats and how the new Trump administration might impact on this engagement.

The XUAR Refugee/Migrant Crisis and Politics in China

The XUAR is located in the northwest of the People's Republic of China (PRC) in the heart of the Eurasian continent. The autonomous region is the country's largest provincial area, occupying 1,664,900 square kilometers of land, and is host to 10.5 percent of China's minority population. The autonomous region also occupies a quarter of the PRC's entire border length, abutting Kazakhstan, Kyrgyzstan, Tajikistan, Afghanistan, Pakistan, Mongolia, Russia and India (Sautman 1998).

Since the end of the 1980s, Xinjiang has been the locus of an increasingly serious ethno-religious conflict. In the summer of 1990, the People's Liberation Army (PLA) specifically delineated the XUAR as the country's "zone of most uncertain control," reflecting the launch of a large-scale insurgency that same year aimed at establishing an independent state to be known as Eastern Turkistan for Uyghur Muslims (Christoffersen 1993; Becquelin 2004). The subsequent two decades saw a series of bombings, uprisings, and assassinations, all of which were justified in the name of a bona fide war of national liberation. The most lethal incident occurred in July 2009 when a series of inter-ethnic riots in the capital city of Urumqi left 184 people dead and more than 1100 injured—the deadliest outburst of public violence since the 1989 Tiananmen Square demonstrations (Eimer 2009a, b; Ramzy 2009).

While this scale of unrest has yet to be repeated, underlying tensions remain palpable as evidenced by reprisal attacks against ethnic Han, communist-approved imams who support the government and local governing officials. Some of the more recent examples include the November 2013 suicide car crash in Beijing's Tiananmen Square (five dead, 38 injured), the March 2014 indiscriminate stabbing incident at the Kunming train station (29 dead and 143 wounded) and the bombing of Urumqi central market two months later (31 dead, 90 injured) (Kaiman 2013, 2014, 2017). Although there has never been validated evidence that a single, organized movement was behind these attacks, China has always insisted that they were the work of the East Turkistan Islamic Movement (ETIM) and perpetrated as part of an anti-PRC jihad undertaken in collusion with al-Qaeda in the past and IS now (Singh 2016).

Background of the XUAR Migrant Crisis

XUAR's problems have in part been due to an upsurge in Uyghur identity politics, historically a flashpoint of social unrest, which has been further exacerbated by the mobilization of exiled political elites and Western sympathizers (some foreign forces) have played a critical role in fermenting these tensions. Their main argument is that unlike China's Hui minority, Uyghurs are distinct from the Han majority, not only in religion but also in language, culture and historical experience. Therefore, Uyghurs deserve a state of their own (Fuller and Lipman 2004). The drive to separate has been heightened by an influx of Han into XUAR—though local people both on account of its prosperity and in response to lucrative incentives offered by Beijing at the same time. This transmigration has generated growing animosity as it has upset the local ethno-religious structure as well as limited Uyghurs in the key political, economic, military, police and economic posts in the region (Singh 2016). The reconstruction of historical elite by knowledge elite also plays a part in this independence movement. The pursuit of independence also coincided with the implosion of the USSR and the formation of the Commonwealth of Independent States. Several of these states border the XUAR (Smith 2002). Many believe that Central Asian influence has been a major factor encouraging the rise of Turkic nationalism and Islamic identity among Uyghur Muslims (Christoffersen 1993).

China has moved to forcefully stem rebel activity in Xinjiang, instituting a regular launch hard campaign against extremism, terrorism and separatism—also known as the "three evils."[2] This activity combined with a growing trend of maintaining stability by the XUAR provincial government.

However, this does not solve the essential problem; instead, it has intensified conflicts between Han Chinese and Uyghur Chinese. In turn, Beijing has introduced ever more draconian internal security legislation, setting in motion a vicious cycle of action and counter-action that has both eroded the prospects for partial, much less genuine, ethno-religious reconciliation and stimulated the "push" to leave XUAR.

The vicious cycle of action and counter-action will almost certainly be entrenched as a result of two recent policies. First was the 2014 announcement by the Xinjiang Communist Party chief that future security work in the region will be conducted under the auspices of the National Security Commission, which will further centralize and streamline security crackdowns in the XUAR (Ng 2014). Second was the ratification of controversial legislation in December 2015 that adopts an array of sweeping measures to combat terrorism. However, it has been broadly criticized for containing no specific safeguards to prevent its clauses from being used to target dissidents and religious minorities, intensifying the contradiction.[3] The impetus for Uyghurs to leave China can be expected because of the two policies.[4]

XUAR to Southeast Asia: Routes and Modus Operandi

Generally, disaffected Uyghurs left Xinjiang via Kyrgyzstan, Kazakhstan and Turkmenistan in Central Asia. This is the most convenient and direct route to transit for Turkey. Moreover, this route also has strong Turkic and Islamic characteristics that are reminiscent of those found in the XUAR (Zenn 2014). However, the institutionalization of the Shanghai Cooperation Organization (SCO) in the early 2000s enabled Beijing to press neighboring countries to repatriate undocumented migrants to Xinjiang.[5] Facing the difficulty of the route from Central Asia, Southeast Asia has become an alternative route for the Uyghurs. The main route passes through Yunnan to Laos, onwards to northern Thailand, down to Bangkok and moves to the southern provinces that share borders with Malaysia. The migrants then head for Kuala Lumpur where they can easily mingle with the large Muslim community before boarding regular commercial flights to Turkey.[6] Total travel time is currently around seven months, although this could be drastically cut in the next five years. Although, under normal circumstances it will be possible to travel seamlessly by train from Kunming to the Malaysian capital.[7]

Typically, the migrants will ditch their identification cards before leaving for southern Thailand and fabricate fake documents for entering Kuala Lumpur. Very high-quality fraudulent passports can be procured in Bangkok for approximately $2000 apiece, while cheaper (and more basic) versions can be obtained in Cambodia, sometimes for as little as $300. However, there is growing speculation that the Turkish government may be complicit in accepting those Uyghurs even without authentic documents. According to some reliable sources in the region, an office at Ankara's consulate facilitates the provision and processing of visas and passports to illegal Uyghur immigrants although it claims to be a non-governmental organization (NGO).[8]

Ankara's alleged involvement in facilitating the illicit movement of Uyghurs via Southeast Asia to Turkey—a number of whom are known to be ultimately seeking covert entry into Syria and Iraq—has generated growing speculation that the Erdogan government may be seeking to develop a deniable paramilitary asset. Uyghur could be used by Ankara as a paramilitary asset, but Ankara does not want to open the links between them. It works at the behest of the intelligence services, for future terrorist/insurgent contingencies in the Middle East, Central Asia and even China.[9] As one report issued by the non-partisan European Information Center on Terrorism (CEI-T) in 2015 observes:

> Startling new evidence has emerged of the "double game" being played by Turkey in the crisis of Islamist radicalism. Senior Turkish embassy officials in Southeast Asia are issuing Turkish identity papers to members of China's Uyghur Muslim minority so they can travel to Turkey and join Islamist gangs fighting in Syria, or train with Islamist terrorists active in China but using Turkey as a safe haven.[10]

The continuing exodus of Uyghurs from XUAR could have implications for future terrorist contingencies in China. Such implications have caused growing concerns in Beijing. It annoys the Chinese government even further when those on exile send the international message that conditions for Muslims in the autonomous region are not good. To ameliorate the situation, the PRC has leveraged both diplomatic and economic pressure to "encourage" main Southeast Asian states where those immigrants transit to immediately repatriate irregular migrants and refugees. However, the requests from Beijing have not yielded significant success, except that 109 Uyghurs were deported from Thailand in 2015 (see Table below).[11]

The explanations for this failure are varied, but there are mainly three reasons: corruption in the local government, incapability of patrolling due to geographical difficulty and the fear of sparking unrest and opposition in a region where there is a high level of sympathy for Muslims in XUAR. The last factor took on more credence in the aftermath of the bombing of the Erawan Buddhist Shrine in August 2015. It is widely believed that this attack, which resulted in more than 20 casualties and more than 100 injured, was an act of terrorist revenge in retaliation for Bangkok's decision to send 109 Uyghurs back to China.[12]

Uyghur Deportations from Southeast Asia (Chen 2016)

Country	*Number deported*	*Date of deportation*
Cambodia	20	2009
Malaysia	11	2011
Vietnam	21	2014
Vietnam	21	2015
Thailand	109	2015

While Southeast Asian states remain aware of the backlash of repatriating Muslims to XUAR, it is expected to see more cooperation to reduce and even crackdown the illicit movement of Uyghurs in the region. One reason is that relations with China play a dominant part in the changing policy. And this chapter argues the security threat posed by the Islamist extremists from XUAR with militants in Southeast Asia also accounts for the policy changes.

Uyghur Militant Activity in Indonesia

In December 2015, the elite Indonesian counter-terrorist unit Densus-88 raided a suspected Islamist safe-house in West Java where they arrested 11 militants who were allegedly planning attacks against high-ranking government officials, Christian churches and Shi'ite mosques in several cities on the main islands of Java, Sumatra and Kalimnatan. Among those detained was a 35-year-old Uyghur identified as Alli. According to police chief Badrodin Haiti, Alli had entered the country with two accomplices (who escaped the dragnet and remain at large) via the island of Bantam after transiting through Thailand and Singapore. The arrestee was being trained as a suicide bomber by a cell of the Mujahidin Indonesia Timur (MIT)—the country's most active and dangerous indigenous terrorist group.[13] Alli has been investigated for complicity in the 2015 Erawan Shrine bombing in Bankok as well as his putative involvement with Bahrun Naim, an Indonesian national who is one of the key leaders of Khatibah Nusantara (a special Malay speaking umbrella unit of 100 men set up in IS) and the plan of January 2016 attacks in Jakarta that left eight dead and 24 injured.[14]

The 2015 incident has raised concerns that militant Uyghurs are now willing to directly support and join forces with local jihadi groups—exacerbating the existing home-grown extremist threat (Singh 2016; Kwok 2015). China's domestic action against terrorism activity have compounded these fears, as has the public pledge of MIT's (now deceased) leader, Santoso (aka Abu Wardah), to accept 100 Uyghurs as part of the movement.[15]

To be sure, MIT has been weakened as a result of a hard crackdown on its activities. It is even weaker after the loss of its founder and leader, Santoso, who died during a gunfight in Poso in July 2016. That said, the group continues to threaten domestic security and is still considered to have a functioning base in the jungles of central Sulawesi. According to Indonesian intelligence officials, MIT still has the willingness and capacity to absorb foreign fighters into its ranks (Gunaratna 2015; Chan 2016).

Uyghurs are known to constitute a component of this external network, with security authorities putting the number of this network at around 14 by mid-2016.[16] Although not large, these militants are important as they are believed to have both ideological and nascent operational/personal ties with IS. This nexus could take on a more practical dimension if combat-hardened, experienced Chinese Muslim volunteers start returning to Asia from the Middle East as a result of the worsening of the war situation.

Between 3000 and 4500 Uyghurs are thought to have joined rebel groups in Syria and Iraq (Ali 2016). Although many are fighting alongside Jabhat Fatah al-Sham (formerly Jabhat al-Nusra, the main al-Qaeda affiliate in the region),[17] a large number are known to be with IS and working closely with Indonesians in Katibah Nusantara.[18] In 2016, Abu Bakr al-Baghdadi's movement saw nearly a quarter (23 percent) of its self-proclaimed "caliphate" recaptured, compounding a 14 percent loss from the year before.[19] Intelligence analysts have warned that, while welcome, this reversal in fortune is liable to trigger an exodus of foreign mercenaries from the Middle East, many of whom will likely seek alternative zones for continuing their violent jihad.[20]

Although Uyghurs would plan to return to XUAR ultimately, for several reasons, Indonesia could also be viewed as a viable option. For one thing, the geographically ungoverned archipelago provides a safe hiding place for the Uyghurs. For another, several radical entities in that area that have openly pledged allegiance to al-Baghdadi provide incentives and interests to the Uyghurs. The most important reasons, however, are the spreading ties that have developed between Uyghurs and Indonesians in Katibah Nusantara. Regional commentators believe this umbrella group is already being used as the main principal vehicle for transporting Chinese militants back from the Middle East and then linking them up with their Islamist brethren in MIT. Naim, who as noted was connected to Alli, is thought to be the principal person facilitating these reverse flows, allegedly operating in conjunction with Amin Baco, a Malaysian who is suspected to be al-Baghdadi's key link man in Southeast Asia.[21]

If Katibah Nusantara is leveraged to entrench an ISIS-affiliated Uyghur presence in this manner, it could have severe ramifications. Within Indonesia, these veterans could help to strengthen a weakened MIT by applying tactics used in Syria and Iraq. This could disrupt the good relations by spearheading attacks on Shi'a Muslims to incite sectarian hatred and violence, as their main goal is not entirely religious extremism. Regionally, they could work to rekindle Southeast Asian transnational Islamic extremism by conducting cross-border strikes in the same manner as Jemaah Islamiyah (JI) did—the group responsible for the worst terrorist atrocities in Southeast Asia.[22]

Uyghur Militant Activity in the Philippines

Besides Indonesia, there is speculation that Uyghurs are also looking to establish a presence in the southern Philippines. Concerns began to emerge in 2014 when five Chinese Muslims traveling on false Turkish passports were arrested in Manila. During their initial interrogation the group claimed they were political refugees from XUAR. However, subsequent investigations revealed that before arriving in the capital, they had first traveled to Basilan and Cotabato City in Mindanao where intelligence authorities believe they had attempted to connect with members of the Abu Sayyaf Group (ASG) and the Bangsamoro Islamic Freedom Fighters (BIFF)—two active (albeit disaggregated)[23] rebel organizations that have both sworn allegiance to IS. Due to strong evidence of their connections with the two active rebel groups, they were deported for violating Philippine immigration laws.[24]

Since then, there have been several social media postings from young members of the ASG expressing support for Uyghurs in Xinjiang. A visual recording of a chant in Mandarin entitled "Mujahid" that was released by the Al Hayat Media Center of IS in late 2015 has also reached followers in the southern Philippines, including those associated with ASG and BIFF—as well as two smaller movements that have similarly pledged loyalty to al-Baghdadi's self-styled caliphate, Ansar Khilafah Philippines (AKP) and Khilafah Islamiyah Mindanao (KIM) (Banlaoi 2016). This affinity could well be indicative of the possible beginnings of an extremist ideology that increasingly co-joins the interests and sympathies of Muslim militants in the Philippines with those in China.

The possible emergence of a Uyghur hub in Mindanao could equally eventuate as a result of the connections that are widely thought to exist between militants in Indonesia and the Philippines, both logistically (in terms of the provision of funds, weapons and safe-haven) and by virtue of blood/family ties. These alleged links have direct relevance, not least because they could avail jihadists fighting in Sulawesi—local and foreign—with an important rear base in Mindanao. Certainly, this is what occurred with JI, which during its most active years conspicuously leveraged the southern Philippines for the triple purposes of refuge, training and arms procurement.[25]

Besides these considerations, there are three facets of Mindanao that could conceivably make it attractive as a hub for Uyghur rebels. First, like Indonesia, porous borders, numerous ungoverned spaces and the presence of active terrorist groups are all characteristic (if not defining) features of the region. Second, democratic sensibilities and memories of past abuses committed under the dictatorship of Ferdinand Marcus. He has worked against the institution of strong counter-terrorist powers in the area (as well as nationally) for fear they could be used to silence legitimate critics of the government.[26] Third, the Duterte administration's current pre-occupation with the war on drugs has greatly impeded the ability of the police and intelligence services to investigate illegal immigrants in the southern Philippines. This is because all resources have now been diverted to the counter-narcotics mission.[27]

To be sure, it would be challenging for Uyghurs to penetrate the region and integrate with the local population without assistance from the locals, as their distinct ethnic features would stand out. To be successful, another entity would be needed to facilitate their entry and in the current regional militant context, there are two possible operational ways. The first is MIT, which is known to have accepted Uyghurs into its ranks and which allegedly works closely with AKP. The second is known as the ASG, and particularly the Basilan-based faction led by Isnilon Hapilon. He is far more outward looking and religiously pious than Radullan Sahiron—the commander of ASG's Sulu-based branch.[28] Hapilon has also been appointed the IS emir in Southeast Asia, which has given him enormous stature as an Islamist "magnet" for attracting jihadists from outside the Philippines. As one former member of the ASG summed up: "If there is going to be a Uyghur connection with the Philippines, it will be to access training camps in Mindanao and it will be forged through the Basilan-based faction of Hapilon."[29]

Effect of Uyghurs Militant Activity Threat to the BRI

The most immediate threat from Uygur militias in Southeast Asia is armed organizations, such as the Turkistan Islamic Party (TIP), that are well trained and have operational experience, such groups might alliance with local terrorist groups now.

There are concerns over cooperation with local terrorist groups, but so far, TIP does not have such plans and the threat remains limited. However, Indonesian ISIS-related groups need to pay close attention because not only are they directly instructed by Syrian Islamic warfare personnel, but they are also trying to bring the Middle East radicalized Uyghur back to the country and recruiting them to their terrorist activities, including using them as suicidal attackers. At the same time, these ISIS members returning from the Middle East in South Africa after a firm foothold are likely to further return to China to carry out suicide attacks. It would be a direct threat to China's social security.

Southeast Asia is an important area of China's BRI. China plans to invest heavily in infrastructure in this region, and there would be a large number of Chinese enterprises and personnel working there. These people and facilities will be an easy target for Uyghur terrorists. It would be a serious impact to the BRI. The risk of terrorist attacks will greatly increase the cost of China's investment in this region and delay China's step to deploy its assets in this region. It is very similar to the problems encountered by China and Pakistan in the China-Pakistan Economic Corridor. Pakistan has invested heavily in security resources in this project, but the construction speed of associated infrastructure has been relatively slow.

On the other hand, the activities of Uyghur terrorists can also cause great political risks. At present, the protection of overseas interests in China depends mainly on local law enforcement agencies and some private local security forces, and Chinese always think the local government should assume responsibility for security. In the face of the threat of terrorist attacks, the Chinese government is often accustomed to using diplomatic means to exert pressure on the local government to enable Chinese enterprises and personnel to obtain better security conditions. However, in many cases, these requirements were hard to fulfill. Many local governments in Southeast Asia have limited capacity to provide adequate security resources. And this diplomatic pressure might become a greater impact on these local governments. Normally, Uyghur terrorists in Southeast Asia will not act alone; they prefer to link local armed groups or extremist forces to form a joint action. Therefore, the local government is not only dealing with the threat of terrorism, but also complex political issues. This would destroy local social balance and weaken political stability. This instability will eventually lead to the deterioration of the local investment environment, halting progress on the important infrastructure of the BRI, thus seriously hindering it.

Finally, Uyghur terrorists may have a long-term impact on Southeast Asia, where they make this region as a long-term settlement area. Southeast Asia may replace the Middle East region as another major place to carry out jihad. It now appears that ISIS terrorists from the Middle East—including Uyghur terrorists—would be a long standing issue in Southeast Asian region. Although it has not yet had a plan to attack China's targets, it does not mean they would not be a threat, and their hostility to the Chinese government will not be declining. As a result, the risk of terrorist attacks in Southeast Asia will gradually increase, which also makes the cost and uncertainty of the BRI far greater than expected.

Conclusion

The growing connections between Uyghur and local terrorist groups in Southeast Asia has posed a problem that is of mutual relevance to China and Southeast Asia. Logically, this mutual threat could be addressed through regional security arrangements such as within the Association of Southeast Asian Nations (ASEAN) and ASEAN Regional Forum (ARF) and ASEAN Plus 3 that include China. However, despite the announcement of various "action plans" and statements of intent, meaningful progress in the general area of counter-terrorism has always been stymied by ASEAN's normative preference for non-interference in internal affairs and unanimity in decision-making.[30] Moreover, the specter of militant Islam is only a concern to a few of the Association's member states and is less of an issue to countries such as Cambodia, Vietnam or Laos. So far, there are no Muslim extremist organizations in these countries to establish strongholds, but as the Uyghurs pass through immigration channels they will face a certain degree of security problems.

Against this background, rigorous regional counter-terrorist cooperation has historically been more bilateral or trilateral in nature, tending not to take the form of concrete policies instituted through the ASEAN framework. While providing a collective response to extremist violence might be weak, this "hub and spokes" model still allows for more limited and narrow action to address common threats. The model is named after a bicycle wheel, which has a strong central hub with a series of connecting spokes. The problem is solved by the direct dialogue between countries, thus greatly simplifying the path of the system. If countries faced a serious threat of terrorism, they might be more willing to engage in counter-terrorism cooperation directly, thus avoiding inefficiencies in complex systems within ASEAN.

To this end, China has steadily stepped up its regional interactions in Southeast Asia to combat what it now portrays as a common threat. The country has increased its counter-terrorist cooperation with Indonesia, particularly in the areas of intelligence sharing, joint investigations, forensics and training. Most of this collaboration takes place through regular bilateral counter-terrorism consultations. On December 4, 2015 these meetings were held and co-chaired by PRC Vice Foreign Minister Cheng Guoping and Saud Usman Nasution, the head of Indonesia's National Counterterrorism Agency (BNPT). During the session, the two sides exchanged views on their respective national security situations, the interaction between militant groupings in XUAR and Sulawesi and the manner by which common threats could best be addressed to the benefit of both countries.[31]

Despite tensions on the South China Sea disputes, the PRC has also stated a willingness to work with the Philippines in fighting terrorism. The potential scope of this engagement has been considerably widened as a result of a restored Sino-Philippines relationship. President Rodrigo Duterte, elected in 2016, made it clear that he not only wants to review parts of Manila's defense ties with the United States, but also is intent on significantly improving Filipino-Sino relations.[32] While the actual substance of this apparent "pivot" is still open to question,[33] it is noteworthy that in October 2016, the two countries pledged to strengthen their law enforcement collaboration to jointly deal with narcotics trafficking and terrorism.[34] It is expected that if Uyghurs are becoming more active with militants in the Philippines, it is likely that this situation will take on a more concrete form, embracing aspects such as information dissemination and capacity building.

China has additionally sought to promote broader action to counter religious extremism, particularly in heightening regional awareness of Internet-based radicalization. As part of this endeavor, Beijing has hosted several international conferences that aim to highlight best practices for countering online extremist messaging and how these can be applied to integrated policies that encapsulate legal tools, education and the reinforcement of positive socio-cultural norms. The most recent event was held in November 2014 and brought together participants from Pakistan, Singapore, Israel, the United States and France.[35]

The threat from Uyghur militants to BRI is far higher than the threat to China. Chinese government has a very mature anti-terrorism and domestic security system in the mainland territory, but the security capacity outside is relatively weak. Although China is gaining more and more influence on the countries involved in the BRI region, it is not enough to support BRI's security demand. Therefore, the Chinese government can only passively face terrorist attacks overseas; such terrorist attacks are likely to delay the smooth development of BRI plans. But this threat does not create sufficient capacity to completely break the BRI program, and the direct attack by Uyghur militants can only cause a significant increase in security risks and costs of BRI. However, the escalation of extremism caused by the security environment in Southeast Asia is very likely to make the goal of BRI difficult to achieve. Therefore, the threat to China was the overall security environment in Southeast Asia rather than simply the problem of armed Uyghur terrorists. As mentioned earlier, the Southeast Asian countries, which have no extremist organization, are relatively less affected by Uyghur militants, and in Southeast Asia foreign militants are unable to gain a foothold in the absence of local support. Therefore, China needs to cooperate with those Southeast Asian countries with extremist issues to upgrade their ability in anti-terrorism and anti-extremism. Increasing the anti-terrorism capability of Southeast Asian countries is a fundamental measure for improving the BRI's overall security environment.

Finally, the PRC has tried to encourage Western nations, including the United States, to support its efforts in blunting the activities of the East Turkestan Islamic Movement (ETIM).[36] Thus far, progress in this direction has been hampered by the continued issue of alleged human rights abuses in XUAR and concerns over the legitimacy of China's new anti-terror laws. It might change, however, as a result of the Trump administration's current priority to eliminate Islamic radicalism in all its forms. As Uran Botobekov observes in *The Diplomat*: "Despite serious contradictions between Beijing and Washington in trade and economic concerns, the firmness of new U.S. President Donald Trump's position on eliminating Islamic radicalism can become common ground." (Botobekov 2017) In this context, the prospect of a more concerted Uyghur militant presence taking hold in Southeast Asia could help pave the way for a joint Chinese-US drive to resuscitate genuine counter-terrorism cooperation in the region. Instituting forceful (but calibrated) collective responses to militant extremism would be a mutually beneficial and politically non-contentious area of collaboration between Beijing and Washington that could also give real meaning to ASEAN's Political and Security Community as it continues to come to fruition in 2017.[37]

Notes

1. See, for example, Christina Lin, "Turkey's Passport Scandal and Settlements in Syria," *The Times of Israel*, October 6, 2015, available online at http://blogs.timesofisrael.com/turkeys-passport-scandal-and-settlements-in-syria/, as of January 26, 2017. Lin reports that more than 50,000 Uyghur had used the route. While this number may have been exaggerated, one of the authors observed that at least 10,000 had traveled to Syria based on sources in the Middle East and propaganda materials released by the so-called Turkistan Islamic Party in al-Sham and IS.
2. See, for instance, Sam Dupont, "China's War on the 'Three Evil Forces,'" *Foreign Policy*, July 25, 2007; and Singh, "Southeast Asian Terrorism: The Rise of the Uighur Factor."
3. The legislation requires technical firms to assist with the decryption of electronic information, severely restricts the right of news media outlets to report on attacks or the authorities' response to such incidents, adopts a very broad definition of terrorism and establishes a new counter-terrorism agency and national intelligence center with significant discretionary pow-

ers. For further details see Zunyou Zhou, "China's Comprehensive Counter-Terrorism Law," *The Diplomat,* January 23, 2016; "China Passes Controversial New Anti-Terror Laws," *BBC News,* December 28, 2015, available online at www.bbc.com/news/world-asia-china-35188137, as of January 18, 2017; and "China Passes Controversial Counter-Terrorism Law," *Reuters,* December 28, 2015.

4. Indeed, official intelligence sources estimate that more than a thousand Uyghur refugees are already currently seeking asylum in just three states—Indonesia, Malaysia and Thailand. See Chen, "Uyghurs' Presence Adds to Southeast Asia's Security Challenges."
5. See, for instance, Weng Loke Yeoh, "Ethnic Unrest in Tibet, Xinjiang and China's Vulnerability to Separatism," available online at https://www.academia.edu/8353539/Ethnic_Unrest_in_China_Tibet_Xinjiang_and_Chinas_vulnerability_to_ethnic_separatism, as of January 17, 2017.
6. A secondary passage runs from the Guangxi Zhuang autonomous region in southwestern China into northern Vietnam and then to Thailand, either via Laos or through Cambodia.
7. Interviews, Bangkok, January 2016.
8. Interviews, Bangkok, January 2016 and Manila, November 2016.
9. Interview, Bangkok, January 2016.
10. See "'Double Game' Turkey Issuing Identity Papers to Islamist Fighters from China," *No-terror,* European Information Center on Terrorism, August 08, 2015, available online at https://www.noterror.eu/en/983/, as of January 08, 2016.
11. Thailand has generally been willing to acquiesce to the demands of China in order to safeguard lucrative trade and investment ties with Beijing.
12. Interviews, Bangkok, January 2016. See also Susan Cunningham, "Bangkok Shrine Bombing—Case (Pretty Much) Closed," *Forbes Asia* (December 23, 2015).
13. MIT mostly acts as an umbrella movement for militants based in the simmering conflict zones of Poso, Palu and Bima and has been directly tied to numerous attacks on the police.
14. Interviews, Manila, November 2017. See also Singh, "Southeast Asian Terrorism: Rise of the Uighur Factor"; and Shannon Tiezzi, "Indonesia Adds 4 Uyghur Militants to Most-Wanted List," *The Diplomat,* March 18, 2016.
15. Interview, Singapore, January 2016. See also Randy Fabi and Augustins Beo Da Costa, "Indonesia Turns To China as Ethnic Uighurs Join Would-Be Jihadis," *Reuters,* January 6, 2016.
16. See "Chinese Uighur Militant Killed By Indonesian Military," *San Diego Union Tribube,* August 19, 2016.
17. On July 28 2016 Jabhat al-Nusra, changed its name to Jabhat Fatah al-Sham and declared that it had formerly split from its parent organization.

The move was widely interpreted as an attempt to remove any "pretext" for the United States and Russia to conduct airstrikes against the movement under the justification of targeting an al-Qaeda affiliate. See Liz Sly and Karen DeYoung, "Syria's Jabhat al-Nusra Splits from al-Qaeda and Changes Its Name," *The Washington Post,* July 28, 2016; and Mona Alami, "Jabhat al-Nusra's Rebranding Is More Than Simple Name Change," *Al-Monitor,* August 15, 2016, available online at http://www.al-monitor.com/pulse/originals/2016/08/jabhat-al-nusra-sever-al-qaeda-focus-local-syria.html, as of January 20, 2017.

18. Interviews, Singapore Manila, November 2017. See also Sing.
19. See "Islamic State Group 'Lost Quarter of Territory' in 2016," *BBC News,* January 19, 2017, available online at http://www.bbc.com/news/world-middle-east-38641509, as of January 20, 2017.
20. See, for instance, Liz Bourke, "Returned Jihadists: The Horror That Comes After Islamic State," *news.com.au,* September 28, 2016, available online at http://www.news.com.au/national/politics/returned-jihadists-the-horror-that-comes-after-islamic-state/news-story/6ffde8f2aa026666 8e3ab9205eb0425f, as of January 20, 2017; and Jo Moir, "Foreign Fighters in the Middle East Could Return to New Zealand as Islamic State Crumbles—John Key," *stuff,* October 24, 2016, available online at http://www.stuff.co.nz/national/politics/85681951/Foreign-fighters-in-the-Middle-East-could-return-to-New-Zealand-as-Islamic-State-crumbles-John-Key, as of January 20, 2017.
21. Interviews, Manila, November 2017.
22. These include the 2002 Bali bombings (202 dead, 209 injured), the 2003 suicide strike attack against the JW Marriott in Jakarta (12 dead, 150 injured), the bombing of the Australian Embassy, again in Jakarta (11 dead, more than 200 injured) and repeat attacks in Bali in 2005 (25 dead, 129 injured). For further details on the operational makeup and activities of JI between 2001 and 2008, see Peter Chalk et al., *The Evolving Terrorist Threat to Southeast Asia: A Net Assessment* (Santa Monica, CA: RAND, 2009), Chapter Five.
23. The ASG is split between two main factions: One led by Isilon Hapilon and based in Basilan and one under the command of Radullan Sahiron in Sulu. They have a combined strength of 500 cadres (2015 estimate) and while cooperating logistically and financially operate independently. BIIF is similarly split between branches: one led by Sheik Muhedeen Animbang (the former Vice Chairman for Military Affairs and Chief of Staff) and one under the charge of Esmail Abu Bakar (the former nominal leader of BIFF). Animbang's group is stronger in terms of numbers (300 compared to 100) and it has a greater capacity to steal weapons as well as manufacture its own. For further details, see Peter Chalk, "Terrorism in Southeast Asia:

Evolving Scope and Dimensions," in Erich Marquadt ed., *Combating Terrorism and Irregular Warfare: The Long War Against al-Qa'ida, the Islamic State* (New York: West Point Military Academy, Counter Terrorism Center, 2017).

24. Interviews, Manila, November 2016.
25. The southern Philippines constituted JI's third regional division (or "mantiqi").
26. The Philippines' chief piece of anti-terrorist legislation is enshrined in the Human Security Act (HSA), which was passed in 2007 (prior to that no specific anti-terror laws existed) and underwrites a range of extrajudicial surveillance and arrest powers for the police. However, the act imposes extremely severe penalties in the event that it is judged to have been employed inappropriately, including a prison term of up to 12 years. In addition, if a person is charged under the HSA and subsequently found to be innocent, he/she has the legal right to demand 500,000 pesos (US $125) compensation for each day of detention—the cost of which is personally borne by the arresting officer. As a result, the law has only been used once since its inception.
27. Interviews, Manila, November 2017.
28. Sahiron is very insular in orientation and mostly focused on criminal endeavors such as kidnapping and extortion.
29. Interview, Manila, 2017.
30. Interviews, Kuala Lumpur, September 2015. See also Peter Chalk, *Black Flag Rising: ISIL in Southeast Asia and Australia* (Canberra: ASPI Strategy Report, December 2015), 25–26.
31. "Vice Foreign Minister Cheng Guoping Chairs the 4th China-Indonesia Counterterrorism Consultation," Ministry of Foreign Affairs of the Peoples Republic of China, December 03, 2015, available online at http://www.fmprc.gov.cn/mfa_eng/wjbxw/t1321795.shtml, as of January 31, 2017.
32. See, for example, "Rodrigo Duterte Wants US Troops 'to Leave Philippines,'" *BBC News,* October 26, 2016, available online at http://www.bbc.com/news/world-asia-37773706, as of January 31, 2017.
33. Many experts believe that the real intention of Duterte's overtures to Beijing has been to boost economic ties and reestablish channels of communication than to institute an entirely new defense partnership with China. Author interviews, Manila, November 2016.
34. "Foreign Ministry Spokesperson Geng Shuang's Regular Press Conference," Ministry of Foreign Affairs of the People's Republic of China, October 10, 2016, available online at http://www.fmprc.gov.cn/mfa_eng/xwfw_665399/s2510_665401/t1404541.shtml, as of January 31, 2017.

35. "Theory and Practice of De-Radicalization in a Counter-Terrorism Context: Global Knowledge and Local Experience," People's Public Security Service University, Beijing, November 14, 2016.
36. "U.S. Says Looking at More Counter-Terrorist Cooperation with China," *Today*, July 26, 2016, available online at http://m.todayonline.com/world/us-says-looking-more-counter-terrorism-cooperation-china, as of January 31, 2017.
37. The Political and Security Community is one of three pillars of the proposed ASEAN Community. Launched in 2015, this institutional initiative is primarily aimed at transforming ASEAN into a more consolidated regional bloc that can take decisive, unified action to address various state and non-state challenges likely to affect Southeast Asia in coming years. For further details see Peter Chalk, *ASEAN Ascending: Achieving 'Centrality' in the Emerging Asian Order* (Canberra: ASPI Strategy Report, March 2015).

References

Mohanad Hage Ali (2016), "China's Proxy War in Syria: Revealing the Role of Uyghur Fighters," *Al Arabiya News*, March 2, 2016, available online at https://english.alarabiya.net/en/perspective/analysis/2016/03/02/China-s-proxy-war-in-Syria-Revealing-the-role-of-Uyghur-fighters-.html, as of January 29, 2017.

Rommel Banlaoi (2016), "Uyghur Militants in Southeast Asia: Should PH Be Worried?" *The Rappler*, July 13, 2016, available online at http://www.rappler.com/thought-leaders/118137-uyghur-militants-southeast-asia-philippines, as of January 22, 2017.

Nicolas Becquelin (2004), "Staged Development in Xinjinag," China Quarterly 178 (2004): 377.

Uran Botobekov (2017), "What's Are China's Stakes in Syria?" *The Diplomat*, January 27, 2017, available online at http://thediplomat.com/2017/01/whats-are-chinas-stakes-in-syria/, as of January 28, 2017.

Francis Chan (2016), "Officials Fear that Militants from China's Xinjiang May Join Local Extremists and Launch Attacks," *Straits Times*, July 21, 2016.

Qingzhedn Chen (2016), "Uyghurs' Presence Adds to Southeast Asia's Security Challenges," *Global Risks Insights*, January 15, 2016, available online at http://globalriskinsights.com/2016/01/uyghurs-presence-adds-to-southeast-asias-security-challenges/, as of January 17, 2017.

Gaye Christoffersen (1993), "Xinjiang and the Great Islamic Circle: Impact of Transnational Forces on Chinese Regional Economic Planning," China Quarterly 133 (1993): 149.

David Eimer (2009a), "As China Reels from 184 Deaths in Urunqi Riots, a Beaten Woman Fears for Her Husband," *The Telegraph*, July 11, 2009.

David Eimer (2009b),"Is China Fraying? Racial Killings and Heavy-Handed Policxy Stirs Up a Repressed and Dangerous Province," *The Economist*, July 09, 2009.

Graham Fuller and Jonathan Lipman (2004), "Islam in Xinjiang," in S. Frederick Starr ed., *China's Muslim Borderland* (Armonk, NY: M.E. Sharpe, 2004), 331.

Rohan Gunaratna (2015), "The Rise of Islamic State: Terrorism's New face in Asia," in *From the Desert to World Cities: The New Terrorism* (Singapore: Konrad Adenauer Stifung, 2015), 15–16.

Jonathan Kaiman (2013), "Islamist Group Claims Responsibility for Attack on China's Tiananmen Square," *The Guardian*, November 25, 2013.

Jonathan Kaiman (2014),"Urumqi: Car and Bomb Attacks Kill Dozens," *The Guardian*, May 22, 2014.

Jonathan Kaiman (2017),"China Mass Stabbing: Deadly Knife Attack in Kunming," *BBC News*, March 02, 2014, available online at www.bbc.co.uk/news/world/asia-china-2640237, as of January 17, 2017.

Yenni Kwok (2015), "Is There a Uyghur Terrorist Build Up Taking Place in Southeast Asia?" *Time*, December 28, 2015.

Teddy Ng (2014), "Xinjiang to Work with National Security Commission to Curb Violence," *The South China Morning Post*, March 07, 2014.

Austin Ramzy (2009), "After Deadly Riots, Ethnic Tension Heats Up in Urumqi," *The Telegraph*, July 07, 2009.

Barry Sautman (1998), "Preferential Politics for Ethnic Minorities in China: The Case of Xinjiang," Nationalism and Ethnic Politics 4/1–2 (1998): 2.

Bilveer Singh (2016), "Southeast Asian Terrorism: The Rise of the Uyghur Factor," *Eurasia Review*, January 05, 2016.

Joanne Smith (2002), "Making Culture Matter: Symbols, Spatial and Social Boundaries Between Uyghurs and Han Chinese," Asia Ethnicity 3/2 (2002): 156.

Jacob Zenn (2014), "Undocumented Uyghur Migrants Find New Route to Southeast Asia," China Brief 14/17, September 10, 2014, https://jamestown.org/program/undocumented-uyghur-migrants-find-new-route-to-southeast-asia/.

CHAPTER 13

Chinese Investments in the Arab Maelstrom

James M. Dorsey

Avoiding the Pitfalls of Diverging Interests

An ongoing Chinese debate on the management of relations with the United States informed China's first articulation of a Middle East policy with the publication in January 2016 of an Arab Policy Paper[1] on the eve of President Xi's visit to the Middle East and North Africa, the first by a Chinese head of state in seven years. The paper shied away from spelling out concrete policies. Instead, it reiterated long-standing principles of Chinese foreign policy like non-interference in the internal affairs of other states, dialogue and win-win modes of cooperation as they applied to the Arab world and emphasised China's key interests in the region: economics,

Dr. James M. Dorsey is a senior fellow at the S. Rajaratnam School of International Studies, co-director of the University of Würzburg's Institute for Fan Culture, and the author of *The Turbulent World of Middle East Soccer* blog, a book with the same title, ***Comparative Political Transitions between Southeast Asia and the Middle East and North Africa***, co-authored with Dr. Teresita Cruz-Del Rosario and ***Shifting Sands, Essays on Sports and Politics in the Middle East and North Africa***.

J. M. Dorsey (✉)
S. Rajaratnam School of International Studies, Singapore, Singapore

Institute of Fan Culture, University of Würzburg, Würzburg, Germany

A. Arduino, X. Gong (eds.), *Securing the Belt and Road Initiative*,
https://doi.org/10.1007/978-981-10-7116-4_13

energy, counter-terrorism, security, technical cooperation and its One Belt, One Road initiative.

In the process, the paper failed to answer influential Chinese blogger Ma Xialing's question: "What's China's strategy in the Middle East?" Xialing argued two years earlier that China does not have a strategy. "Strategy, for one, depends on theory. In this regard, China still follows the general principle set out by Deng Xiaoping – we don't really care too much about outside developments, for now we just make our economy stronger. In Zhongnanhai (the headquarters of the Chinese Communist Party), leaders don't care much about Middle East, but about China's domestic interest. Moreover, even in the times of (former president) Hu Jintao and Xi Jinping, China does not aim to develop strategy, but rather short-term policies. That is why China will not play an important role in the Middle East… China is hesitant to get deeply involved in the Middle East, as it is very complex and a troublesome place. China is not prepared for the risks that could be encountered there. Often, Chinese political leaders and scholars say that the Middle East is a graveyard for empires, as many big empires through history collapsed after getting involved and failing in the Middle East," Xialing noted.[2]

If Ma Xiang's criticism seemed reasonable in 2016, it looks very different in 2017 with the rise of Donald J. Trump as president of the United States. What seemed then failure to develop a policy, allows China in the era of Trump to keep its options open amid uncertainty about what US policy will be not only in the Middle East and North Africa but also towards China itself.[3] Trump has promised to adopt a much tougher stand on issues of trade and the South China Sea. Already, Trump initiated a more hostile attitude towards Iran, a key Chinese partner in the Middle East, imposing sanctions on the Islamic republic in his first weeks in office.[4]

While China has exploited Trump's apparent isolationism and inclination to back away from the US role as a champion of liberal values to project itself as the guarantor of globalisation, it remains reluctant to inherit the US mantle of the world's policeman. That is particularly evident in the Middle East and North Africa, were China maintains its hesitancy to become embroiled in the region's pitfalls even though facts on the ground inevitably push Chinese leaders towards greater engagement. And the stakes for China are rising as its interests in the region mushroom.

Energy and resource security are key to China's continued economic growth and rising standards of living on which the legitimacy of the

Communist Party of China (CCP) rides. Add to that the geo-strategic importance of Middle Eastern and North African states as hubs for access to African and European markets and their centrality to China's One Belt, One Road strategy is obvious.

Finally, as was evident in China's complex compliance with past United Nations sanctions against Iran and Xi's visit to the Middle East, balancing Chinese relations with rival Middle Eastern states as well as the United States as they relate to the region is increasingly resembling the act of a dancer on a tightrope.

China has sought to enhance its energy security within the limitations of its inter-dependency with the United States and its continued reliance on the US defence umbrella in the Gulf by investing significantly in resource-related sectors in Middle Eastern and North African states.

The region's increased economic and security importance to China is reflected in the fact that an estimated 60 per cent of Chinese exports travel through the Suez Canal. As a result, China has invested heavily in the channel's ports. Investments include a US $186 million joint venture to operate a container terminal in Port Said, a US $219 million expansion of the port's quay and the construction of a US $1 billion quay and US $416 million container terminal in Al-Adabiyya.[5]

China has also moved to ensure robustness by investing in a rail line that links the Israeli Red Sea port of Eilat with the Mediterranean Sea that would enable Chinese exports to circumvent the canal[6] as well as Israeli ports. Shanghai International Port Group won in 2015 a tender for the management of Haifa port[7] while China Harbour Engineering Co is building Israel's first private port in Ashdod at a cost of US $876 million.[8]

The need for robustness symbolised by the Israeli backup to the Suez Canal was driven home when Suez Canal ports experienced backlogs and closures in the wake of the 2011 popular revolt that toppled Egyptian President Hosni Mubarak and again in 2013 when a vessel in the canal belonging to China Ocean Shipping Group Company was hit by rocket-propelled grenades.[9]

Israel is but one toe in China's footprint and associated interests that are evident across the Eurasian landmass that it envisions as part of its One Belt, One Road initiative. In 2010, China overtook the European Union as Iran's largest trading partner,[10] and has more recently agreed to press ahead with the construction of a natural gas pipeline linking Iran with Pakistan.[11] The pipeline is part of a US $46 billion infrastructure spending plan in Pakistan, China's largest planned investment to date in any one single country.[12]

China's plans to invest in an array of Pakistani projects, including a 1700-mile trade route to the Gulf, illustrate the politics of its One Belt, One Road Initiative. Xi Jinping believes that he can achieve Chinese dominance through investment and inter-connected infrastructure. In doing so, China is convinced that it can succeed where the United States has failed. It expects its massive investment will serve as an incentive for Pakistan to step up its crackdown on Pakistani militants and to end the support of the country's intelligence service, Inter-Services Intelligence (ISI), for radical Islamist groups. China hopes moreover that Chinese-built transport infrastructure could spur economic development in its troubled northwestern province of Xinjiang where harsh measures against the cultural practices of the Uighurs have fuelled Islamist violence. A job boom in Xinjiang would allow the government to further dilute Xinjiang's Uighur population through the immigration of non-Uighurs.

Sun Degang Sun, the deputy director of Shanghai International Studies University's Middle East Institute, argued that China could afford to adopt its economically focussed approach because of its insistence on non-alignment and non-interference and differences in definitions of national interest between the West and China. In contrast to the West, which sees terrorism, proliferation of weapons of mass destruction and other great powers seeking political and military dominance in the Middle East as national security threats, China prioritises protection of its economic, trade and energy interests.[13]

Underlying the Chinese approach is the notion that rising living standards will enhance domestic stability and the security of the regime. These different definitions constitute the backbone of One Belt, One Road, described by Wu Jianmin, a member of the Chinese Foreign Ministry's foreign policy advisory group, a senior research fellow with the State Council of China and former ambassador to the United Nations and various European countries, as "the most expansive Chinese initiative ever."[14] Wu argued that the initiative was needed given that "the epi-centre of war and conflict is the Middle East and North Africa" and that "Iraq, Afghanistan and Libya prove that war does not solve problems."[15]

China's vast investments across Eurasia are rooted in a belief that geopolitics and economics ultimately mitigate in its favour. The era of a primary economic focus of oil-rich Gulf States on the United States and Europe ended in 2013 with a shift in trading patterns that pushed the

United States to second place in the Gulf and saw India moving Japan out of third place. "It's a shift from the old industrialised powers to the newly industrialised powers," said Tim Niblock, a renowned expert on Gulf-Asian relations.[16]

If the traditional US approach towards the Middle East and North Africa is rooted in the Washington Consensus, a set of value-oriented free market economic ideas, supported by international organisations such as the IMF and the World Bank, China's approach amounts in the words of political scientist Mojtaba Mahdavi to a non-ideological Beijing Consensus, a mercantilist policy that is "another form of neo-liberalism with Chinese characteristics"[17] focussed not only on securing resources and global transportation routes but also on access to consumer export markets and access to innovative technologies.

Leaving aside the sheer audacity and scope of Xi's Silk Road project that focusses on integrating the enormous swath of territories between China and the Middle East by concentrating on infrastructure, transportation, energy, telecommunications, technology and security, applying China's lofty principles is easier said than done and raises a host of unanswered questions. Its insistence on multi-polarity as opposed to US dominance in the Middle East implicitly means that the status of the United States would have to change before Washington would be willing to entertain the Chinese approach. The Trump era could well usher in an opportunity with the president's potential willingness to share the burden of guaranteeing regional security and insisting that the beneficiaries of a US shield pay what he describes as their fair share.

The Middle East: Testing the Boundaries of Non-Interference

The contours of China's policy debate as it relates to the Middle East and North Africa has been evident in the way Chinese officials, policy analysts and former ambassadors to the Middle East conceptualise China's approach in discussions with their scholarly Western and Arab colleagues. The debate is coloured by what appear to be generational differences. Often, older current and former Chinese officials appear to attribute greater importance to the formal aspects of political processes rather than political realities on the ground. One expression of that view is their emphasis on the outcomes of elections irrespective of whether they were free and fair and represent a voluntary expression of popular will. A case in point are Chinese official statements supporting the re-election in June 2014 of Syrian President Bashar al-Assad despite the fact that the vote lacked legitimacy or credibility in a country in which the government no longer is in control of all of its territory and has demonstrated a willingness to retain power irrespective of cost.

This approach camouflages Chinese support for autocratic regimes in the Middle East and North Africa behind a veil of declared non-interference in a country's domestic affairs and recognition of a government legitimately constituted in nominal terms. It is, despite Chinese denials, a policy akin to the US emphasis on stability in the region rather than adherence to liberal American values. It is a policy for which the United States, Europe and the international community have paid dearly given that it produced the violent and often brutal undercurrents of change that are sweeping the Middle East and North Africa as well as the emergence of jihadism, forces that increasingly also threaten Chinese interests.

Current and former Chinese officials often frame the debate by emphasising external rather than domestic drivers of crisis in the Middle East. To be sure, Chinese policymakers and politicians do not have to take into account powerful ethnic and national lobbies like the Israel, Gulf, Turkish, Armenian and Greek groupings that play an important role in the formulation of policy in the United States.

Yet, in the spirit of all foreign policy being a function of domestic policy, China is not void of domestic drivers that play an increasingly important role in its foreign policy making. Those drivers stem from evolving definitions of national interest and the increased number of players in China's foreign policy debates as China's global economic footprint expands.[18] These players include major state-owned enterprises such as national oil companies whose interests in the Middle East and North Africa have mushroomed. The oil companies argue that China's lack of engagement and insistence on non-intervention deprive the People's Republic of leverage needed to negotiate pricing and supply in energy contracts in a market that is virtually inelastic.[19] China's ambassador to Saudi Arabia, Li Chengwen, highlighted the scale of China's stake in the Middle East and North Africa when he noted in 2013 that 140 Chinese companies were involved in contracts worth US $18 billion in Saudi Arabia's construction, telecommunications, infrastructure and petrochemical sectors.[20]

The domestic drivers of Chinese foreign policy further involve popular insistence that the government ensure the safety and security of the growing number of Chinese nationals and jobs in the region. Of the Chinese companies active in Saudi Arabia, 70 employ a total of 16,000 Chinese workers.[21] Dubai boasts the Middle East's largest Chinese expatriate community with 200,000 nationals and an estimated 3000 companies.[22] China has framed its need to protect its expatriate nationals as humanitarian aid and used it to project itself as a global power[23] and justify its mushrooming military budget.[24]

A further driver of Chinese policy towards the Middle East and North Africa is mounting concern that jihadist groups like the Islamic State (IS) could fuel unrest among Uighurs, a Turkic-speaking people that has long felt culturally more akin to the region's Turkic trading partners than to the majority Han Chinese and Hui Muslims.[25]

These domestic drivers and the growing realisation that China will at the very least have to be opportunistic about adherence to its policy principles have helped to narrow the gap between hardliners and moderates. Hardliners favour a more assertive policy already visible since 2009 in China's soft military approach to the Middle East and North Africa as opposed to proponents of a more conservative policy that harks back to former Chinese leader Deng Xiaoping's maxim of keeping a low profile that would allow China to avoid challenging US regional hegemony and benefit from conflicts sapping US strength.[26] The gap is narrowed by the fact that China has de facto already let go of Deng Xiaoping's maxim.

Sun Degang acknowledged this by arguing that "the further expansion of China's soft military presence overseas is necessary to protect its growing foreign commercial investments and other interests, not to mention the safety of Chinese expatriate workers." He was referring to China's evacuation in 2011 of 35,000 workers from Libya with the help of Chinese naval vessels and Air Force aircraft diverted from anti-piracy operations off the Horn of Africa[27] as Col. Muammar Qaddafi's efforts to repress mass-anti-government protests turned violent. Sun Degang was also making reference to subsequent kidnappings of Chinese nationals in Sudan and Egypt's Sinai desert. The Libyan evacuation prompted President Hu in 2012 to identify the protection of nationals overseas as one of three new diplomatic priorities in his work report to the 18th Party Congress.[28] "You need to protect your overseas interests. We will do that in a cooperative way… It is not a zero-sum game," added Wu Jianmen, the foreign ministry advisor.[29]

The Middle East and North Africa's violent convolutions have persuaded some Chinese analysts that the region has become a testing ground for an inevitable adjustment of Chinese policy principles, including the notion of non-intervention. Their views are rooted in realities on the ground as well as Mao Zedong's belief that the Middle East and North Africa was a key arena for the struggle against the hegemony of superpowers.[30] Mao's assessment, like Chinese approaches to the region today, was driven by China's definition of its national security interests rather than a desire to resolve the Middle East and North Africa's seemingly intractable problems.

As a result, these scholars warn that China cannot afford to further avoid factoring into its policies profound processes that are shaking the fundaments of the Middle East and North Africa's nation state structure, post-colonial borders and security architecture. Scholars like Israel expert Yiyi Chen noted that protection of Chinese economic interests had already forced Beijing to become more flexible in its adherence to the notions of mutual respect for sovereignty and territorial integrity, mutual non-aggression, non-interference in each other's internal affairs, equality and mutual benefit and peaceful coexistence that were adopted in 1954 in a joint statement on peaceful cooperation by the leaders of China, India and Burma.[31] Chen cited as an example Chinese shuttle diplomacy between Sudan and South Sudan on the back of Chinese investments in Sudanese oil fields and South Sudanese infrastructure.[32] Similarly, Chen argued that it was not a question of if but when China would seek to mediate in the Israeli Palestinian conflict.[33] China has also unsuccessfully sought to arbitrate in Afghanistan and Syria.

Changing patterns in China's foreign policy driven by events in the Middle East and North Africa were evident in the constructive role China played in UN deliberations that led to the adoption of the principle of the right to protect provided the use of force had been endorsed by the Security Council[34] and in the evolution of Chinese defence policy. A Chinese defence white paper identified in 2013 the protection of overseas energy resources and Chinese nationals abroad as a major security concern to be shouldered by the Chinese military.[35] The shift in Chinese policy was facilitated by the fact that China had never clearly defined what would constitute intervention in the domestic affairs of another country,[36] a vagueness that allowed China in the 1950s and 1960s to support revolutionary movements in Africa, South America and Southeast Asia.[37]

Building on the evolution of China's positions, Middle East scholar Liu Zhongmin warned that "the deep political changes in the Middle East, the restructuring of the regional system and the strategy adjustment of the U.S., Europe and other Great Powers…suggests that it is urgent for China to work out a mid-term and long-term diplomatic strategy toward the Middle East and corresponding mechanism and measures."[38] This, Liu argued, would have to involve adhering to the principle of non-intervention "with an innovative mind" that would "enrich the connotation of the principle from time to time."

Liu suggested China could increase its influence in the region through increased aid, investment and efforts to mediate in disputes. China should "dare to propose to the related states more practical and specific resolutions in line with international morality" and expand its contact with opposition groups in the region, Liu argued. In line with the near consensus among Chinese scholars and officials that puts the Middle East in the context of China's relations with the United States and determines the international posture China should adopt, Liu maintained that China for a considerable time to come would have to compensate for structural limitations of its power and political disadvantages. These limitations include the lack of the kind of soft and hard power available to the United States and persistent tension with the Uighurs.

China's limitations notwithstanding, some analysts suggest that China has no choice but to position itself as a global power sooner rather than later. Renmin University international relations professor Pang Zhongying, one of China's most outspoken scholars on the issue, argued that "China should declare clearly that China intervenes globally, regionally, and multilaterally, but conditionally" adding that "a global China . . . has to intervene."[39]

In a variation on the theme, Peking University international relations scholar Wang Yizhou speaking to the Beijing Review sought to address the issues posed by non-interventionism by developing the concept of "creative involvement" that would allow it to participate in efforts to resolve conflicts with "cautious, creative and constructive mediation"; create institutions; and provide global public goods, "imprinting the future world with (China's) contributions." Wang argued that "creative involvement is a concept that focuses on diplomatic, commercial and military fields and stresses improving flexibility and skills of foreign affairs-related departments. It can be considered as a new direction for China's diplomacy. It will be a new option for China's diplomacy based on its new position and strength as well as its culture and traditions. It will bring a Chinese style to the world stage during the process of the peaceful development of the country."[40]

Christina Y. Lin, a former US government official and China expert, noted that China's commercial and financial muscle gave it a leg up on the United States. China was not only armed with a larger war chest, but also able to neutralise market forces by skipping over tenders and ignoring the rules of level-playing field competition. "In addition to bilateral agreements, China…provides competitive package deals that may include military aid in addition to concessional loans," Lin said.[41]

Expanding China's Naval Horizons

Doubts about US reliability in the Middle East that were first bolstered by President Barak Obama's declared pivot towards Asia and then by the rise of Trump reinforce Chinese concerns that differences with Washington over disputes in the South and East China Seas or Taiwan could prompt a US naval blockade of the Malacca Straits through which much of China's energy imports flow. These concerns constitute a basis for China's gradually more assertive military policy in the Middle East as well as its massive investment in naval modernisation. They also explain the creation of a string of ports that link China to commercial and refuelling facilities in the Indian Ocean and the Gulf and a network of railways that could play a key military transport and logistics role once China decides to project power across Eurasia,[42] and pipelines connecting it to Central Asia and the Middle East.[43]

Like the Middle East's multiple conflicts and geostrategic relevance, China's gradual emergence as a global naval power threatens the integrity of its principle of non-interventionism. The challenge was reflected in a Chinese defence white paper published in 2015 that outlined significant changes in the role assigned to the military that was expanded among others to include protection of Chinese interests abroad.[44] Military analysts suggest that it is at best a matter of time until China will have the capability to act in line with the paper once it has completed the training of troops tasked with protecting overseas investments and Chinese nationals and put in place the necessary transportation and logistics infrastructure. Meanwhile, China in situations of emergency will likely have to limit itself to smaller-scale hostage rescue missions.[45]

The change in China's defence and foreign policy posture will probably be further fuelled by its future acquisition of additional aircraft carriers that in turn will heighten the need for overseas bases. This, cautioned US Naval War College scholar Nan Li, could "contradict China's desire to project the image to the world that, unlike the rise of other great powers, China's rise will be peaceful."[46]

The change in China's approach became formal with the 2015 defence white paper that emphasised China's intention to improve and project its naval capabilities far beyond its coastline.[47] The International Business Herald, a paper published by the Xinhua News Agency, reported that China was likely to establish over the next decade three strings of "overseas strategic support bases" totalling 18 facilities: a North Indian Ocean supply line with bases in Pakistan, Sri Lanka, Myanmar; a Western Indian Ocean supply line with bases in Djibouti, Yemen, Oman, Kenya, Tanzania and Mozambique; and a central-south Indian ocean supply with bases in Seychelles and Madagascar.[48] In addition to its naval strategy, China has sought to forge broader military relations with various Middle Eastern and North African nations through joint exercises and closer cooperation.

Navigating Regional Rivalries

Xi's January 2016 visit to the Middle East illustrated the increasing degree to which China is walking a tightrope in its efforts to avoid being bogged down and mired in the region's numerous wars, conflicts, disputes and animosities. That is proving to be a gargantuan, if not impossible task. While Xi made sure that he visited both Riyadh and Tehran, he left little doubt that the lifting of international sanctions allowed China to reinforce ties with Iran with which it has far more in common than with Saudi Arabia.

Xi's visit to the kingdom was accompanied by talk of brotherly relations and strategic cooperation. The rhetoric, however, did little to mask serious differences on issues ranging from Syria to Saudi propagation of Wahhabism, a puritan interpretation of Islam that many fear breeds jihadism, and a relative decline in Chinese reliance on Saudi oil and the fact that the Gulf plays a secondary role compared to Iran in the One Belt, One Road initiative. The overland component if One Belt, One Road passes in its current conception through Iran rather than the Gulf while the maritime touches the Gulf only on the Red Sea approach to the Suez Canal.

Chinese officials worry that alleged Saudi funding of Islamic schools or madrasahs in Xinjiang may be encouraging Uighur militants who have staged several attacks in a low-intensity campaign for equal rights and autonomy, if not independence. Saudi officials have assured their Chinese counterparts that they do not support the violence despite the fact that the Uighurs, some of whom have joined IS, are Turkic-speaking Sunni Muslims. Those assurances appear to have done little to put Chinese concerns to rest. "Our biggest worry in the Middle East isn't oil – it's Saudi Arabia," a Chinese analyst told the Asia Times.[49]

Chinese media in 2002 questioned Saudi Arabia's ability to cope with the threat of Wahhabism breeding radicalism[50] and hinted at Xinjiang's potential in becoming an irritant in Chinese-Arab relations. In response to the media reports, Saudi Arabia's Arab News rankled China's ire in an editorial that compared China to Israel in the way it dealt with Xinjiang. The Arab News referred to Xinjiang as East Turkestan, the anti-Chinese Uighur reference to the region.[51] In his PhD thesis, Martin Harrison cautioned that "a prolonged downturn in the Xinjiang security situation would have consequences to which Riyadh could not long tum a blind eye."[52]

Religious affinity is not something China has to worry about with Shiite-majority Iran, which has long projected itself as a revolutionary not a sectarian power. China moreover supports the Iranian-backed regime of Syrian President Bashar al-Assad and favoured Russian intervention in Syria to prop up the Assad regime—a position that puts it at odds with Saudi Arabia that backs the rebels and has hinted at intervening militarily on their behalf. Russian and US airstrikes against Saudi-backed Islamist rebels have allowed Syrian and Kurdish forces to gain increasing control of much of Syria's borders, making it more difficult for Uighurs from northwest China to find their way to Syria.

China's subtle shift towards Iran is also visible in the oil market. Iran is determined to win back Chinese market share with the lifting of the sanctions. Iran expects to boost oil exports by 500,000 barrels a day, much of which it hopes will go to China. Iran's oil plans put it in direct competition with Saudi Arabia, which had emerged as one of China's largest suppliers. That has begun to change with China apparently shifting its reliance on oil away from Saudi Arabia. Chinese oil imports from the kingdom rose a mere 2 per cent in 2015 while its purchase of Russian oil jumped almost 30 per cent. The shift is likely to create an opening for Iran at Saudi Arabia's expense.[53]

Despite the lofty pledges of increased trade during Xi's visit, Chinese self-centeredness in its management of economic ties called in question in Middle Eastern and North African minds China's sincerity and commitment. Iran cancelled in 2014 a US $2.5 billion contract with the China National Petroleum Corporation (CNPC) for the development of the South Azadegan oil field citing repeated delays as well as the high cost and poor quality of Chinese equipment and services.[54] Iranian businessmen were cautious on the eve of Xi's visit, raising questions about the degree to which China would benefit from the lifting of international sanctions against the Islamic republic. The businessmen charged that Chinese banks and businesses had exploited the sanctions to charge them high commissions and delay deliveries in the knowledge that they had no choice but to buy Chinese products.

The stakes for Chinese companies are high. Iran has said that with sanctions lifted it would need up to US $50 billion in foreign investment in energy; road, rail and air transportation; agriculture; and industries such as household, textile and ceramics.[55] In a symbolic gesture, the first train loaded with Chinese products to traverse China's One Belt, One Road land expanse arrived in February 2016 from China's eastern Zhejiang province in Tehran within weeks of Xi's visit. Mohsen Pourseyed Aqayi, the head of Iran's railway company, greeted the train, which will operate on a once-a-month schedule in the presence of the ambassadors of China and Turkmenistan with the words: "The revival of the Silk Road is crucial for the countries on its route."[56]

In a speech during his Middle East tour to the Arab League in Cairo, Xi argued that "dialogue and development" offered the solution—a tough proposition in a part of the world in which opposing parties either refuse to talk to each other or only go through the motions to ensure that they are viewed as being constructive with no intention of arriving at a negotiated resolution. Xi suggested that China would succeed where others had failed by building a "cooperative partnership network for win-win outcomes" in the framework of One Belt, One Road and the establishment of the AIIB, the Chinese-led infrastructure bank.[57]

The list of failed Chinese initiatives involves many of the region's major disputes. It includes efforts to bridge the gap between Sudan and South Sudan in 2011 and 2014,[58] half-hearted Chinese attempts in 2012 and 2013 to negotiate a political solution in Syria,[59] and an Israeli-Palestinian peace deal. The Israeli-Palestinian and Syrian efforts were based on four-point plans put forward by Beijing. The Israeli-Palestinian one died a quiet death after it was rejected by Israel[60] while the Syrian plan failed to generate serious interest.[61] The Sudanese, Israeli-Palestinian and Syrian initiatives constituted nonetheless an early testing of concepts of "constructive" or "creative" intervention put forward in 2010 and 2011 by scholars Zhao Huasheng and Wang Yizhou.[62]

The failures notwithstanding, Chinese Foreign Minister Wang Yi signalled his country's recognition that it will progressively have to move from non-interference to active engagement in a speech in 2013 to the United Nations General Assembly. China intended to play a "more proactive and constructive role" in the world's hot spots and provide "public goods to the international community,"[63] Wang said. Wang was building on President Hu's statement in 2004 that Chinese diplomacy should "enhance the capability of protecting interests overseas, improve relevant laws and regulations, strengthen the early-warning and fast-response system, improve the style of work and enthusiastically serve Chinese citizens and legal persons in foreign countries."[64]

China's recognition of changing realities on the ground was also on display in its shifting approach towards Afghanistan, a prime case study for how domestic issues make it increasingly difficult for China to remain aloof to developments beyond its borders, insist on the principle of non-interference and attempt to make economics and investments the core drivers of its foreign policy. Stability in Afghanistan is of vital interest to China. The Central Asian country's eastern tongue, the Wakhan Corridor, barely touches China's borders, but it potentially could serve as a route into Xinjiang for Uighur rebels abroad who take advantage of the region's porous borders.

Chinese engagement in Afghanistan is further driven by the withdrawal of the bulk of NATO forces from the country and the United States' more limited military commitment to a country in which China has invested heavily. China has poured money into the world's second largest copper mine in Afghanistan as well as an oil field in the country. "Chinese companies can't go there without U.S. security. We hope the U.S. keep their troops in Afghanistan. The U.S. can't just leave after 14 years of killing," said Pan.[65]

China's concern is heightened by the fact that the scala of jihadist and Islamist groups operating in Afghanistan includes not only the Taliban, IS and Al-Qaeda but also the East Turkestan Islamic Movement (ETIM). East Turkistan is the name nationalist Uighurs and pan-Turkists use to identify Xinjiang. China's effective support for autocratic governments or governments whose legitimacy is contested under the guise of non-interference has reinforced perceptions among Uighur nationalists and Islamists and their jihadist allies of China as a pillar of the status quo.

China blames the increasingly real threat emanating from instability in Afghanistan on US and Saudi mismanagement of Islamist forces that fought the Soviets in the 1980s and the US invasion of Afghanistan in 2001. "We gave a lot of aid to the mujahedeen in Afghanistan. They fell into the hands of jihadists," said Pan. Pan was referring to the anti-Soviet Islamists who spawned jihadist groups across Asia, the Middle East and North Africa.[66]

To achieve its goal in Afghanistan, China has stepped up its contacts with the government and invited Taliban and former Taliban for visits to the mainland. In one instance China brought former Taliban officials with close ties to Pakistan's intelligence agency together with an Afghan government envoy in Urumqi[67] for what Foreign Minister Wan termed an "Afghan-led, Afghan-owned" reconciliation process.[68] On an earlier visit to Kabul, Wan announced China's intention to help Afghanistan become a "unified, stable, developing, and friendly" country. [69]

Conclusion

Volatile, often brutal and bloody political transition in the Middle East and North Africa that is characterised by sectarianism and national aspirations of ethnic and ethno-religious groups challenges long-standing principles of Chinese foreign and defense policy, including notions of non-interference, win-win economically driven policies and a rejection of the development of a foreign military presence. The challenge in the framework of China's rising global posture as a superpower is forcing China in deed rather than word to gradually compromise if not abandon its lofty principles in a bid to secure its increasingly massive investments in the Middle East and North Africa and ensure the safety of rapidly growing Chinese expatriate communities.

Notes

1. Xinhua, Full text of China's Arab Policy Paper, 13 January 2016, http://news.xinhuanet.com/english/china/2016-01/13/c_135006619.htm.
2. Ma. Xiaolin, #38 Event Report: Islamic Caliphate in Iraq: What Can China Do? thinkINchina, 22 October 2014, http://www.thinkinchina.asia/38-event-report/.

3. Tom Phillips, Trump keeps China on hold with letter but no phone call for Xi Jinping, The Guardian, 9 February 2017, https://www.theguardian.com/us-news/2017/feb/09/trump-china-letter-no-phone-call-xi-jinping.
4. US Department of the Treasury, Iran-related Designations; Non-proliferation Designations; Counter Terrorism Designations; Balkans Designation Update, 3 February 2017, https://www.treasury.gov/resource-center/sanctions/OFAC-Enforcement/Pages/20170203.aspx.
5. Emma Scott, China's Silk Road: A Foothold in the Suez Canal, but Looking to Israel, China Brief 14, no. 19, 2014, http://www.ccs.org.za/wp-content/uploads/2014/11/CCS_Commentary_Suez_and_China_ES_2014.pdf.
6. Ibid., Scott.
7. Avi Bar-Eli, Chinese company to run new Haifa port, Haaretz, 24 March 2015, http://www.haaretz.com/business/.premium-1.648483.
8. Rami Amichai and Ari Rabinovitc, Chinese firm starts work on new Ashdod port, as Haifa workers strike, 28 October 2014, Haaretz, http://www.haaretz.com/news/national/1.623216.
9. David Barnett (7 September 2013). *Al Furqan Brigades claim 2 attacks on ships in Suez Canal, threaten more*, The Long War journal, http://www.longwarjournal.org/archives/2013/09/al_furqan_brigades_claim_two_a.php.
10. Najmeh Bozorgmehr, China overtakes EU to become Tehran's largest trading ally, The Irish Times, 9 February 2010, https://www.irishtimes.com/news/china-overtakes-eu-to-become-tehran-s-largest-trading-ally-1.619509.
11. Saeed Shah, China to Build Pipeline from Iran to Pakistan, The Wall Street Journal, 9 April 2015, http://www.wsj.com/articles/china-to-build-pipeline-from-iran-to-pakistan-1428515277.
12. Saeed Shah and Jeremy Page, China Readies $46 Billion for Pakistan Trade Route, The Wall Street Journal, 16 April 2015, http://www.wsj.com/articles/china-to-unveil-billions-of-dollars-in-pakistan-investment-1429214705.
13. Sun Degang, China's Soft Military Presence in the Middle East, Middle East Institute, 11 March 2015. http://www.mei.edu/content/map/china%E2%80%99s-soft-military-presence-middle-east.
14. Wu Jianmin, One Belt and One Road, Asia's Stability and Prosperity, RSIS Distinguished Public Lecture, 12 March 2015.
15. Ibid., Wu Jianmin.
16. Tim Niblock, The Gulf, the West and Asia: Shifts in the Gulf's Global Relations, Lecture at 4th International Forum on Asia and the Middle East: International Conference on Great Powers and the Middle East Political & Social Transformation, Shanghai, 10 September 2014.

17. Mojtaba Mahdavi, Is China Becoming a New Hegemony in the Middle East? International Conference on China in the Middle East, Indiana University and Peking University, Beijing, 17–18 March 2015.
18. Linda Jakobsen and Dean Knox (2010). *New Foreign Policy Actors in China*, Stockholm International Peace Research Institute, http://books.sipri.org/files/PP/SIPRIPP26.pdf.
19. Chaoling Feng, Embracing Interdependence: The Dynamics of China and the Middle East, Brookings Doha Center, 2015, http://www.brookings.edu/~/media/research/files/papers/2015/04/28-middle-east-china-feng/en-embracing-interdependence-pdf.pdf.
20. Ash-Sharq Al-Awsat, Saudi–Chinese trade increases by 14 percent, 20 November 2013, http://english.aawsat.com/2013/11/article55323012/saudi-chinese-trade-increases-by-14-percent.
21. Naser M. Al-Tamimi, China-Saudi Arabia Relations, 1990–2012: Marriage of Convenience or Strategic Alliance? London: Routledge, 2014, p. 126–143.
22. Dania Thafer, After the Financial Crisis: China-Dubai Economic Relations, Middle East-Asia Project (MAP), 15 September 2013, http://www.mei.edu/content/after-financial-crisis-dubai-china-economic-relations.
23. Chengqiu Wu, Sovereignty, Human Rights, and Responsibility: Changes in China's Response to International Humanitarian Crises, Journal of Chinese Political Science/Association of Chinese Political Studies Vol. 15:1, p. 71–97.
24. Ministry of National Defense Chinese Ambassador to India: New security concepts should be nurtured, 24 April 2009, http://eng.mod.gov.cn/Opinion/2015-04/24/content_4581804.htm.
25. Enrico Fardella, China's Debate on the Middle East and North Africa: A Critical Review, *Mediterranean Quarterly*, Vol. 26:1, p. 5–25.
26. Globalsecurity.org. *Deng Xiaoping's "24-Character Strategy*, http://www.globalsecurity.org/military/world/china/24-character.htm.
27. Shaio H. Zerba, China's Libya Evacuation Operation: A New Diplomatic Imperative: Overseas Citizen Protection, Journal of Contemporary China, Vol. 23:90, 2014, p. 1093–1112.
28. Xinhua. 2012. Full text of Hu Jintao's report at 18th Party Congress, November 17, http://news.xinhuanet.com/english/special/18cpcnc/2012-11/17/c_131981259.htm.
29. Ibid., Wu Jianmen.
30. Yitzhak Shichor, The Middle East in China's Foreign Policy, 1949–1977, Cambridge: Cambridge University Press, 1977 p. 160–161.
31. Ministry of Foreign Affairs of the People's Republic of China, China's Initiation of the Five Principles of Peaceful Co-Existence, http://www.fmprc.gov.cn/mfa_eng/ziliao_665539/3602_665543/3604_665547/t18053.shtml.

32. Yiyi Chen, Will China Interfere in the Israeli-Palestinian Conflict? Middle East Institute, 6 May 2015, http://www.mei.edu/content/map/will-china-interfere-israeli-palestinian-conflict.
33. Ibid., Chen.
34. Gareth Evans, Responding to atrocities: the new geopolitics of intervention, SIPRI Yearbook, Oxford: Oxford University Press, 2012, p. 30.
35. Chinese State Council, The Diversified Employment of China's Armed Forces, Defence White Paper, Beijing, April 2013, http://eng.mod.gov.cn/Database/WhitePapers/.
36. Mathieu Duchatel, Oliver Braunel, and Zhou Hang, Protecting China's Overseas Interest: The Slow Shift Away from Non-interference, Stockholm International Peace Research Institute, June 2014, http://books.sipri.org/files/PP/SIPRIPP41.pdf.
37. Mikhail Barabanov, Vasiliy Kashin and Konstantin Makienko, *Shooting Star*, China's Military Machine in the 21st Century, Minneapolis: East View Press, 2012, section 3.1.
38. Liu Zhongmin, Political Unrest in the Middle East and China's Response in Sun Sun Degang and Yahia H. Zoubir (eds), *Building a New Silk Road: China and the Middle East in the 21st Century*, Shanghai: World Affairs Press, 2014, p. 106–125.
39. Pang Zhongying, Through Chinese eyes: Pang Zhongying (part 1), The Interpreter, 22 December 2012, http://www.lowyinterpreter.org/post/2011/12/22/Through-Chinese-eyes-Pang-Zhongying-(part-1).aspx.
40. Beijing Review, New Direction for China's Diplomacy, 8 March 2012, http://www.bjreview.com.cn/world/txt/2012-03/05/content_439626.htm#.
41. Christina Y. Lin, China's Strategic Shift Toward the Region of the Four Seas: The Middle Kingdom Arrives in the Middle East, IDC Herzliya Rubin Center for Research in International Affairs, 2013, http://www.rubincenter.org/2013/03/chinas-strategic-shift-toward-the-region-of-the-four-seas-the-middle-kingdom-arrives-in-the-middle-east/.
42. Pakistan Defence, China's Military Railway Transport, 24 June 2010, http://defence.pk/threads/china%C2%92s-military-railway-transport.62935/.
43. John McLaughlin, The Great Powers in the New Middle East in John B. Alterman (ed), Rocky Harbours: Taking Stock of the Middle East in 2015, Washington: Center for Strategic and International Studies, 2015.
44. The State Council Information Office of the People's Republic of China, China's Military Strategy, May 2015, http://www.chinadaily.com.cn/china/2015-05/26/content_20820628.htm.

45. John Calabrese, Fate of the Dragon in the Year of the Red Fire Monkey: China and the Middle East 2016, Middle East Institute, 3 February 2016, http://www.mei.edu/content/map/fate-dragon-year-monkey-china-and-middle-east-2016.
46. Nan Li, The Evolution of China's Naval Strategy and Capabilities: From "Near Coast" and "Near Seas" to "Far Seas," Asian Security, Vol. 5:2, p. 144–169.
47. Xinhua, Full Text: China's Military Strategy, 26 May 2015, http://en.people.cn/n/2015/0526/c90785-8897779-7.html.
48. China Defense Mashup, Chinese paper advises PLA Navy to build overseas military bases, 8 January 2013, http://www.china-defense-mashup.com/chinese-paper-advises-pla-navy-to-build-overseas-military-bases.html.
49. David P. Goldman, Saudi Arabia stews in policy hell: Spengler, Asia Times, 3 January 2016, http://atimes.com/2016/01/saudi-arabia-in-policy-hell/.
50. China Daily, Saudis face dilemma over Islamic militancy, 2 February 2002, http://www.highbeam.com/doc/1P2-8785765.html.
51. Arab News, Uighurs, 24 March 2002.
52. Martin Harrison, Relations between the Gulf Oil Monarchies and the People's Republic of China, 1971–2005, Lancaster University, Unpublished PhD thesis, 2006.
53. Bloomberg News, Russia Races Past Saudi Arabia in Tussle for Chinese Oil Market, 21 October 2015, http://www.bloomberg.com/news/articles/2015-10-21/russia-races-past-saudi-arabia-in-tussle-for-chinese-oil-market.
54. Benoit Faucon Iran Cancels $2.5 Billion Contract with Chinese Oil Company, The Wall Street Journal, 29 April 2014, http://www.wsj.com/articles/SB10001424052702303939404579531111999051656.
55. Charles Clover, Heba Saleh, Najmeh Bozorgmehr and Simeon Kerr, Xi faces diplomatic test on first Middle East visit, Financial Times, 18 January 2016, http://www.ft.com/cms/s/0/6ce8bb08-bdbf-11e5-846f-79b0e3d20eaf.html?ftcamp=published_links%2Frss%2Fworld_asia-pacific_china%2Ffeed%2F%2Fproduct#axzz3xcDnbvIw.
56. Agence France Press, First 'Silk Road' train arrives in Tehran from China, 16 February 2016, https://news.yahoo.com/first-silk-road-train-arrives-tehran-china-134703954.html?soc_src=mail&soc_trk=ma.
57. Xi Jingping, Work Together for a Bright Future of China-Arab Relations, China Daily, 22 January 2016, http://www.chinadaily.com.cn/world/2016xivisitmiddleeast/2016-01/22/content_23191229.htm.
58. Shannon Tiezzi (6 June 2014). *In South Sudan Conflict, China Tests Its Mediation Skills*, The Diplomat, http://thediplomat.com/2014/06/in-south-sudan-conflict-china-tests-its-mediation-skills/.

59. Xinhua, China announces new proposal on Syria, 31 October 2012, http://news.xinhuanet.com/english/china/2012-10/31/c_131942913.htm.
60. Xinhua (6 May 2013). *Chinese President makes four-point proposal for settlement of Palestinian question*, http://news.xinhuanet.com/english/china/2013-05/06/c_132363061.htm.
61. Amrutha Gayrathi, China Signals Greater Role in Global Affairs but Sticks to Principle of Mutual Non-Interference, Associated Press, 11 September 2012, http://www.ibtimes.com/china-signals-greater-role-global-affairs-sticks-principle-mutual-non-interference-866668.
62. Ibid., Fardella.
63. Andrew Small (26 March 2015). *Chinese Foreign Policy Comes of Age*, The New York Times, http://www.nytimes.com/2015/03/27/opinion/chinese-foreign-policy-comes-of-age.html?_r=2.
64. Permanent mission of China to the UN at Geneva(Undated). The 10th Conference of Chinese diplomatic envoys stationed abroad held in Beijing, http://www.china-un.ch/eng/xwdt/t156047.htm.
65. Pan Guang, Keynote Speech at International Conference on China in the Middle East, Indiana University and Peking University, Beijing, 17–18 March 2015.
66. Ibid., Pan Guang.
67. Edward Wong, Taliban and Afghan Peace Officials Have Secret Talks in China, The New York Times, 26 May 2015, www.nytimes.com/world/taliban-and-afghan-peace-officials-have-secret-talks-in-china.html.
68. Li Jing, China stands by Afghanistan, China daily, 28 September 2015, http://www.chinadaily.com.cn/world/2015xivisitus/2015-09/28/content_22000357.htm.
69. Foreign Ministry of the People's Republic of China, Foreign Minister Wang Yi arrived in Kabul to begin a visit to Afghanistan, 22 February 2014, http://www.gov.cn/gzdt/2014-02/22/content_2619024.htm.

PART VI

The European Union: The Belt and Road Terminus

CHAPTER 14

Beyond Ports and Transport Infrastructure: The Geo-Economic Impact of the BRI on the European Union

Alessia A. Amighini

Since Xi Jinping first announced it in 2013, the China-led Belt and Road Initiative (BRI)—a network of land and sea trade and communication corridors eventually linking China to Europe through Central Asia, the Middle East, North and Eastern Africa—has inspired a plethora of studies by scholars from all over the world, speculating about its rationale, its development and its implications on international economic and political affairs.[1]

As the terminal point of both the overland and the maritime routes envisioned within China's action plan (NDRC 2015), the European Union faces significant geo-political, economic and geo-strategic consequences from the BRI (European Parliament Research Service 2016). This chapter reviews the state of the art in the scholarly and policy debates as well as in the policy actions and activities taken so far by the European Union as a response to the BRI.[2]

The most evident influence of the BRI on the European Union will be on the sometimes-cumbersome EU-China bilateral relations. As

A. A. Amighini (✉)
University of Piemonte Orientale, Vercelli, Italy

Catholic University of Milan, Milano, Italy

A. Arduino, X. Gong (eds.), *Securing the Belt and Road Initiative*,
https://doi.org/10.1007/978-981-10-7116-4_14

the original focus of China's action plan was on physical connectivity, the initial EU response to the BRI was a proposal, in 2015, to establish a policy forum—the EU-China Connectivity Platform—to achieve consistent objectives with its own infrastructure policy. Recognising the importance of infrastructure for growth, transport infrastructure has always been at the heart of EU policies for the completion of the single market.[3] In the most radical overhaul of EU infrastructure policy since its inception in the 1980s, the Trans-European Transport Network (TEN-T) launched in 2013 established a core transport network built on nine major corridors (two North–South corridors, three East–West corridors and four diagonal corridors) that will act as a backbone for transportation in Europe's single market and revolutionise East–West connections within the European Union, with a triple budget for the period 2014–2020 (€26 billion) compared to the past. To be completed by 2030, the core network will improve connections among different modes of transport and contribute to the European Union's climate change objectives.

What has been partly overlooked in the design of the EU TEN-T corridors—whose aim is mainly to improve connectivity within the European Union—is the likely impact of the future transport network on the external economic and trade relations of the Union. Although around two thirds of EU trade is intra-EU, that is, trade flows among member states, the share of extra-EU trade is increasing in both directions, with neighbouring countries and faraway countries alike. This means that future goods trade and economic relations with EU partners will also depend on the efficiency of the transport network linking member states with its major trade partners. China is the European Union's main import partner (providing 17.6% of total EU imports) and the second largest export partner after the United States (accounting for 9.3% of total EU exports). Almost all EU exports to China (96.4% of total value) travel by sea. Similarly, the European Union is China's main import partner, accounting for 12.5% of total Chinese imports, and the second largest export partner after the United States, as the destination for 15.6% of Chinese exports. The vast majority of these exports (92.3% of the total value) travel by sea, leaving very little to air, rail and road transport. Although seaborne trade is by far more convenient than any other mode of transport, some major trade routes are inefficient, most notably the routes of EU-China trade. As the two world largest trading nations, the European Union and China share a common interest in reducing the transport costs of shipping their goods abroad, an important part of which is accounted for by time-to-destination.

Transportation costs of bilateral China-Europe trade are significantly higher than the world's average. The average shipping time from China to European partners is 730 hours, 20% more than China's average shipping time (about 610 hours, which is much longer than the world average of 406 hours). Switching to railway transport has great potential for saving transport time: according to data provided by GEFCO, infrastructure construction would reduce railroad travel time from China to Europe to 16–21 days (depending on departure and arrival location), compared to 37–45 days for sea freight, port to port.[4] This explains why in some high-tech sectors (such as electronics) international freight forwarding agencies are already switching to railroad, for example, Hewlett-Packard is planning to rely solely on railway transport by 2017 for shipping its made-in-China PCs to Europe. This runs counter to recent trends and near-future expectations, and has prompted shipping agencies and major port authorities to redesign sea lanes to reduce shipping times and improve the interconnectedness between the ports and the inland railway network.

However, switching to railway transportation entails a trade-off between time and cost. In fact, China's average cost of shipping by sea to European countries is only US$922 for a 40-foot container, about half as much as China's average shipping cost, while railway transport is three times as expensive as maritime transport (DB Schenker 2012). Given that it can lead to a large decrease in transit times and the fact that technology now allows for a reduction in railroad costs, BRI has the potential to become a game changer in international trade by moving large volumes of commerce from sea to land lanes. Formulating scenarios is not easy, however, as it is widely acknowledged that in choosing among alternative modes, firms consider predictability in transport costs a valuable feature. Therefore, a further element that can affect the trade-off between cost and time in different transport modes is the high volatility of sea freight rates compared to rail tariffs. This is because sea freight rates depend on the overall trade volumes much more than rail tariffs, which is why sea freight rates volatility has increased dramatically since the beginning of the world trade slowdown associated with the economic crisis since 2009. Although there is still no precise information about the cross-border infrastructure projects financed under the BRI, it is quite evident from the progress made so far that most of them aim to increase the prospects for land connectivity between China and Europe. This is why an important goal of the projects funded within the BRI is trimming average travel times: documents must include statistics on the reduction in travel time and cost expected from project completion.

Compared to the intense sea lanes between China and Europe (accounting for more than 90% of bilateral trade flows), land routes have been almost totally irrelevant in EU-China trade. The extremely low degree of connectivity within Central Asia is one the major reasons why the bulk of world trade (more than 90%, and 60% of China's trade in value, and a much higher share in volume) travels by sea, due not only to the lower transport costs associated with international shipments compared to railway transport but also the lack of infrastructure for land transport across Central Asia. While economics acknowledges the importance of efficient and peaceful trade relations in global growth, the understanding of geographic patterns of international trade remains sketchy. The literature has extensively analysed the determinants of individual countries' access to international markets and bilateral trade flows, and has found support for the hypothesis that trade and infrastructure costs are important, but not the choice of transport modes, let alone the efficiency of the global network of trade routes (Amighini 2017).

The common interest by the European Union and China to reduce travel time between one another is all the more relevant as Europe is gaining a prominent role in global trade routes even far beyond the routes of EU trade itself. A massive reshuffling of both land and seaborne trade routes on a global scale is expected soon to occur due to two major developments. First, the relative expansion of the Suez Canal compared to the Panama Canal will make the China-Europe maritime corridor increasingly important for China's trade with its other main trade partner, the United States. Container shipping between China and the North American east coast increasingly makes use of the Suez Canal. Because the Panama Canal is narrower than the Suez Canal and not wide enough for the largest container vessels, there is a shift from the trans-pacific to the trans-atlantic route for container traffic between Asia and the North American east coast. In 2014, the container capacity from Asia to the US east coast through the Suez Canal surpassed that of the Panama Canal for the first time. Although the Panama Canal is in the process of being widened, once this is completed it will still not be able to accommodate the largest container vessels that are currently in use. Second, the ongoing expansion of Special Economic Zones (SEZ) in several Central Asian and CEE countries that will serve as gateways in otherwise landlocked territories can potentially alter the current relative dominance of sea compared to land shipping. At the moment, only limited low-volume, high-value items are being shipped by train, but this is largely subsidised by the Chinese SEZ in China as well as along the way to increase the financial viability of the new railways, which are working most westbound than eastbound.

Despite the broader policy implications of the BRI on the future geo-economic role of the European Union, the only bilateral dialogue on the BRI today is still the EU-China Connectivity Platform, with the aim to promote cooperation on infrastructure, including financing, interoperability and logistics. Nevertheless, there is a growing sense of urgency to move forward to more substantive policy dialogues to create synergies between EU policies and projects and China's BRI. At the "Belt and Road Forum" held in Beijing on May 14–15 2017 Vice-President Katainen of the European Commission set out the European Union's vision for improving Europe-Asia connectivity, which is a step forward in EU-China cooperation on a common policy objective. It confirms the European Union's willingness to "support co-operation with China on its Initiative on the basis of China fulfilling its declared aim of making it an open initiative which adheres to market rules, EU and international requirements and standards, and complements EU policies and projects, in order to deliver benefits for all parties concerned and in all the countries along the planned routes."[5] However, and not surprisingly, given the technical nature of the Connectivity Forum, at the 19th EU-China Summit held in Brussels on June 2 2017, the progress acknowledged on "policy exchange and alignment on the principles and the priorities in fostering transport connections between the EU and China, based on the TEN-Ts framework and the Belt and Road initiative, and involving relevant third countries," in fact has boiled down to having agreed upon a list of infrastructural projects of common interest.

Within the current governance structure of EU-China relations, there is a **need for matching the technical dialogue within the Connectivity Platform with a high-level policy dialogue** on a broader range of issues. As the BRI goes far beyond physical connectivity to encompass a variety of policy areas, it has raised awareness of a need to give a boost to parallel dialogues on a large number of issues on which the European Union and China have been handling meetings under the umbrella of the EU-China Summit since 1998, within more than sixty substantive and sectoral dialogues (including cooperation on climate, competition, customs, energy and investment). Acknowledging the BRI as a simple "repackaging of the many initiatives and projects that China was already carrying out well before 2013" (Makocki 2016, p. 68), it should today be widely accepted that none of its implications for the European Union were in fact raised, either directly or specifically, by the BRI itself. If an issue has been genuinely raised by the BRI, that issue is certainly the need to define **a comprehensive response by the European Union** to the increasing Chinese influence in its territory as well as in neighbouring countries. Such response **should not be confined to just trade and investment issues, but should also encompass foreign policy, political and security issues in a comprehensive way.**

This is even more important, as the technical dialogue within the Connectivity Platform tends to cover only the new projects lying at the "common borders" between the TEN-T and the BRI, which are obviously located in member states at the southern and eastern borders of the European Union.[6] Instead, any other issue arising from infrastructure projects across non-EU member states or independent from the joint financing efforts envisaged for the projects included in the draft list is out of the scope of the Platform, despite having potential implications on the smooth and efficient functioning of the overall European transport network. The focus on improving infrastructure—the hardware of globalisation—lies behind an approach to regional integration that widely "differs from EU-style regionalism. Rather than using multilateral treaties to liberalise markets, China promises to facilitate prosperity by linking countries to its continuing growth through hard infrastructure such as railways, highways, ports, pipelines, industrial parks, border customs facilities, and special trade zones; and soft infrastructure such as development finance, trade and investment agreements, and multilateral cooperation forums." (Leonard 2016, p. 21). Because truly multilateral cooperation fora and dialogues are missing, the building of new networks of physical infrastructure are somehow calling for the building of new fora of institutional infrastructure.

Besides the Connectivity Platform, the EU response to BRI so far has consisted in formal statements with extremely limited follow-up in terms of policy actions and dialogues. Until the end of 2015, there had not even been an official EU position on One Belt, One Road. Only in its 16 December 2015 resolution on EU-China relations did the European Parliament take note "... of the launch of the 'One Belt, One Road' initiative aimed at constructing major energy and communication links across Central, West and South Asia as far as Europe." It stressed "that given the geostrategic relevance of this initiative it should be pursued in a multilateral way" and "that it is of the utmost importance to develop synergies and projects in full transparency and with the involvement of all stakeholders." It urged "the Commission to reflect on the impact of China's global investment policy, as well as its investment activities in the EU and its Eastern Neighbourhood." It was only during the first "Belt and Road Forum" in Beijing on May 14–15 2017 that an official message was delivered confirming the EU support of the BRI, while at the same time calling for "a level-playing field for trade and investment based on full adherence to market rules and international norms [as] a critical condition ... to maintain the political momentum for better connectivity in Asia and between Europe and Asia."

The need for improved institutional infrastructure has been increasingly apparent following the initial workings of the Connectivity Platform. Although discussions have not been confined to the coordination of infrastructure development plans in the European Union and China, related issues such as market rules for public procurement and reciprocal access for investments in the respective markets have not yielded any substantive progress, which is hardly surprising given the political nature of those issues, which are supposed to be discussed at a policy rather than a technical level. Possibly the most evident case witnessing the urgent need for an effective policy dialogue on the broad range of issues raised by the BRI, extending far beyond the practical aspects of infrastructure coordination, is the Belgrade-Budapest rail project. Regarded as a flagship project within the BRI, it is currently being reviewed by Brussels for potential infringements of the European Union's requirement that public tenders are offered for such large-scale infrastructure projects. The latter case shows that the differing degrees of adherence to market rules in countries involved in the BRI is a source of inevitable frictions that can act as bottlenecks in the progress towards an effective transport network, and at the same time divert public opinion and policy dialogue away from substantive issues. A further related issue that should deserve an effective dialogue is the financial viability of infrastructure projects along the BRI. Currently, the need to make the new transport routes (railways linking different cities in China to diverse European cities) attractive compared to the much cheaper seaborne trade has led Chinese authorities to subsidies firms with the aim to divert trade from sea to land. This approach acknowledges the need to reach a sufficient trade volume in order for the rail company to be profitable, while today the new transport routes are mainly working on the westbound direction compared to the eastbound. However, it runs against the market rule principles prevailing in the European Union and therefore prevents mutual benefits for Chinese firms exporting to Europe, compared to European firms exporting to China as well as, in both cases, possibly also to other countries along the route. Enduring the lack of progress on a broad range of policy issues related to the BRI—mainly investment framework, market rules, market access and public procurement—allows avoiding serious dialogue, but paves the way to confrontational matters that may be even harder to handle.

Far beyond bilateral EU-China relations, the impact of the BRI on the European Union is manifold and multifaceted, to the extent that the BRI will spread over a large number of countries, up to and potentially more than the current 64 countries included in the action plan. The BRI will also affect the European Union through the European Neighbourhood Policy (ENP) towards its southern and eastern bordering countries, many of which are essential participants in the BRI. Moreover, and more importantly, the BRI will require the European Union to take a comprehensive attitude about its engagement beyond traditional diplomacy, security and defence policies towards an entire range of new diplomacy areas, including cultural diplomacy, energy diplomacy, maritime diplomacy and "rail diplomacy" (Kratz and Pavlicevic 2016), consistently with the strategic priorities included in the Global Strategy for the European Union's Foreign and Security Policy.[7] Finally, the increasing Chinese influence in some member states with a central position in the BRI might call for a strengthening of EU internal cohesion policies and the overall attention towards peripheral member states.

The BRI marks a milestone in "China's traditional diplomacy based on economic and commercial calculations to embrace a broader political and security engagement with the countries involved by the initiative." (Arduino 2016, p. 4). The rising weight of China in many countries' economic and trade relations has increased their dependence on the former and therefore also its geo-strategic influence. The BRI—together with the establishment of its funding institutions, namely the Asian Infrastructure Investment Bank (AIIB) and the Silk Road Fund—signal China's willingness to take a more active role in regional and global governance, compared to the key principle of China's foreign policy over the past decades, that is, a "peaceful rise with a low profile." As a result, the BRI is potentially a game changer for global governance as China's influence on international economic and political affairs has increased altogether (Loesekrug-Pietri 2015). More specifically related to EU-China relations,

China's previous focus on the large EU member states has recently been complemented by growing attention by Beijing diplomacy to the CEECs and Southern Europe, which implies a need for the European Union to look for a firmer balance in the Union's foreign policy, between the diplomatic and economic power of larger member states and the rising power of peripheral member states.

The growing diplomatic profile China has recently set, both bilaterally with an increasing number of countries, and multilaterally within existing international organisations and newly funded Chinese-led ones, perfectly confirms the view that in "the new age of geo-economics" (Leonard 2016, p. 22), "countries use economic asymmetries to achieve geo-political goals" (Schwarz 2016, p. 10). This is hardly a brand new age to all those following the international exposure of China over last two decades, as political and economic objectives have invariably been deeply intertwined in China's foreign policy; they do not simply reinforce each other, but are in fact two sides of the same coin. **China's foreign investment to acquire stakes in firms, banks, ports and utilities, many of which are in Europe** (both EU and non-EU), aimed at fostering economic alliances and partnerships, **resulted** at the same time **in a comparatively massive "investment in influence"** (ECFR 2015) **that is unevenly distributed across member states**. Although the bulk of Chinese investment in Europe over the last decade has undoubtedly gone to some of the largest European countries (United Kingdom, Germany and Italy) (Amendolagine et al. 2017), some other CEECs (Hungary) and countries in Southern Europe (most notably Greece) have been targeted by Chinese firms for massive inflows of greenfield investment and acquisitions. Therefore, some of the latter have been gaining a prominent effective bilateral position within Europe-China relations, a position that has not yet been matched by a common position in the European Union's relations with China. The resulting instrumental use of those differing degrees of economic dependence on Chinese capital for geo-political ends has been depicted by some scholars as an attempt by Beijing diplomacy to design China's shadow world order (Rudolf 2016). In this scenario, the BRI has initially been regarded as a comprehensive strategy to increase foreign dependence on China, most notably to expand Chinese influence in Eurasia and to alter the global patterns of interdependence in its favour.

However, despite being supported by ample evidence on the wide range of subtle tools of China's soft diplomacy to legitimately increase the effectiveness of its foreign diplomatic activities, this argument underplays the (more active and assertive) role the international community, and the European Union in particular, should take in the BRI. In fact, the essence of the BRI goes far beyond "Beijing's key geostrategic attempt to alter Eurasian trans-regional trade in its favour" (Rudolf 2016, p. 86), to encompass the improvement of a multi-layered infrastructure network including physical (i.e., transport, energy and telecommunication) infrastructure, but also institutional infrastructure (i.e., funding institutions) to the common benefit of a vast number of countries. Infrastructure, notably a precondition for industrialisation and economic development across all ages and continents,[8] has today undoubtedly become "the most innovative geo-economic tool" (Leonard 2016, p. 23) at the core of the BRI. The improvement of infrastructure per se should not be considered a self-oriented objective of the Chinese leadership as it does not accrue benefits to isolated countries, but to all countries being connected into a network. In this spirit, China's action plan refers to the formal purpose of the BRI as China's contribution to international economic development by strengthening connectivity through an improvement of transport, energy and telecommunication infrastructure in Asia, Africa and Europe with the ultimate aim of linking those continents together into a comprehensive network. Improving connectivity between Asia, Europe and Africa will potentially be beneficial to prosperity in all the regions involved, conditional on the ability of each region to link the new infrastructure to their own development goals and priorities.[9]

The single most evident case of potential divergence between the BRI and national development priorities is the progress taken by the "16+1" cooperation framework since the launch of the BRI. The 16+1 mechanism is a platform created in April 2012 by the Chinese leadership that seeks a stronger connection between China and the 16 CEECs, namely Albania, Bosnia and Herzegovina, Bulgaria, Croatia, Czech Republic, Estonia, Hungary, Latvia, Lithuania, Macedonia, Montenegro, Poland, Romania, Serbia, Slovak Republic and Slovenia. Nowadays, many previously agreed-upon joint 16+1 projects were given the BRI label, which may pave the way for diverging perceptions towards EU internal integration policies. CEECs have shown that they are able to adopt an active policy of cooperation with China and an issue has been raised about the status of Central Europe within the region and in the European Union. There are evident discrepancies between EU and non-EU members, especially in terms of rules and procedures related to investments and infrastructural projects. This poses serious challenges to the extent that EU and non-EU member countries develop common interests under the China-led 16+1 mechanism but perceive the divergent rules and regulations in EU vs. non-EU members as a source of bottlenecks in their development process.

This cooperation framework is not just paving the way to divergent perceptions and positions on the power of the European Union to set rules and standards within its own borders and in neighbouring countries, but as well as on its ability to convey a unified position in international decisions. The increasing Chinese economic and commercial influence in some member states, together with a timely diplomatic push from Beijing, "has boosted its capacity to influence the choices of European states and has complicated EU diplomacy .... Following the pronouncement of the Permanent Court of Arbitration in The Hague on the status of land masses in the South China Sea in July 2016, for instance, the stances of Hungary and Greece – key countries for China's OBOR initiative – resulted in a more convoluted European position on the ruling" (van der Putten et al. 2016, p. 10). The BRI has further exacerbated the inconsistencies in the 16+1 framework and confirmed the need for three-party cooperation between the European Union, China and the CEECs, a region that is central in the overall BRI and from which will depend the smooth and efficient functioning of the entire international land transport network in Eurasia.

Besides the CEECs, the BRI is dramatically changing the geo-strategic environment in Eurasia. It is widely accepted that the region where the highest impact of infrastructure is expected is Central Asia. Currently, Central Asia is the least accessible and connected area in the world. All Central Asian countries except Pakistan are landlocked (i.e., they have no direct access to the sea), a major disadvantage insofar as the lack of a direct maritime connection is associated with a handicap in terms of export value (Amighini 2017) and plays an important role in determining trade costs (Arvis et al. 2013). More precisely, the absence of a direct maritime connection has been estimated to have the same impact on freight rates as an increase in distance between two countries of 2612 km (Wilmsmeier and Hoffman 2008). By facilitating landlocked countries' access to the sea, the BRI has the potential to improve connectivity and therefore promote socio-economic development in a vast region that is expected to become the next emerging region.

Because infrastructure improvement will affect all cargo plying these transport routes, the BRI is of interest to countries along the routes, but also to countries beyond the designated Silk Road routes. Therefore, a further trade creation effect is likely to take place through new trade routes that will unlock potential trade ties with new trading partners. The most unexploited potential trade seems to be between Central Asian countries and their largest neighbouring economies, that is, China and Europe. Central Asia is a fast-growing emerging region, according to the World Bank, with promising demographic (with a projected 4.45% of world population by 2030) and economic prospects (4% average GDP growth projected through 2017). Poor connectivity and expensive logistics rank high in the list of factors that act as obstacles to growth, because all of the countries (except Pakistan) are landlocked. Pakistan has in fact the highest potential, and its economy is projected to become 16% larger than Italy's by 2050 according to PricewaterhouseCoopers. At the other extreme, Uzbekistan is one of the only two countries in the world that are "double landlocked," that is, surrounded entirely by one or more landlocked countries and requiring the crossing of at least two national borders to reach a coastline.

As already indicated, improving infrastructure across Central Asia would increase connectivity and allow the region to exploit further trade potential with both China and the European Union, its main trading partners. Currently, the European Union shows much higher import and export values than China's trade with the region, but the (both Central and South Asia) STANs' imports from China have been growing very rapidly since 2010, so the region's trade balance with China has progressively deteriorated. Better infrastructure will intensify trade with China, with the STANs selling similar goods and therefore expected to face even stronger competition with one another in the region in the future. This is partly a source of concern for the STANs as a group, as it could lead to an excessive dependence on China for consumption and capital goods.

Moreover, a further source of geo-economic competition is the fact that some Central Asian countries—most notably Kazakhstan—are part of other regional initiatives, such as the Eurasian Economic Union (EEU), an economic union of five states in northern Eurasia (Belarus, Kazakhstan, Russia, Armenia and Kyrgyzstan), which might become a competitor in the global economic space. However, the trade complementarity of these countries vis-à-vis one another is rather low (according to the United Nations Conference on Trade and Development [UNCTAD]) (i.e., their export profiles do not match the import profiles of any others within the group), which means that a preferential trade agreement would not lead to any significant trade expansion or creation, and at the same time would not divert any of the trade of these Central Asian countries with other major trade partners.

The European Union has an historical responsibility to open a high-level dialogue on current competing initiatives for regional integration in Eastern Europe and Central Asia. In fact, the BRI is a regional integration effort alternative to the EUU and an important absence in the BRI is the lack of relationships between the EUU and the European Union. The BRI could open new opportunities for the European Union to pursue its geo-strategic ambitions in Central Asia by deepening the EU-China strategic partnership through cooperation in security fields, possibly paving the way to EU-Russia reconciliation. At the same time, China, Russia, Ukraine and the European Union have some common economic and security interests in Eurasia that they could follow together in spite of different approaches. Under these conditions, it is better for European countries to try to find a common language with former Soviet republics and China than to passively observe how the existing order is being replaced by something unfamiliar to European values and interests.

Improving infrastructure along the land-based Silk Road Economic Belt has the potential to contribute to economic development and regional stability in Eurasia from which both China and the European Union could benefit in terms of new markets and energy security. One Belt, One Road thus opens opportunities for the European Union to pursue its geo-strategic ambitions in Central Asia by deepening the EU-China strategic partnership through cooperation in non-traditional security fields, possibly paving the way to EU-Russia reconciliation. The maritime trajectory of OBOR will sooner or later require the EU to take a more outspoken position on maritime disputes in the South China Sea in favour of an international rules-based order.

Concluding Remarks

The BRI aims at integrating China into the global economy along much deeper avenues—far beyond trade and investment flows—than ever before. Along with the flourishing of bilateral agreements signed by the Chinese government with individual partner countries since the 1990s (now up to 202 international investment agreements and 14 free trade agreements), the BRI intends to build a great Eurasian continent along lines that are very different from any other traditional paradigm of regional integration. While the world has so far experienced rule-based regional integration arrangements, the Chinese way to regional integration tends to be less rule-based and more coalition-based along country-specific interests. Although the BRI should be appreciated and not disregarded, Europe's historical responsibility is to make multilateralism prevail against closed and competing initiatives towards regionalism. The BRI will likely contribute to economic development and regional stability in Eurasia from which both China and the European Union could benefit in terms of new markets and energy security. Overall, the BRI presents the European Union with a unique opportunity to re-enter the "Great Game" (Arduino 2016), not just in Central Asia, but also in a series of new or renewed games. Therefore, Europe should consider the BRI as a much broader vision than the simple improvement of physical and digital connectivity.

As regards digital connectivity, the Internet is the software of globalisation, as transport links are its hardware. Part of the BRI is to create the so-called digital Silk Road, that is, an Internet community that would facilitate cross-border e-commerce and Internet banking. According to Ren Xianliang, vice minister of the Cyberspace Administration of China, the expansion should be undertaken in addition to implementing the country's Internet Plus plan, whereby everything will be connected to a superfast broadband network.[10] One of the main obstacles towards a digital Silk Road is the still high level of China's services trade barriers, including licensing requirements, complex regulations and product quotas.[11] Moreover, "Like physical infrastructure links, the virtual infrastructure of the internet is also being weaponised by states competing for power." (Leonard 2016, p. 21). As a consequence, "countries such as Australia, France, South Korea, India, Indonesia, Kazakhstan, Malaysia, and Vietnam have already moved to keep certain types of data on servers within their national borders. Deutsche Telekom has suggested a German-only "Internetz", while the EU is considering a virtual Schengen area (Leonard 2016, p. 22)." The digital revolution … has sparked a new "Great Game", analogous to the race for control of Asia in the nineteenth century (Hobbs et al. 2016).

Moreover, the European Union should seriously consider the consequences of the lack of a common framework for bilateral investment with China. In fact, the BRI will further accelerate Chinese investment activity in various infrastructure projects in European countries. Before the BRI was announced, China's infrastructure investment in Europe targeted individual EU countries and many non-EU members in Central and Eastern Europe, mainly in the manufacturing and services sectors.

Recently, Chinese firms have started to invest in large infrastructure projects backed by their inclusion in the BRI project list. Coalition building around individual projects now tends to prevail over the legal rules and procedures that are at the heart of the EU competition policy, as the core principles around which the internal market has been developed.

As most powerfully expressed, "Beijing's diplomacy is very transactional in nature and the respect it accords foreign counterparts and adversaries depends on their ability to bargain hard and get results" (de Jonquières 2015, p. 3). Time has come for the European Union to bargain hard to get results that will allow the Chinese BRI to become a game changer to the mutual benefits of all the countries involved.

Notes

1. Major comprehensive reports on the BRI and its significance to the European Union are Amighini (2017), van der Putten et al. (2016). For a more comprehensive analysis of the potential impact of China's foreign policy (including OBOR) on the European Union, please see China's foreign policy and external relations, Burnay et al. (2015).
2. It is beyond the scope of this chapter to dig into individual member countries' bilateral activities with China, which have widely differed in size and scope.
3. European Commission Vice-President Siim Kallas, responsible for transport, said: "Transport is vital to the European economy. Without good connections Europe will not grow or prosper. This new EU infrastructure policy will put in place a powerful European transport network across 28 Member States to promote growth and competitiveness. It will connect East with West and replace today's transport patchwork with a network that is genuinely European." Available at https://ec.europa.eu/transport/themes/infrastructure/news/ten-t-corridors_en.
4. The Yuxinou Railway, in particular, runs from Chongqing to Duisburg in Germany in only 288 hours.
5. EU common messages at the Belt and Road Forum, available at https://eeas.europa.eu/delegations/china/26051/belt-and-road-forum-eu-common-messages_en.
6. Of the 12 projects currently included in the draft list agreed upon by the EU-China Connectivity Platform, four are in Poland, three in Slovakia, three in Bulgaria and two in Italy.
7. "A Global Strategy for the European Union" available at https://europa.eu/globalstrategy/en.

8. For a comprehensive review of the impact of infrastructure in development, see Sawada (2015).
9. This is the same perspective that has been recently embraced and highlighted in the EU message at the "Belt and Road Forum" in Beijing on May 14–15 2017.
10. China Daily, http://www.chinadaily.com.cn/world/2015-07/07/content_21202745.htm.
11. Bergsten et al. 2014 and https://www.oecd.org/trade/services-trade/STRI_CHN.pdf.

References

Amendolagine, V., Amighini, A. and Rabellotti, R. (2017), Chinese Multinationals in Europe, in Beretta, S., Berkofski, A. and Zhang, L. (Eds), *Understanding China Today*, Springer.

Amighini, A. (Ed.) (2017), China's Belt and Road: A Game Changer?, ISPI, available at http://www.ispionline.it/it/EBook/Rapporto_Cina_2017/China_Belt_Road_Game_Changer.pdf

Arduino, A. (2016), China's One Belt One Road: Has the European Union Missed the Train?, RSiS Policy Report, available at https://www.rsis.edu.sg/wp-content/uploads/2016/03/PR160307_China-One-Belt-One-Road.pdf

Arvis J. F., Duval Y. and Utoktham C. (2013), Trade Costs in the Developing World: 1995–2010. Policy Research Working Paper Series No. 6309, The World Bank.

Bergsten C., Hufbauer G. C., & Miner, S. (2014). *Bridging the Pacific: Towards Free Trade and Investment Between China and the United States*. Washington: Peterson Institute for International Economics.

Burnay, M., Carbonnet, A., Raube, K. and Wouters, J. (2015), China's Foreign Policy and External Relations, University of Leuven.

DB Schenker (2012), Rail Based Transports between China and Europe, available at http://www.iccwbo.org/Data/Documents/Transport-and-logistics/6-Rail-based-transports-between-China-and-Europe/

de Jonquières, G. (2015), The European Union's China Policy: Priorities and Strategies for the New Commission, ECIPE Policy Brief No. 3, available at http://www.ecipe.org/app/uploads/2015/04/The-European-Union%E2%80%99s-China-Policy.pdf

ECFR (2015), China's Investment in Influence: The Future of 16+1 Cooperation, available at http://www.ecfr.eu/page/-/China_Analysis_Sixteen_Plus_One.pdf

European Parliament Research Service (2016), One Belt, One Road (OBOR): China's Regional Integration Initiative, available at http://www.europarl.europa.eu/RegData/etudes/BRIE/2016/586608/EPRS_BRI%282016%29586608_EN.pdf

Hobbs, C., Puddephatt, A. and Torreblanca, J. I. (2016), The Geo-Economics of the Digital, in Leonard (Ed.), *Connectivity Wars*, ECFR, available at http://www.ecfr.eu/page/-/Connectivity_Wars.pdf

Kratz, A. and Pavlicevic, D. (2016), China's High-Speed Rail Diplomacy: Riding a Gravy Train?, Lau China Centre Working Paper Series, available at https://www.kcl.ac.uk/sspp/departments/lci/documents/working-papers/Lau-China-Institute-Working-Papers-1.pdf

Leonard, M. (2016), Introduction, in Leonard, M. (Ed.), *Connectivity Wars*, ECFR, available at http://www.ecfr.eu/page/-/Connectivity_Wars.pdf

Loesekrug-Pietri, A. (2015), Why Europe Can't Afford to Ignore China's New Silk Road, available at https://www.weforum.org/agenda/2015/11/europe-china-new-silk-road/

Makocki, M. (2016), The EU Level: 'Belt and Road' Initiative Slowly Coming to Terms with the EU Rules-Based Approach, in ETNC (2016), *Europe and China's New Silk Roads*, ETNC Report, available at https://www.clingendael.nl/sites/default/files/Europe_and_Chinas_New_Silk_Roads_0.pdf

NDRC (2015), Vision and Actions on Jointly Building Silk Road Economic Belt and 21st-Century Maritime Silk Road, available at http://en.ndrc.gov.cn/newsrelease/201503/t20150330_669367.html

Rudolf, M. (2016), China's Shadow World Order, in Leonard, M. (Ed.), *Connectivity Wars*, ECFR, available at http://www.ecfr.eu/page/-/Connectivity_Wars.pdf

Sawada, Y. (2015), The Impacts of Infrastructure in Development: A Selective Survey, ADBI Working Paper Series No. 511, available at https://www.adb.org/sites/default/files/publication/154248/adbi-wp511.pdf

Schwarz, M. (2016), Introduction, in Leonard, M. (Ed.), *Connectivity Wars*, ECFR, available at http://www.ecfr.eu/page/-/Connectivity_Wars.pdf

van der Putten, F.-P. et al. (Eds) (2016), The Role of OBOR in Europe-China Relations, in ETNC (2016), *Europe and China's New Silk Roads*, ETNC Report, available at https://www.clingendael.nl/sites/default/files/Europe_and_Chinas_New_Silk_Roads_0.pdf

Wilmsmeier G. and Hoffman J. (2008), Liner Shipping Connectivity and Port Infrastructure as Determinants of Freight Rates in the Caribbean. *Maritime Economics and Logistics*, 130–151.

CHAPTER 15

China's Belt and Road Initiative and the 16+1 Platform: The Case of the Czech Republic

Alica Kizeková

This chapter examines China's activities in Central and Eastern European Countries (hereinafter referred to as 'CEECs'), with a specific reference to the 16+1 platform, during a time of the emerging Belt and Road Initiative (BRI). In Europe, this initiative has been looked upon with suspicion and referred to as a 'divide and conquer' strategy, aiming to potentially disrupt the workings of the European Union. The argument presented here is that the cooperation between China and the CEECs has not been a one-sided activity. Some countries did not hide their enthusiasm for forging closer partnerships with China and embracing the China-led 16+1 platform, as well as BRI. The Czech Republic is a case in point; however, it still questions the benefits of opening up to China and what the real outcomes of promised investments domestically and in the wider region are. In response to the criticisms, the Chinese leadership has reassured the Europeans that China is acting peacefully under a win-win premise for all parties involved and that the activities within the 16+1 take in consideration the existing projects, such as China-EU cooperation and the EU infrastructure projects.

A. Kizeková (✉)
Institute of International Relations Prague, Prague, Czech Republic

A. Arduino, X. Gong (eds.), *Securing the Belt and Road Initiative*,
https://doi.org/10.1007/978-981-10-7116-4_15

Introduction

China's recent expansion of activities in Central and Eastern European Countries (CEECs) should be understood in the context of its overall strategy of becoming a more active player in Europe and worldwide. Without doubt, China is seeking to equalize its economic power with its global political position. It means focusing on development and security of its projects abroad especially through corridors across Europe, Central Asia, South and Southeast Asia.

Since 2017, the world has had several opportunities to learn about China's view of its global standing and its approach to relations with other countries.[1] President Xi Jinping's speech at the Davos World Economic Forum in January 2017 promoted globalization and clearly contrasted President Donald Trump's economic protectionism. President Xi argued that China had opened and gained the second rank thanks to the global economy within the last 38 years. As such, he provided an alternative to exclusive economic systems by suggesting that the China-led initiatives were more inclusive and open to all (Xi Jinping 2017a). He shared the same ideas during the Belt and Road Forum for International Cooperation hosted by Beijing in May 2017 (Xi Jinping 2017b).

In preparation for the Forum, the organizers prioritized focusing on infrastructure development, financial integration, policy coordination, trade promotion and closer people-to-people bonds as a counterbalance to growing protectionism and pushback against globalization or fragmentation. The Joint Press Communiqué provided specific figures for each segment, including some assistance for refugees in collaboration with the United Nations (Joint Press Communiqué 2017).

Nevertheless, this initiative on globalization is not an immediate response to the current US administration. It was introduced during President Barack Obama's so-called pivot to Asia and the Trans-Pacific Partnership (TPP) and the Transatlantic Trade and Investment Partnership (TTIP) negotiations. What is undeniable is that China has recently become more proactive in presenting its narrative and the country is arguably moving from the position of a 'norm-taker' to a 'norm-shaper' or 'institution-creator' (Reilly 2011; Alden and Large 2015; Huijskens 2016).

Not everyone accepts this change of status quo. Some believe that in Europe, China uses a 'divide and conquer' approach by successfully institutionalizing the 16+1 cooperation and thus weakens the unity of the European Union.[2] The European Union has not been pleased that Beijing created a format of cooperation, which involves the EU and non-EU member states, at the time when the EU representatives have been trying to work out a more coordinated EU strategy towards China. Brussels' concerns relate to bilateral agreements between China and individual EU member states, especially in the CEECs. There is an argument that the logic of economics rules over the logic of political ideals—democracy and human rights.[3]

It is premature to conclude that China would be the primary divider of the European Union. When, in 2015, China's National Development and Reform Commission (NDRC), the Ministry of Foreign Affairs and Ministry of Commerce published the *Vision and Actions plan on 'One Belt One Road' (OBOR), now Belt and Road Initiative (BRI)*, it became clear that China was not seeking a 'one-size-fits-all' type of cooperation. The focus was to be on finding the best suitable model for a specific bilateral relationship, to ensure a win-win scenario for both parties involved.

In fact, the current disruptions have come from the internal disagreements within the European Union. The member states have struggled to find their common voice in various areas, such as the refugee crisis and, more importantly, the supranational entity is facing a major challenge of its unity by conducting negotiations with the United Kingdom over Brexit. Some insecurities were dispelled after the presidential elections in France, where Emmanuel Macron, the independent and pro-European centrist, won the elections in May 2017. At the time of writing (December 2017), Brussels has been in anticipation for the new German government, which has not been formed since the German Federal Elections took place in September 2017.

Additionally, in short to medium terms, differences of opinions among CEECs will prevent the framework from becoming a major divider (Grieger 2016; Stanzel et al. 2016). One of the key concerns of the participating countries is that the promises of large investments in specific countries have not been translated into tangible results. There has been some criticism over purchases by Chinese companies into real estate, media and sports clubs, which would not bring adequate benefits for host countries. Instead, the expectations had been for China to invest in sustainable employment (Góralczyk 2017).[4]

This chapter undertakes the task to examine the 16+1 framework in the context of the increasingly bolder China and how the Czech Republic responds to this development. The focus is going to be on possibilities and risks. The argument presented here is that the cooperation between China and CEECs has not been a one-sided activity. Some countries did not hide their enthusiasm for forging closer partnerships with China and openly embraced the China-led 16+1 platform, as well as BRI. However, there is a growing pragmatism in assessing specific investments—promises verses the actual outcomes. This is quite visible in the Czech Republic where the wider expert community and media have scrutinized the results of the Chinese investments so far.

The 16+1 Initiative: Expectations and Disappointments

The official beginning of the 16+1 is linked to the summit in Warsaw in 2012. By then, China's former Prime Minister Wen Jiabao had already proposed the development of trade, investments, infrastructure projects, fiscal and financial cooperation and people-to-people ties during the Business Forum in Budapest in 2011. In the aftermath of the global financial crisis, the 16 countries welcomed China's initiative with open arms and their expectations of real investments were certainly high.

In his speech, former Prime Minister Wen described the interaction between China and the CEECs as 'traditional' by making a reference to the ancient Silk Road, which linked Asia and Europe. In his words, the CEECs were uniquely strong in aircraft manufacturing, auto-making, brewing, bio-pharmacy, sewage treatment and shipbuilding while China was presented as having advantages in infrastructure construction, manufacturing and processing. He mentioned specific investments, such as Huawei's decision to set up its European supply center in Hungary (Wen 2011).

It was made clear that those CEECs that were part of the European Union would be viewed as viable bridges to Western markets and important to the EU-China cooperation. According to former Prime Minister Wen, there was an incentive in investing in CEECs. It would cut costs for Chinese enterprises and thus CEECs were to become a strategic priority in the context of China's going global.

Former Prime Minister Wen made five specific suggestions to enhance: (1) bilateral trade; (2) two-way investment; (3) infrastructure construction cooperation; (4) fiscal and financial cooperation; and (5) people-to-people and cultural exchanges. His speech was a call for an active participation in China's development through concrete projects. Thus, the Chinese leadership presented their plans for the development of the CEECs' area prior to the establishment of the 16+1 platform and without consulting the CEECs in advance.

The formalization of the CEECs cooperation with China took place the following year in Warsaw at the First Summit of 16+1. Upon gaining an overwhelming support from the participating countries, this China-led initiative turned into *Twelve Measures for Promoting Friendly Cooperation with Central and Eastern European Countries.*

Drawn from the *Measures*, the first step towards the 16+1 institutionalization was setting up a secretariat at China's Ministry of Foreign Affairs. This Chinese institution oversees daily affairs. It communicates and coordinates activities between China and the CEECs, including preparations for meetings and forums. Each participating country has a national coordinator who is the primary contact point and facilitator of discussions for their respective country with the 16+1 secretariat.

China suggested establishing a USD 10 billion special credit line, an investment cooperation fund, trade and investment promotion missions, currency swaps, the establishment of bank branches, advisory committees, cultural forums, scholarships and an active support for Confucius Institutes, tourism promotion and young political forum (Twelve Measures 2012).

The following summits in Bucharest and Belgrade, in 2013–2014, were no longer one-sided China-led events. The European countries contributed to the final guidelines. In Bucharest, further planning of activities took place, and new associations were set up. It should be noted that joining them by relevant Chinese and CEECs' agencies and businesses is on a voluntary basis. Additionally, the Belgrade Guidelines, based on the theme *New Driving Force, New Platform and New Engine,* included an update on the progress made towards the implementation of the *Measures* of the Bucharest Guidelines in the previous year.

Both guidelines dealt with the question of EU-China relations to reassure the critical voices in Europe that the 16+1 cooperation was 'in concord with China-EU comprehensive strategic partnership' (Bucharest Guidelines 2013), and stressed that it would contribute 'to the implementation of the EU-China 2020 Strategic Agenda for Cooperation', as well as be 'in accordance with their respective laws and regulations, and in the case of EU member states, the EU legislation, regulations and policies stemming from their membership' (Belgrade Guidelines 2014).

While the first three summits took place in Europe, China hosted the fourth summit in Suzhou in November 2015. The circle of additional attendees at the meeting expanded by representatives from the European Union, Austria and the European Bank for Reconstruction and Development. The group stated its support for the China-EU Connectivity Platform, BRI and the Investment Plan for Europe. In terms of planning, a document called *the Medium-Term Agenda for Cooperation between China and Central and Eastern European Countries* was issued, for the period of 2015–2020. Influenced by the bold BRI, the summit was themed *New Beginning, New Domains, Vision.*

Although, the participating countries concluded that bringing the platform to life was successful, some CEECs pointed out that there had not been many visible results. Often, the unsuccessful infrastructure project of the Chinese firm COVEC in Poland was mentioned as a discouraging example, and the fact that many states had relatively developed infrastructure and if not, most 16 states could access the EU funding for infrastructure projects, and the construction would be done under requirements of high standards within the European Union.

The Riga Summit in Latvia in November 2016, themed *Connectivity, Innovation, Inclusiveness and Common Development,* concluded that the 16+1 mechanism became 'more mature and ready to harvest' (Riga Guidelines 2016). A commitment was made to complement the EU-China Connectivity Platform and more observers could join the meeting, such as Greece and Switzerland. Special attention was paid to the joint Adriatic-Baltic-Black Sea Seaport Cooperation and an extension of the shipping route network of inland waterways and ports. The Riga Declaration called for 'greater synergy between the BIR, development strategies of CEECs and the EU's Trans-European Transport Network' (Riga Declaration 2016).

In five years of its existence, the 16+1 platform has evolved into a functioning mechanism and improved the coordination of discussions among specific ministries. It is clear now that states aim for a lasting set-up and want to achieve realistic outcomes. Some obstacles remain. On a broader scale, China has not fully convinced the wider EU community that its intentions of investing in the CEECs are benign.

Some believe that Beijing is driven by the desire to gain more influence and sway decision-makers in respective EU member states towards China, and therefore, counteract the unity of the European Union. This could be the case of the European Union's statement on legal ruling related to the South China Sea, which avoided a reference to China (Emmott 2016; EU Statement 2016). Additionally, Beijing could have an impact on the five Western Balkans countries that participate in the 16+1 to even abandon the idea of joining the European Union if their accession process is too prolonged (Long 2014).

For now, the real challenge to China's cooperation in the CEECs is that individual states differentiate in their degree of support of the current 16+1 mechanisms. A 'cooperation vacuum' has been created in countries where the enthusiasm faded in response to the gap between the hyped expectations and the lack of tangible results from promised investments, as well as the lack of support from the public (Long 2016; Stanzel et al. 2016).

The Polish decision makers, for instance, share a very positive approach to BRI, a position that remained unchanged after the presidential and general elections in 2015. The local government in Łódź has also taken up the initiative, having the cargo connection from Chengdu, and wants to become a logistical and technological hub to facilitate trade. In contrast, Slovakia's participation in BRI has been minimal. While previously the government of Prime Minister Robert Fico lobbied for more economic cooperation with China, such as a hydropower plant, an establishment of a Chinese bank or a direct flight between Slovakia and China, the inability to materialize these projects, as well as being outside the main Silk Road corridors, led to a decreased enthusiasm and a lack of media coverage in the Slovak news outlets (Szczudlik-Tatar 2016; Pleschova 2016).

Another obstacle in gaining more support from the 16+1 countries is the redistribution of Chinese investments. In 2016, it was reported that the European Union was China's favorite destination for investments, with an increase of 75% from 2015, totaling EUR 35 billion (approx. USD 40.8 billion) of completed outbound foreign direct investment (FDI). However, more than half of total incoming investment was directed to Germany (EUR 11 billion, USD 12.8 billion) and United Kingdom (EUR 7.8 billion, USD 8.16 billion) (Hanemann and Huotari 2017). The investment in Central and Eastern Europe is still rather limited. It might take some time for the projects to materialize and generate some revenues.

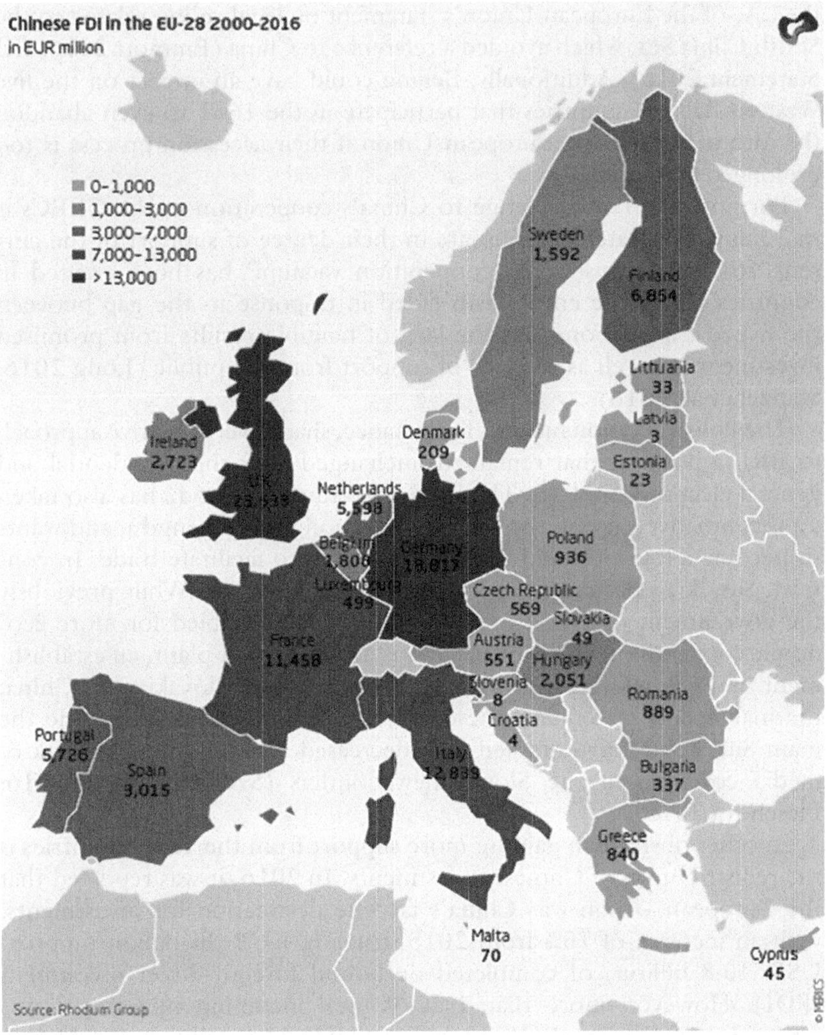

Source: Hanemann and Huotari (2017, p. 10)

It is important to note that the distribution of investments within the 16+1 grouping is uneven. Based on data, six out of 16 European countries—Bulgaria, the Czech Republic, Hungary, Poland, Slovakia and Romania account for 95% of 16+1 investment.

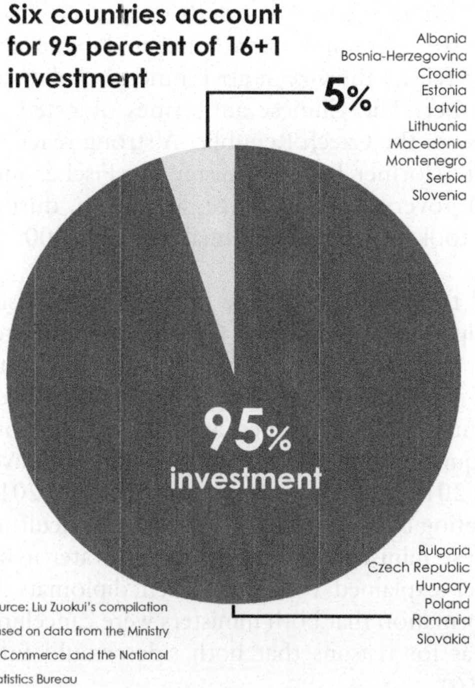

Source: Liu in Kratz (2016, p. 8)

The Case of the Czech Republic

The Czech Republic, which is one of the top destinations of China's investments among CEECs, has successfully managed to maintain an active exchange of high-profile delegations in the past three years. The efforts of the current Czech government to strengthen the economic and political ties with China culminated with the historical visit of President Xi Jinping and the signature of forging a strategic partnership in March 2016.[5]

There is no question that the political ties between the Czech and Chinese counterparts are mainly supported by President Miloš Zeman. His visit to China for the Belt and Road Forum in May 2017 was his third trip to China since taking up his office. Also, by then, he had already met the Chinese president six times within the last three years.

It should be noted that during the previous periods—especially from the early 1990s until 2004—the communication between Prague and Beijing was quite limited, affected by the Czech government's policy on human rights, Taiwan and Tibet. The Chinese authorities objected to regular visits of the Dalai Lama in the Czech Republic. A strong reaction from China came in 2009 after former Prime Minister Jan Fischer met the Dalai Lama in his official government residence, and again, during the most recent visit, which took place at the annual Forum 2000[6] in October 2016.

The previous instances led to reduced exchange of high-profile visits and the cancellation of participation of the former Czech prime minister at the Shanghai Expo 2012. It was in 2014 when the first most significant Chinese investment contract was signed in Beijing—the Slovak-Czech J&T Financial Group and Chinese CEFC, valued at USD 750 million, which led to subsequent acquisitions in the Czech Republic in travel industry and real estate (Fürst 2015). The latest incident in October 2016 led to the cancellation of a meeting between Czech Minister of Agriculture Marian Jurečka and the Chinese ministers of agriculture and water management. The Czech minister explained that the Czech diplomats in Beijing had had "received information that both ministers were cancelling the meetings…and that it was for reasons that both sides would fully understand" (Willoughby 2016).

In response to these tensions, the four highest constitutional leaders—the president, the prime minister and the speakers of the Senate and the Chamber of Deputies—issued an unpopular Joint Statement to reassure China that the Czech Republic continued to respect the sovereignty and territorial integrity of the People's Republic of China (hrad.cz 2016). As such, the Czech leadership has not been deterred from participating in BRI. Yet, if another case of criticism of human rights or sensitive political issues from the Czech side comes up, there is a high probability that the Chinese leadership will use various means of pressure towards the Czechs, notwithstanding economic tools.

When it comes to supporting the BRI and the 16+1 platform, the Czech leadership has continued to develop the bilateral relationship while mentioning the 'vision' and platform in a majority of key speeches and during negotiations with top-ranking Chinese officials. Recently, Prime Minister Bohuslav Sobotka attended the Local Leaders Meeting of 16+1 and opened the Summit of Health Ministers in Suzhou while primarily focusing on aviation, healthcare and financial sectors within the agreed framework (vlada.cz 2016).

Nonetheless, after China and the Czech Republic agreed on a bilateral collaboration under the umbrella of BRI during the 16+1 Riga Summit in November 2016, several Czech experts on China, politicians, media and public argued that this document was a paper tiger and there had not been enough tangible investments to justify the invested political capital (Agenda 2017). However, the Czech representation has not stated that BRI would overshadow other forms of collaboration. The latest 'vision' and added activities would have to complement the existing China-EU partnership and the bilateral relations (CT 2015; Sobotka 2016).

There are several opportunities for the Czech Republic's cooperation in the context of BRI. The Czech Republic's strategic location in Central Europe could serve as a 'gateway' for China vis-à-vis the Western European markets; further, logistics, infrastructure, air industry and travel, production of small planes, smart cities, services, environment, advanced technologies, automobile industry and machinery, as well as energy (AMO 2016).

Being labeled as China's gateway or 'bridge to Europe' can lead to great expectations, yet it can also end up in some disappointments. Initially, Poland and Hungary were frontrunners to serve as viable 'bridges'. Prime Minister Viktor Orban stated that Central Europeans could use the opportunity of CEECs-China gatherings to understand the thinking of Chinese politicians and the Chinese political system (Orban 2016).

The reconstruction of the Budapest-Belgrade railway has become the most advertised project linked to the Chinese-Hungarian relations. It is already estimated that the construction will not be accomplished on time, however, once finalized, the line will serve as an important connection to Central, South and Western Europe. It would also serve as an important reference point for future projects that China might want to achieve in the European Union (Matura 2016).

Nevertheless, the project has been under revision by Brussels for possible infringements of the EU guidelines on public tenders. The focus is on Hungary (a EU member state). The failure to comply with the European procurement law would most likely lead to fines and proceedings to reverse infringements. The rules for Serbia are looser since it is only a prospective candidate for EU membership. Prolonged delays and possibly breaches of the European law would cause a diplomatic embarrassment to China (Kynge et al. 2017).

In Poland, China experienced different outcomes of its initiatives: a successful one by investing in a steel works and industrial heavy machinery company in Stalowa Wola, and a failed one, a highly criticized construction of a highway that would connect Łódź and Warsaw (Cienski 2011). There are a few outstanding problems for Poland to achieve a real strategic cooperation: a huge negative trade balance in favor of China, asymmetry in market access, the volume of investments in Poland—the interest in Greenfield investments that would create jobs versus the Chinese side acquiring existing plants. In general, there is a problem of reciprocity when the benefits would be a real win-win scenario (Szczudlik-Tatar 2015). The Polish policy-makers seem to be optimistic that BRI will help to resolve some of the issues. The government eagerly joined the Asian Infrastructure Investment Bank (AIIB) and expressed its interest in the Silk Road Fund (Szczudlik-Tatar 2016).

Similarly, the Czech government certainly believes that there is a great potential to become and remain an important partner for China among the CEECs. It has a pro-EU orientation with quite non-confrontational ties with Moscow, and the GDP per capita is ranked highly in the region. Moreover, Czech President Zeman has made it clear on several occasions that he directly supported China and BRI, and as the sole EU leader attended the V-Day parade in Beijing in September 2015.

However, there are two specific sectors where the Chinese investors might find it harder to reach: nuclear power and telecommunications. A recent comparative study of the Central European attitudes towards Chinese energy investments, which was conducted in the Czech Republic, Poland and Slovakia, found that these investments were viewed more negatively than those in other sectors. This is due to the strategic nature of these investments (Turcsányi 2016).[7]

It should be noted that monitoring of foreign investments into sectors of critical infrastructure, to avoid disruptions of operations or use of power to promote foreign economic or political interests at the expense of the Czech Republic, are not unique to China. The Czech Security Strategy clearly outlines the reasons behind protecting the energy, information and communication technology sectors from any players who have a potential to cause cyber-attacks, economic crime or politically motivated manipulation of supplies of raw materials (Security Strategy 2015).

Energy, Telecommunications and Security Risks

Nuclear energy in the Czech Republic plays an important role and the government is committed to its future. It issued an updated State Energy Policy in 2015. The following year, a new committee was set up by the Ministry of Industry and Trade, which was tasked to coordinate a new construction, the supply chain, wastes and legislation in the nuclear sector. The Czech government declared the intention to build two nuclear units in 2015—one at the Dukovany plant and one at the Temelin plant. The anticipated price of both units is 300 billion Czech crowns (approximately USD 13.8 million). Dukovany is a priority since the nuclear reactors there will most likely close in 2035 (MPO 2015). There is a projection for nuclear energy to become the primary source of electricity production, with an increase from 32.5% to 46% to 58% by 2040 (IEA 2016).

There are several foreign investors who expressed their interest in participating in a public tender for the construction of two additional nuclear reactors: the Russian company ROSATOM; the French EDF; the American-Japanese Westinghouse Electric Company; the joint project between Areva and Mitsubishi, Atmea; the Korean company KHNP; and China General Nuclear Power. The Chinese expression of interest in participating in nuclear cooperation with the Czech Republic was incorporated into the Belgrade Guidelines in 2014 (Belgrade Guidelines 2014).

The Czech Republic is still assessing the submitted proposals. It is also working out the right model and it is considering three different priority scenarios of financing. The first scenario counts on the CEZ Group and its partner company CEZ a.s., an integrated energy group, with the largest shareholder—the Czech Republic with a nearly 70% stake in the company's share capital. The second scenario would entail the purchase of the partner company from CEZ Group by the Czech Republic and subsequently the company would be responsible for constructing the new units in Dukovany. The third scenario entails the Czech Republic taking over a part of CEZ Group—including nuclear power plants—and this part would be 100% owned by the state and would then oversee the Dukovany project (HN 2017).

There is a widespread opinion that if the public tender would go ahead and a foreign investor would be invited to undertake the construction in Dukovany, then the selected foreign supplier would be required to invite Czech firms to join similar projects in the third countries. There are those foreign investors that are more willing to comply with the request and those that are not.

Former Minister of Industry and Trade Jan Mladek explained that the Russian company ROSATOM and partially the Korean Electric Power Corporation (KEPCO) were the most willing to comply, while Japanese-American Westinghouse and China General Nuclear Power were not. According to him, the Chinese representative was rather surprised that the Czechs would participate in Chinese projects. There was an expectation that the Chinese would use their own workers, engineers and material (Sinopsis 2016).

China Nuclear Power Engineering Company (CGN) bets on getting some help from a media company that would facilitate building a positive image of CGN as a reliable and long-term partner of the Czech nuclear industry. The aim is to forge more trust and increase the company's competitiveness on the market.

In relation to telecommunications and security risks, the Czech security services identified Russia and China as 'security threats' in the last three years. The annual report of the Security Information Services for 2015 stated that their intelligence services were the most active in the Czech Republic. They stated that in China's case, diplomats, intelligence officers and economic entities were building on previous successes and strengthened their influence in the Czech economy and politics (BIS 2016).

The 2013 report specifically mentioned the Chinese companies Huawei and ZTE as posing a 'potential threat' to the Czech Republic, based on experiences from other countries who had excluded Huawei from public tenders on the grounds of cooperation with Chinese security services and being involved in spying activities. The concerns were linked to ignoring error reports and mistakes that could enable illegal remote access to devices (BIS 2014).

Recently, Huawei has made some headlines in the Czech press for being declined by the Ministry of Interior due to security risks (Reflex 2016). The company has operated in the Czech Republic since 2003 and has since become one of the most successful sellers of smart phones on the market. For marketing purposes, the company smartly picked the most famous and popular Czech ice hockey player, Jaromir Jágr, as the promotional 'face' of their campaigns in the Czech Republic.

For the Czech intelligence community, the biggest fear is that the Chinese agents could use the network technology and software to 'eavesdrop' sensitive communication or they could implant technology, which could enable China, in cases of a hypothetical conflict, to block selected systems (BIS 2014, 2016; Sinopsis 2016).

There are signs of a more pragmatic and strategic approach to investments—in specific sectors and in terms of the level of entry. It is, however, clear that the Czechs are not always united in their positions. The failure to join the AIIB is a case in point. The hesitance to become one of the founding members has kept the Czechs away from becoming better involved in institution, which has become the center of the financial dimension of the BRI.

The pragmatic approach will most likely be seen in different sectors in the future. The Czechs have sided with others within the 16+1 in their appeals to improve the situation for the entry of agricultural products to the Chinese market. The most criticism has been directed towards AQSIQ, the bureau for approving the procedures, for extremely long waiting periods of several years.

The Chinese counterparts were asked, that being members, to follow the rulings of the World Organization for Animal Health, instead of their own decisions, and not duplicate the processes. For the EU member states, including the Czech Republic, it is also more viable to use the European Union as a platform for joint negotiations—especially in terms of unified internal veterinary and phytosanitary guidelines and the common market.[8]

For now, both governments embrace the momentum. The latest visit of Czech President Zeman led to Beijing, Nanjing and Shanghai in May 2017. In anticipation of the visit, the Chinese media printed articles in the *China Daily* where President Zeman was quoted as stating that BRI was the 'greatest infrastructure project in history' and that he was pleased the plan to connect China with Europe includes the Czech Republic (Li 2017). Another article suggested that the Czech Republic hoped to become a 'regional financial center'. Ambassador Ma Keqing admitted that the outmost priority was to institutionalize the platform and 'design suitable projects' (Fu 2017).

There are three direct flights between Prague and Beijing, Shanghai and Chengdu. There is a plan to add Kunming to the list. More headway has been achieved in the air industry. The Czech producer of ultralight Direct Fly signed an agreement with Wanfeng in April 2016. The plan is to produce planes with Czech know-how in China. However, Wanfeng has also been planning to purchase more than 30 planes from various Czech producers.

One thing that is going to be crucial for the Czech Republic and other members of the 16+1 platform is to find the common view of the initiative. At one specific meeting on 27 March 2017, the general director of the International Relations Department at China's Foreign Affairs Ministry, Sui Pengfei, declared that the Chinese side would consider and present the 16+1 as one 'region'—and the reason behind this was to increase the value of the small CEE states in the eyes of Chinese investors. This, however, has not been taken positively by all representatives from the 16 countries.

Some argued that the states were way too different and it would be unreal to expect a common approach in many questions. The Czech Republic would be at a disadvantage if it were separated from the more developed member states of the European Union. As such, it will most likely continue with viewing the platform as an added tool to strengthen bilateral ties and in some respects, it will want to be viewed as an EU member state first, before considering the initiatives of the 16+1.[9]

The Chinese investments will also need to be evaluated in relation to other incoming investments from East Asia into the Czech Republic. According to the governmental statistics by CzechInvest, 235 projects valued at 239 billion Czech crowns (approx. USD 10.4 million) took place with Asian countries between 1993 and 2016. When it comes to ranking of foreign investors, Japan came in second place, South Korea came in fourth, Taiwan came in tenth and China came in twentieth. It is expected, however, that China's position is going to rise in the upcoming years (CzechInvest 2017).

Chinese investors are gradually changing their approach and investing into building new factories. Yangeng Automotive Interior invested around USD 230 million into building two factories in Žatec and Planá nad Lužnicí. The latter was opened with a promise of employment for 588 people (MPO 2017).

In the future, the Czechs will need to find the right balance between the decision-makers in their approach to China. It is vital to stay united, consistent and predictable even after the parliamentary elections in October 2017. In a recent interview, the president of the New Silk Road Institute Prague, former Minister of Foreign Affairs Jan Kohout, pointed out that it was primarily up to the Czechs to opt for projects that have some added value and there should be an effort to prepare the right conditions domestically for such projects (Kohout 2017).

Conclusions

The evolving relations between China and the 16+1 CEECs have generated some interest and provided an opportunity to assess the flows of Chinese investments, not just in the CEECs but Europe-wide. While the mechanism facilitates interactions, it helps in identifying areas of collaboration, and it has already brought some practical results, China's intentions are still questioned, as well as the long-term validity of such a diverse platform. It is difficult to predict how much impact there will be on the workings of the European Union if the institutionalism of the 16+1 platform deepens. The ideal scenario would be if the processes were complementary with the European Union's goals.

The Czech Republic belongs to the group of CEECs that have benefited and used the framework to increase its position in gaining more potential investment opportunities from China vis-à-vis other CEECs. So far, the results have been mixed, and the public as well as some political opposition and expert community are calling for a more sober and pragmatic approach to investment projects. They want the Czech interests to come first and focus on areas such as gaining a better access to the Chinese market and protection of the Czech investments there.

It is recommended that the Czechs remain active in BRI, however, they also participate in shaping priorities. Two-way benefits should be seen. For the Czechs, the benefits are still marginal. It is widely expected that investments will lead to new spheres, regions with higher unemployment and that the Czech companies will be more involved. More protection of knowledge internally and on the EU level is necessary. One area that still needs improvement is passing the right legislation that would protect strategic infrastructure, which would better separate the political and economic interests. It would subsequently increase the confidence in foreign investors in the Czech Republic. This mechanism should be consulted within the European Union to make sure that there is no doubt about the Czech Republic's commitment to the agreed processes.

Notes

1. For a good assessment of China's ambitions read François Godement's 'Expanded Ambitions: Shrinking Achievements: How China Sees the Global Order', Policy Brief, European Council on Foreign Affairs, March 2017.
2. The EU member states: Bulgaria, Croatia, the Czech Republic, Estonia, Hungary, Latvia, Lithuania, Poland, Romania, Slovakia and Slovenia.

Non-EU member states: Albania, Bosnia and Herzegovina, Macedonia, Montenegro and Serbia.

3. The author attended an international workshop 'European Perspectives on China's New Silk Road' at the European Economic and Social Committee of the European Parliament in Brussels on 14–15 September 2015 where some of these concerns were raised by the majority of speakers.
4. Czech China experts, affiliated with the Czech Institute of East Asian Studies at the Charles university in Prague, have set up a special portal, 'Sinopsis', in the Czech language in response to the lack of critical assessment of the Chinese investments in the Czech Republic. They translate media reports and official statements from Chinese and other languages to provide a more balanced view of China and the interactions with the Czech Republic. See: https://sinopsis.cz/.
5. The author attended the meeting between the Chinese President Xi Jinping and the Czech Speaker of the Chamber of Deputies Jan Hamáček on 29 March 2016. During this meeting President Xi mentioned the dire situation of global economy, China's support for the EU integration, the complementarity of the Czech Republic and China and the potential of the Czech Republic—thank to its industry—to play a role in Central Europe in the context of BRI.
6. This platform was jointly founded by the former Czech President Vaclav Havel, Japanese philanthropist Yosei Sasakawa and the Nobel Peace Prize Laureate Elie Wiesel in 1996. The purpose is to openly debate about democracy, civil society, cultural and ethnic tolerance, as well as human rights.
7. Relevant comparative research has already been done in terms of China's interests in investing in nuclear power and telecommunications in Scandinavia (Denmark, United Kingdom, Norway), Pakistan, Saudi Arabia or Ukraine by Yang Jiang, Aki Tonami, Adam Moe Fejerskov, DIIS Report 2016, http://pure.diis.dk/ws/files/727852/DIIS_RP_2016_8_WEB.pdf.
8. The author consulted the issue with the Czech diplomatic staff in informal interviews in Prague in April 2017.
9. The author verified the information about the meeting with the Czech diplomatic staff and consulted the views on the 16+1 platform in an informal interview in Prague in April 2017.

Bibliography

Agenda (2017), 'Agenda for Czech Foreign Policy', AMO, 24 June 2017, https://www.amo.cz/en/agenda-for-czech-foreign-policy/, accessed 28 June 2017.

Alden, C. and Large, D. (2015), 'On Becoming a Norms Maker: Chinese Foreign Policy, Norms Evolution and the Challenges of Security in Africa', *The China Quarterly*, 221, 123–142.

AMO (2016), 'Nová Hedvábná cesta: výzvy a příležitosti' (New Silk Road: Challenges and Opportunities), Research Paper 1/2016, https://www.amo.cz/wp-content/uploads/2016/03/amocz_RP_1_2016_web.pdf, accessed April 2016.

Belgrade Guidelines (2014), 'The Belgrade Guidelines for Cooperation Between China and Central and Eastern European Countries', Ministry of Foreign Affairs of the People's Republic of China, http://www.fmprc.gov.cn/mfa_eng/zxxx_662805/t1224905.shtml, accessed 10 September 2016.

BIS 2014 (2015), 'Annual Report of the Security Information Service for 2014', Intelligence Service of the Czech Republic, https://www.bis.cz/vyrocni-zpravaEN6c8d.html?ArticleID=1096, accessed 10 June 2017.

BIS 2016 (2017), 'Annual Report of the Security Information Service for 2016' (In Czech), Intelligence Service of the Czech Republic, https://www.bis.cz/vyrocni-zprava6c88.html?ArticleID=1117, accessed 10 June 2017.

Bucharest Guidelines (2013), 'The Bucharest Guidelines for Cooperation Between China and Central and Eastern European Countries', http://gov.ro/en/news/the-bucharest-guidelines-for-cooperation-between-china-and-central-and-eastern-european-countries, accessed 10 September 2016.

Cienski, J. (2011), 'China Group Sees Collapse of Poland Ambitions', *Financial Times*, 16 June 2011, http://www.ftchinese.com/story/001039121/en/?print=y, accessed 15 May 2017.

CT24 (2015), 'Nova hedvábná stezka povede i přes Česko' (The New Silk Road Will Also Go Through the Czech Republic), Report from the Prime Minister Bohuslav Sobotka's Visit of China in November 2015, http://www.ceskatelevize.cz/ct24/svet/1625320-nova-hedvabna-stezka-povede-i-pres-cesko, accessed 10 January 2017.

CzechInvest (2017), M. Krejčí, 'Současný stav asijských investic v České republice' (The Current Status of Asian Investments in the Czech Republic), Asia Business Conference, the Chamber of Deputies of the Parliament of the Czech Republic, Prague, 25 May 2017, http://asbuco.cz/wp-content/uploads/2017/05/martin-krejci-czechinvest.pdf, accessed 15 June 2017.

Emmott, R. (2016), 'EU's Statement on South China Sea Reflects Divisions', Reuters, 15 July 2016, https://www.reuters.com/article/southchinasearuling-eu/eus-statement-on-south-china-sea-reflects-divisions-idUSL8N1A130Y, accessed 15 June 2017.

EU Statement (2016), Declaration by the High Representative on Behalf of the EU on the Award Rendered in the Arbitration Between the Republic of the Philippines and the People's Republic of China, Council of the EU, 15 July 2016, http://www.consilium.europa.eu/en/press/pressreleases/2016/07/15/south-china-sea-arbitration/pdf, accessed 20 July 2016.

Fu, J. (2017), 'Czech Republic Looks to Strengthen Ties', *China Daily*, 10 May 2017, http://www.chinadaily.com.cn/beltandroadinitiative/2017-05/10/content_29281851.htm, accessed 11 May 2017.

Fürst, R. (2015), 'Czech-China Relations: Accelerated Ice Melting', in *Mapping Europe-China Relations: A Bottom-Up Approach*,' Report, M. Huotari, M. Otero-Iglesias, J. Seaman and A. Ekman (eds.), 15–19.

Fürst, R. (2016), 'The Czech Republic: New Strategic Partnership with China, yet Little Real OBOR Touch,' in *Europe and China's New Silk Roads*, Report, F.-P. van der Putten, J. Seaman, M. Huotari, A. Ekman and M. Otero-Iglesias (eds.), 12–16.

Fürst, R. (2017), 'Partnerství EU-ČLR vyžaduje update', (The EU-PRC Partnership Requires an Update), Policy Paper, Institute of International Relations Prague.

Góralczyk, B. (2017), 'China's Interests in Central and Eastern Europe: Enter the Dragon', *European View*, https://link.springer.com/article/10.1007/s12290-017-0427-9, accessed 1 July 2017.

Grieger, G. (2016), 'One Belt, One Road (OBOR): China's Regional Integration Initiative', Briefing, *European Parliamentary Research Service.*

Hanemann, T. and Huotari, M. (2017), 'Record Flows and Growing Imbalances: Chinese Investment in Europe in 2016', MERICS and Rhodium Group, no. 3, 10 January 2017, http://rhg.com/reports/record-flows-and-growing-imbalances-chinese-investment-in-europe-in-2016, accessed 10 February 2017.

Herrero Garcia, A. and Xu, J. (2016) 'China's Belt and Road Initiative: Can Europe Expect Trade Gains?' Working Paper, Issue 5, http://bruegel.org/wp-content/uploads/2016/09/WP-05-2016.pdf, accessed 22 December 2016.

HN (2017), 'Stavbu nového bloku Dukovan by měl financovat ČEZ nebo stát. O konečné variantě rozhodne vláda příští rok' (CEZ or the State Should Finance the Construction of the New Bloc in Dukovany. The Government Will Decide About the Final Scenario Next Year), Hospodářské noviny, https://byznys.ihned.cz/c1-65768720-stavbu-noveho-bloku-dukovan-by-mel-financovat-cez-nebo-stat-tvrdi-sobotka-o-finalni-variante-rozhodne-vlada-pristi-rok, accessed 20 July 2017.

Hrad.cz (2016), 'Společné prohlášení nejvyšších ústavních činitelů České republiky' (Joint Statement of the Highest Constitutional Figures in the Czech Republic), https://www.hrad.cz/cs/pro-media/tiskove-zpravy/aktualni-tiskove-zpravy/spolecne-prohlaseni-nejvyssich-ustavnich-cinitelu-ceske-republiky-12953, accessed 10 January 2017.

Huijskens, F. (2016), 'From Norm-Taker to Institution-Creator: China's Growing Role in International Institutions', PRIMO Working Paper no.7, http://www.primo-itn.eu/PRIMO/wp-content/uploads/2015/07/WorkingPaper-7_PRIMO_Fleur-Huijskens2.pdf, accessed 10 July 2017.

Huotari, M., Otero-Iglesias, M., Seaman, J. and Ekman, A. (eds.) (2015), 'Mapping Europe-China Relations: A Bottom-Up Approach,' Report, (The European Think-Tank Network on China (ETNC), http://www.iai.it/sites/default/files/2015_etnc_report.pdf, accessed 22 December 2016.

IEA (2016), 'The 2016 IEA Review of the Czech Republic's Energy Policies', International Energy Agency, https://www.iea.org/countries/membercountries/czechrepublic/, accessed 20 January 2017.

Kaczmarski, M. and Jakobowski, J. (2015), 'China and Central-Eastern Europe: '16+1' as Seen from Beijing,' Commentary No. 166 (Center for Eastern Studies, https://www.osw.waw.pl/sites/default/files/commentary_166.pdf, accessed 3 March 2017.

Kohout, J. (2017), Interview: 'Vyvarujme se servility vůči Číně' (Lets Avoid the Servility vis-à-vis China), Interviewed by Kateřina Menzelová, Lidové Noviny.

Kopecky, V. and Rezkova, A. (2016), 'Česká zahraniční politika vůči Číně: Možnosti, priority a rizika' (*Czech Foreign Policy Towards China: Opportunities, Priorities and Risks*), Policy Paper 28, http://www.amo.cz/wp-content/uploads/2016/10/AMO_Ceska-zahranicni-politika-vuci-Cine_-moznosti-priority-a-rizika.pdf, accessed 1 November 2016.

Kratz, A. (2016), 'The Best of Both Worlds? CEE's Place in China-Europe Economic Relations', in China's Investment in Influence: The Future of 16+1 Cooperation, ECFR.eu, http://www.ecfr.eu/publications/summary/chinas_investment_in_influence_the_future_of_161_cooperation7204, accessed 15 December 2016.

Kynge, J., Beesley, A. and Byrne, A. (2017), 'EU Sets Collision Course with China over 'Silk Road' Rail Project', *Financial Times*, https://www.ft.com/content/003bad14-f52f-11e6-95ee-f14e55513608, accessed 20 March 2017.

Le Corre, P. (2016), 'Sino-EU Relations, a Post-Brexit Jump into the Unknown ?', https://www.brookings.edu/blog/order-from-chaos/2016/07/11/sino-eu-relations-a-post-brexit-jump-into-the-unknown/, accessed 10 December 2016.

Li, W. (2017), 'Czech President's Praise for Initiative', *China Daily*, 12 May 2017, http://europe.chinadaily.com.cn/epaper/2017-05/12/content_29314819.htm, accessed 13 May 2017.

Long, J. (2014), Relations Between China and CEE Countries: Development, Challenges and Recommendations. China Institute of International Studies, http://www.ciis.org.cn/english/2014-11/21/content_7388215.htm, accessed 10 January 2017.

Long J. (2016),'Opportunities and Challenges of the Belt and Road Initiative in Central and Eastern Europe', (一带一路'倡议在中东欧地区的机遇和挑战', Yidai yilu changyi zai zhongdongou diqu de jiyu he tiaozhan), Guoji guancha, no.3, 118–130.

Matura, T. (2016), 'Hungary: Along the New Silk Road Across Central Europe', in *Europe and China's New Silk Roads*, Report, F.-P. van der Putten, J. Seaman, M. Huotari, A. Ekman and M. Otero-Iglesias (eds.), 35–37.

MPO (2015), 'State Energy Policy of the Czech Republic', Ministry of Industry and Trade of the Czech Republic, https://www.mpo.cz/dokument161030.html, accessed 20 December 2017.

MPO (2017), 'MPO navrhlo vládě podpořit investiční akci, která vytvoří téměř 600 nových pracovních míst' (Ministry of Industry and Trade Recommended the Government Supports an Investment Which Would Create Almost 600 new jobs), BusinessInfo.cz, 22 May 2017, http://www.businessinfo.cz/cs/clanky/mpo-navrhlo-vlade-podporit-investicni-akci-ktera-vytvori-temer-600-novych-pracovnich-mist-90485.html, accessed 20 June 2017.

Mrazek, F. (2016), 'Je i v českém zájmu plán Hedvábné stezky?' (Is the Silk Road Plan also in the Czech Interest?), Právo, accessed 19 September 2016.

Noesselt, N. (2016), 'One Belt, One Road: A New Roadmap for a Sinocentric World?' *The Asan Forum*, http://www.theasanforum.org/one-belt-one-road-a-new-roadmap-for-a-sinocentric-world/, accessed 10 January 2017.

Orban, V. (2016), 'Viktor Orbán's Speech at the Conference "China-CEE Political Parties Dialogue", Cabinet Office of the Prime Minister, http://www.miniszterelnok.hu/viktor-orbans-speech-at-the-conference-china-cee-political-parties-dialogue/, accessed 15 June 2017.

Pleschova, G. (2016), 'Slovakia: Disconnected from China's New Silk Road', in *Europe and China's New Silk Roads*, Report, F.-P. van der Putten, J. Seaman, M. Huotari, A. Ekman and M. Otero-Iglesias (eds.), 53–55.

Reflex (2016), 'Čínská Huawei nesmí na české vnitro' (The Chinese Huawai Cannot Access the Czech Ministry of Interior), 3 September 2016, https://www.respekt.cz/tydenik/2016/36/cinska-huawei-nesmi-na-ceske-vnitro, accessed 10 October 2016.

Reilly, J. (2011), 'A Norm-Taker or a Norm-Maker? Chinese aid in Southeast Asia', *Journal of Contemporary China*, 21(73), 71–91.

Riga Guidelines. (2016), 'The Riga Guidelines for Cooperation Between China and Central and Eastern European Countries', *China Daily*, http://www.chinadaily.com.cn/world/2016liattendsSCOCCEEC/2016-11/06/content_27286311.htm, accessed 10 January 2017.

Security Strategy (2015), 'Security Strategy of the Czech Republic 2015', http://www.army.cz/images/id_8001_9000/8503/Security_Strategy_2015.pdf, accessed 17 January 2017.

Sepulchre, A. and Le Corre, P. (2016), *China's Offensive in Europe (Geopolitics in the 21st Century)* (Brookings Institution Press).

Sinopsis (2016), 'Český tisk o Číně: Bezpečnost na vnitru, jaderná energetika a družba zvířatek v zoo' (The Czech Press About China: Security at the Ministry of Interior, Nuclear Energy and Friendship of Animals at the Zoo), https://sinopsis.cz/cesky-tisk-o-cine-bezpecnost-na-vnitru-jaderna-energetika-a-druzba-zviratek-v-zoo/, accessed 10 October 2016.

Sobotka, B. (2016), Opening Remarks by Prime Minister of the Czech Republic, Mr. Bohuslav Sobotka at the Discussion Seminar 'New Silk Road and the Czech Republic' on 19 January 2017, Senate of the Czech Republic.

Stanzel, A., Kratz, A., Szczudlik, J. and Pavlicevic, D. (2016), 'China's Investment in Influence: The Future of 16+1 Cooperation', http://www.ecfr.eu/publications/summary/chinas_investment_in_influence_the_future_of_161_cooperation7204, accessed 22 December 2016.

Suzhou Guidelines (2015), 'The Suzhou Guidelines for Cooperation Between China and Central and Eastern European Countries', Ministry of Foreign Affairs of the People's Republic of China, http://www.fmprc.gov.cn/mfa_eng/zxxx_662805/t1318039.shtml, accessed 10 September 2016.

Szczudlik-Tatar, J. (2015), 'Poland-China Relations: Forging a Strategic Partnership?' in *Mapping Europe-China Relations: A Bottom-Up Approach*, M. Huotari, M. Otero-Iglesias, J. Seaman and A. Ekman (eds.), 56–61.

Szczudlik-Tatar, J. (2016), 'Poland on the Silk Road in Central Europe: To Become a Hub of Hubs?' in *Europe and China's New Silk Roads*, Report, F.-P. van der Putten, J. Seaman, M. Huotari, A. Ekman and M. Otero-Iglesias (eds.), 45–48.

Turcsányi, Richard Q. (2016), 'Central European Attitudes Towards Chinese Energy Investments: The Cases of Poland, Slovakia and the Czech Republic', *Energy Policy.*

Twelve Measures (2012), 'Twelve Measures for Promoting Friendly Cooperation with Central and Eastern European Countries', http://www.fmprc.gov.cn/mfa_eng/topics_665678/wjbispg_665714/t928567.shtml, accessed 10 June 2017.

Wen, J. (2011), 'Strengthen Traditional Friendship and Promote Common Development', Speech at the China-Central and Eastern European Countries Economic and Trade Forum, Budapest, http://www.chinaembassy.cz/cze/xwdt/t834966.htm, accessed 10 June 2017.

Willoughby, I. (2016), 'Beijing Cancels Czech Minister's Visit as Dalai Lama Visit Fallout Continues', Radio Praha in English, http://www.radio.cz/en/section/curraffrs/beijing-cancels-czech-ministers-visit-as-dalai-lama-visit-fallout-continues, accessed 15 July 2017.

Xi, J. (2017a), 'Jointly Shoulder Responsibility of Our Times, Promote Global Growth' Keynote Speech at the Opening Session of the World Economic Forum Annual Meeting 2017, Davos, http://news.xinhuanet.com/english/2017-01/18/c_135991184.htm, accessed 25 March 2017.

Xi, J. (2017b), 'Work Together to Build the Silk Road Economic Belt and The 21st Century Maritime Silk Road' Speech at the Opening Ceremony of The Belt and Road Forum for International Cooperation, http://www.fmprc.gov.cn/mfa_eng/wjdt_665385/zyjh_665391/t1465819.shtml, accessed 10 June 2017.

Index[1]

[1] Note: Page numbers followed by 'n' refer to notes.

A. Arduino, X. Gong (eds.), *Securing the Belt and Road Initiative*, https://doi.org/10.1007/978-981-10-7116-4

The manufacturer's authorised representative in the EU is Springer Nature Customer Service Centre GmbH, Europaplatz 3, 69115 Heidelberg, Germany. If you have any concerns regarding our products, please contact ProductSafety@springernature.com

Printed and bound by CPI Group (UK) Ltd, Croydon, CR0 4YY
30/09/2026
02225451-0014